This book explores the past and future of central bank cooperation. In today's global economy, the cooperation among central banks is a key element in maintaining or restoring monetary and financial stability, thereby ensuring a smooth functioning of the international financial system. Or is it? In this book, economists, historians, and political scientists look back at the experience of central bank cooperation during the past century, at its goals, nature, and processes, and at its successes and failures, and draw lessons for the future. Particular attention is devoted to the role played by central bank cooperation in the formulation of minimum capital standards for internationally active banks (the Basel Capital Accord, Basel II) and in the process of European monetary unification and the introduction of the euro.

Claudio Borio is Head of Research and Policy Analysis at the Bank for International Settlements (BIS), where he has worked since 1987, covering various responsibilities in the Monetary and Economic Department. Dr. Borio was formerly a Lecturer and Research Fellow at Brasenose College, Oxford, and an economist at the Organisation for Economic Co-operation and Development (OECD). He holds a D.Phil. and an M.Phil. in economics from Oxford and has published extensively in the fields of monetary policy, banking, finance, and issues related to financial stability.

Gianni Toniolo is Research Professor of Economics and History at Duke University, Durham, NC; a Research Fellow of the Centre for Economic Policy Research (CEPR), London; and a member of the Academia Europæa. He was previously Professor of Economics at the University of Rome, Tor Vergata, and at Ca' Foscari, the University of Venice. He is a former President of the European Historical Economics Society. Toniolo's books include *An Economic History of Liberal Italy, 1850–1918* (1990); *Central Bank Cooperation at the Bank for International Settlements* (Cambridge University Press, 2005, with the assistance of Piet Clement); and *The International Economy Between the Wars* (2008, with Charles H. Feinstein and Peter Temin).

Piet Clement is Head of Library, Archives, and Research Support at the Bank for International Settlements. He holds a Ph.D. in history from the Catholic University of Leuven, Belgium, and has published on the history of international cooperation and of the BIS.

Studies in Macroeconomic History

SERIES EDITOR: Michael D. Bordo, *Rutgers University*

EDITORS: Marc Flandreau, *Institut d'Etudes Politiques, Sciences Po, Paris*
Chris Meissner, *University of California, Davis*
François Velde, *Federal Reserve Bank of Chicago*
David C. Wheelock, *Federal Reserve Bank of St. Louis*

The titles in this series investigate themes of interest to economists and economic historians in the rapidly developing field of macroeconomic history. The four areas covered include the application of monetary and finance theory, international economics, and quantitative methods to historical problems; the historical application of growth and development theory and theories of business fluctuations; the history of domestic and international monetary, financial, and other macroeconomic institutions; and the history of international monetary and financial systems. The series amalgamates the former Cambridge University Press series Studies in Monetary and Financial History and Studies in Quantitative Economic History.

Other books in the series:

Howard Bodenhorn, *A History of Banking in Antebellum America*

Michael D. Bordo, *The Gold Standard and Related Regimes*

Michael D. Bordo and Forrest Capie (eds.), *Monetary Regimes in Transition*

Michael D. Bordo and Roberto Cortés Conde (eds.), *Transferring Wealth and Power from the Old to the New World*

Richard Burdekin and Pierre Siklos (eds.), *Deflation: Current and Historical Perspectives*

Trevor J. O. Dick and John E. Floyd, *Canada and the Gold Standard*

Barry Eichengreen, *Elusive Stability*

Barry Eichengreen (ed.), *Europe's Postwar Recovery*

Caroline Fohlin, *Finance Capitalism and Germany's Rise to Industrial Power*

Michele Fratianni and Franco Spinelli, *A Monetary History of Italy*

Continued after the index

Past and Future of
Central Bank Cooperation

Edited by

CLAUDIO BORIO
Bank for International Settlements

GIANNI TONIOLO
Duke University

PIET CLEMENT
Bank for International Settlements

CAMBRIDGE
UNIVERSITY PRESS

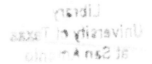

CAMBRIDGE UNIVERSITY PRESS
Cambridge, New York, Melbourne, Madrid, Cape Town, Singapore, São Paulo, Delhi

Cambridge University Press
32 Avenue of the Americas, New York, NY 10013-2473, USA

www.cambridge.org
Information on this title: www.cambridge.org/9780521877794

First published 2008

Printed in the United States of America

A catalog record for this publication is available from the British Library.

Library of Congress Cataloging in Publication Data

Borio, C. E. V.
Past and future of central bank cooperation / Claudio Borio, Gianni
Toniolo, Piet Clement.
p. cm. – (Studies in macroeconomic history)
Includes bibliographical references and index.
ISBN 978-0-521-87779-4 (hbk.)
1. Banks and banking, Central – International cooperation.   I. Toniolo, Gianni, 1942–
II. Clement, Piet.   III. Title.   IV. Series.
HG1811.B66   2008
332.1′5–dc22   2008000500

ISBN   978-0-521-87779-4 hardback

Contents

Contents

Acknowledgments

The editors would like to thank the series editor, Michael D. Bordo, and Scott Parris and Adam Levine at Cambridge University Press. Thanks are also due to Tenea Johnson for efficiently coordinating the editorial work, and to Antonio Rossi at the BIS for his indispensable support.

Contributors

Claudio Borio, Bank for International Settlements, Basel, Switzerland

Piet Clement, Bank for International Settlements, Basel, Switzerland

Richard N. Cooper, Harvard University, Cambridge, Massachusetts

Ethan B. Kapstein, INSEAD, Fontainebleau, France

Alexandre Lamfalussy, Catholic University of Louvain, Belgium

Tommaso Padoa-Schioppa, Former Member of the Executive Board of the European Central Bank, Frankfurt, Germany

Beth A. Simmons, Harvard University, Cambridge, Massachusetts

Gianni Toniolo, Duke University, Durham, North Carolina

Introduction

Past and Future of Central Bank Cooperation

While the oldest central banks in the world claim a lineage stretching back to the late 1600s, central banking in the modern sense is a relatively recent phenomenon, making its first appearance in the second half of the nineteenth century. Even then, not that many central banks were around. In 1900, there were no more than eighteen (Capie 2003: 373). By that time, what constituted a central bank had come to be defined by a common set of core functions. These included a responsibility for monetary (i.e., price and exchange rate) stability, support for financial stability (if necessary, by acting as lender of last resort), and, in some cases, the domestic note-issuing monopoly. The rise and spread of modern central banking was closely intertwined with the process of nation building and political emancipation throughout the nineteenth and twentieth centuries. As new nation-states were created, setting up a central bank was often part of defining their identity. By the beginning of the twenty-first century, the number of central banks had reached almost 180, nearly as many as there were independent states, and ten times as many as 100 years earlier.

---

[1] Historian, Bank for International Settlements. The views expressed in this chapter are those of the author and do not necessarily reflect those of the BIS.

Central bank cooperation is as old as modern central banking itself. To be sure, the mandate of each central bank – to preserve monetary and financial stability – is by definition a domestic one. But in an increasingly interdependent world economy, the international dimension plays a key role, particularly for the smaller economies. For the past 130 years or so, central banks have cooperated with one another, bilaterally or multilaterally, *ad hoc,* sporadically, or within a more or less regular and formalized framework.

This cooperation is the subject of the current volume. Rather than discussing the desirability of international central bank cooperation as such – and whether a positive or normative case can be made for it – the volume deals primarily with the history and future of central bank cooperation in action: How did/does it operate? What has it achieved? Under what circumstances has it been successful or not? What are the main factors fostering or hampering cooperation? As central bank cooperation is only part of the wider area of international financial cooperation, which includes intergovernmental cooperation – for instance, through the International Monetary Fund, the World Bank, or the G8 – and private sector cooperation, this broader context features prominently in the following pages. The main focus, however, remains on central bank cooperation.

The contributions contained in this volume were originally prepared for a conference held in Basel, Switzerland, to mark the seventy-fifth anniversary of the Bank for International Settlements (BIS), the "central banks' bank." The book provides a comprehensive overview of the history of central bank cooperation through the BIS and otherwise (chapters 1 and 2); offers an in-depth analysis of two major episodes in the recent history of monetary and financial cooperation, namely the agreements on international capital standards reached between financial supervisors (chapter 3), and the European monetary unification process as it has unfolded after Maastricht (chapter 4); and looks at some of the key issues that are likely to shape central bank cooperation in the future (chapters 5 and 6).

Introduction: Past and Future of Central Bank Cooperation

A specific characteristic of this book is that it considers central bank cooperation from a multidisciplinary angle. In bringing together economists, historians, and political scientists, a conscious attempt has been made to break away from a purely economic analysis of central bank cooperation and place more emphasis on other determinants such as history, culture, institutional developments, and political processes. It is hoped that this approach not only enriches the analysis of and debate on central bank cooperation as such, but also provides some significant pointers to its potential future development.

Chapters 1 and 2 look at the history of central bank cooperation over the past 130 years, partly from a BIS perspective. Both Claudio Borio and Gianni Toniolo (in chapter 1), and Richard Cooper (in chapter 2) provide a chronology in which central bank cooperation can be seen to have waxed and waned. During the first globalization era (1870–1914), the international monetary system based on the gold standard performed remarkably well. Central bank cooperation was limited. As Borio and Toniolo point out, the main banks of issue were able to focus on their high-profile domestic role as "guarantors of convertibility," while problems relating to international imbalances were largely left to sort themselves out through automatic adjustment, facilitated by high levels of capital mobility and by the relatively low political costs of deflation and unemployment (given the limited representative character of nineteenth-century democracy). Even so, the classical gold standard could not guarantee continuous domestic financial stability, and in a handful of severe banking crises, central banks cooperated by extending emergency credits to one another in order to prevent risks of contagion. This cooperation, however, was essentially of a bilateral and *ad hoc* nature. The abandonment of the gold standard at the outbreak of World War I and the difficult process of returning to gold convertibility in the 1920s markedly increased the scope and demand for central bank cooperation. It was "tirelessly preached" (Borio and Toniolo) by leading central bankers such as Bank of England Governor Montagu Norman. A culminating point was reached in 1930 with the foundation of the BIS, intended to settle Germany's World War I reparations. The main central banks involved in the reparations issue took the opportunity of this institutional innovation to turn the BIS into an instrument of their cooperation and an expression of their independence (as they effectively owned and ran the institution). However, the creation of the BIS could not prevent the breakdown of the international monetary and financial system during the Great Depression as "events overwhelmed the limited capacity of central banks to cooperate" (Cooper). The unsuccessful attempt to counter the 1931 financial crisis through multilateral action and international lending was followed by a rapid descent into protectionism, currency manipulation, and isolationism (Eichengreen 1992).

The post-World War II period, in contrast, saw enhanced central bank cooperation, but in a profoundly different monetary and financial environment (Borio and Toniolo). The Bretton Woods system was designed to avoid the "mistakes" of the interwar period. It provided for fixed but adjustable exchange rates pegged to gold (or to the gold-backed dollar) and allowed foreign exchange and capital controls to safeguard the greatest possible autonomy for domestic macroeconomic policymaking. By and large, governments were in charge of the Bretton Woods system, with central banks acting *de facto* as agents of government. Nevertheless, there was scope for intensive central bank cooperation, which manifested itself first and foremost through the European Payments Union (EPU, 1950–58) – an elaborate scheme designed to help war-ravaged European countries restore current account convertibility and "one of the great success stories in international monetary cooperation" (Borio and Toniolo). Intensive cooperation continued after the end of the EPU, as it quickly became clear that the Bretton Woods system, now fully operational, required a good deal of international coordination and even intervention. The key was the protection of the gold-dollar convertibility that formed the basis of the system, and a number of joint central bank initiatives were developed to this end, including the Gold Pool, central bank swap arrangements, and sterling support. Thus, "the 1960s saw the real birth of multilateral central bank cooperation envisioned but still-born in 1930" (Cooper). After 1968, however, with the demise of the Gold Pool and the return of the United States to a policy of "benign neglect" of the dollar, multilateral cooperation to shore up the Bretton Woods system lost momentum. The fixed exchange rate regime collapsed in 1971–73, making way for the era of floating.

The end of Bretton Woods had a profound impact on central bank cooperation. In a context of floating rates, economic stagnation, and rising inflation, "macroeconomic policy coordination took a back seat as central banks became increasingly reluctant to sacrifice monetary orthodoxy on the altar of global cooperation" (Borio and Toniolo). However, at a regional level, macroeconomic and thus monetary policy coordination remained attractive as a way to better insulate a group of already well integrated economies from external or global shocks. This was the path taken by the countries of the European Community, leading, in the 1990s, to "the ultimate form of central bank cooperation" (Cooper) among them, namely that of monetary union. At the same time, the gradual liberalization and deregulation of financial markets from the 1970s sealed the shift in the objectives of central bank cooperation away from monetary stability toward financial stability issues. The strong growth of global financial markets, spurred on by rapid advances in information and communications technologies, and epitomized by the surge of the eurocurrency market from the 1960s, created a high degree of financial interdependence between countries. Financial innovations, such as derivatives and securitization, contributed to a better distribution of risks and improved market efficiency, but also added sources of potential instability to the system. These developments highlighted the importance of sound and efficient payment and settlement systems. They also gave rise to concerns that if a financial crisis were to occur, it might more easily take on a global dimension as a result of contagion effects. Such considerations supported the view that active cooperation between central banks was required in order to develop and promote the adoption of minimum standards in the fields of banking supervision and of clearing and settlement systems (thereby contributing to a level global playing field), and, more generally, in order to preserve systemic stability (Lamfalussy 1994). The case for cooperation was further reinforced by the need to integrate the fast-growing emerging markets into the international financial system. As far as central bank cooperation through the BIS is concerned, these developments led to a broadening of its geographical and institutional reach that is still ongoing (Borio and Toniolo).

In assessing the historical experience of central bank cooperation, Borio and Toniolo and Cooper agree that it has grown extensively, if fitfully, over the past century. Both chapters provide important insights into why this should have been the case. First, of course, the nature of the international financial and monetary system itself has strongly influenced the scope and pattern of central bank cooperation. This refers in particular to the shifting balance between fixed and floating exchange rate regimes, and to the extent of international capital mobility. Thus, under Bretton Woods, "in a context of domestic financial repression and constraints on external capital flows, financial stability concerns did not figure prominently on the policy agenda" (Borio and Toniolo). By contrast – and as noted above – after Bretton Woods, the transition from a government-led to a market-led financial system with rapidly increasing capital mobility raised financial stability concerns, prompting central banks to intensify cooperation in this field. As a result, after 1973 financial cooperation basically followed two paths: on the one hand, the strengthening of international prudential regulation and of payment and settlement systems following the high-profile collapse of a number of individual financial institutions; and, on the other, the strenuous efforts to address emerging market countries' debt crises, notably after the 1982 Mexico default. By the end of the 1990s, Borio and Toniolo argue, these two trajectories had fully converged in the concerted attempt to strengthen the international financial architecture, following the 1997 Asian crisis.

Introduction: Past and Future of Central Bank Cooperation

It is clear that the scope and intensity of central bank cooperation are not only determined by prevailing financial and monetary conditions, but also, to a considerable extent, by the broader political and institutional environments. Borio and Toniolo conclude that "central bank cooperation was more intense in periods when international relations were friendlier and oriented to multilateral rather than bilateral cooperation, when the reputation and independence of central banks was high, and when the issues requiring a cooperative approach were such that the technical expertise of central banks would make a difference." At first sight, it may appear that the increased independence most central banks enjoyed from the 1980s, together with their strong focus on domestic price stability, would have acted as something of a brake on international cooperation. It may have done so as far as cooperation on exchange rates was concerned, but in the cooperative efforts in the field of prudential regulation, Borio and Toniolo underline, this newly found central bank autonomy has proven a valuable asset.

To better understand the evolution of central bank cooperation, it is not enough to analyze its context and its shifting targets. Also, the different tools that have been and are being employed to achieve these targets have to be looked at in a systematic manner. Richard Cooper provides a useful distinction between the different possible ways in which central banks may cooperate. These range from simple information exchange (what Beth Simmons calls "shallow cooperation" in chapter 5) to the "most demanding form" (Cooper) of commonly agreed actions. While information exchange and standardization of concepts and even of regulations (Basel Capital Accord) are widely held to be beneficial, joint monetary policy actions – including joint market interventions – are much more controversial (Bordo and Schwartz 2000).

In terms of the instruments of cooperation, it is useful to single out two significant developments over the period considered in this volume. The first one refers to the role of the BIS. The institutionalization of central bank cooperation through this organization has certainly helped, the authors of this volume agree, to foster useful information exchange and the building of a conceptual consensus among central banks. Second, within the framework of the BIS, a particular form of cooperation has sprung up from the 1970s onward that has since proven its merits. The more or less informal committees first set up among the G10 central banks to discuss and monitor the eurocurrency markets (1971) and to exchange information on domestic banking regulations and supervisory practices after the Herstatt episode (1974) have provided an interesting model for effective cooperation in the financial field (Borio and Toniolo). Information exchange was usually followed by discussions on the commonality in the different national approaches and eventually by the development of common codes and standards – for cross-border banking supervision or for the sound functioning of payment and settlement systems. However, the codes and standards developed through this process were implemented not as the outcome of legally binding agreements ("hard law"), but rather through voluntary adoption in national law and regulations as the result of a mixture of peer pressure and market forces ("soft law"). This successful approach has been copied many times since.

In all of this, of course, the authors do not intend to suggest that central bank cooperation has always been successful or has gone unchallenged. In recent decades, monetary cooperation – if defined as the international coordination of monetary policy action, for example, through agreed interest rate adjustments or foreign exchange market interventions – has not been an unqualified success and its usefulness has been repeatedly called into doubt. However, Cooper reminds us that during the past half-century there has in fact been "little cooperation in framing monetary policy *per se*" and that, at least where the Federal Reserve is concerned, "international factors were rarely decisive in determining policy." In other words, the evidence points to the fact that, even at the height of international cooperation, central banks have always safeguarded their ability and freedom to act independently. Thus, according to Cooper, international monetary cooperation has not been quite as "dangerous" as its detractors have sometimes depicted it. Criticism has also been leveled at the role of central bank cooperation in times of financial crisis, as emergency credits and lender of last resort-type actions have raised alleged moral hazard issues (as the likelihood of a public bailout may not be the best incentive for prudent market behavior). Cooper argues, though, that the concerns voiced with regard to central bank cooperation have generally been overstated and that, at least in theory, "cooperative solutions to policy choices in interdependent systems can lead to superior outcomes to non-cooperative choices in the same environment."

In chapters 3 and 4, Ethan Kapstein and Alexandre Lamfalussy, respectively, illustrate and discuss two major examples of central bank cooperation "at work." Kapstein retraces in more depth the recent history of international cooperation among financial regulators, with specific reference to banking supervision and the so-called Basel process. The first steps toward global standards in banking supervision were taken by the G10 Basel Committee on Banking Supervision from the mid-1970s onward in the wake of highly publicized bank collapses (Herstatt, Franklin National). The cooperation among central banks and financial regulators in this field eventually yielded the 1988 Basel Capital Accord, a set of minimum capital standards for internationally active banks that became globally accepted. Its successor, known as Basel II, was formally endorsed by the G10 central bank Governors and heads of supervision in June 2004. In Kapstein's words, cooperation in this field over the past thirty years has been rewarded with the "undeniable – and even unexpected – achievement of these regulators in crafting a more robust financial system," even though much remains to be done. He credits this success partly to the ability of financial supervisors to "depoliticize the systemic risk environment and to transform crisis management into a technocratic exercise," thereby simplifying the decision-making process.

To Kapstein it is clear that it will not be possible to simply recreate this successful model going forward. For one thing, the "Basel process" has outgrown its original G10 framework and – particularly in the wake of the 1997 Asian crisis – has had to become more generally inclusive of systemically important constituencies worldwide. Second, as Kapstein argues, the central banks' and supervisors' concern with financial stability has not been the only driving force behind the Basel Capital Accord and Basel II. Competitive concerns to "level the playing field" have also played a decisive role. Naturally, with private sector interests at stake, and voiced ever more strongly, national and political interests too (re-)enter the field. The challenges posed by the rapidly evolving risk environment itself point in the same direction. Kapstein draws attention to the apparent paradox that in today's financial system risk seems to have become at the same time more consolidated and more atomized: more consolidated through the emergence of large, complex financial institutions, which operate on a global scale and may have become "too big to fail"; and more atomized because these same institutions have passed on at least part of their risk exposure to other players, including firms and households, for instance, through securitization and credit derivatives. These developments, Kapstein believes, raise the stakes and will further strengthen the linkage between regulators and legislators, already apparent in the Basel II process. Finally, while it is true that the Basel process has helped to improve the resilience of the financial system, this cannot be considered shockproof. The high public cost of recent financial crises, in terms of bailouts financed with taxpayers' money, has again highlighted the issue of the democratic legitimacy of a process that is essentially driven by independent, technocratic institutions and unelected officials. It thus remains to be seen whether the framework engendered by the Basel process will be sufficiently robust to cope with the challenges posed by a widespread politicization of banking regulation. Kapstein thinks it inevitable that central bankers and financial regulators will have to work more closely with elected officials on these issues.

As a former General Manager of the BIS and former President of the European Monetary Institute, Lamfalussy is particularly well placed to discuss the process of European monetary unification up to the establishment of the European Central Bank (ECB). In chapter 4, he argues that effective international cooperation in the monetary and financial field is almost without exception the result of a close partnership between central banks and governments. Lamfalussy attributes the undeniable success of the European monetary unification process to an exceptional concurrence of favorable facts and influences. The most important ones were: the strong political commitment of the governments concerned; the trust placed in central bank experts in preparing the 1992 Maastricht Treaty; the incremental momentum resulting from the tight timetable; and, last but not least, the prevailing favorable macroeconomic conditions. In the run-up to achieving European Monetary Union (EMU), Lamfalussy assigns a crucial role to the convergence criteria spelled out by the Maastricht Treaty. These criteria not only proved a very effective tool in aligning national monetary and macroeconomic policies, they also helped to further consolidate central bank independence in the participating countries (in fact, it can be argued that central bank independence became an additional convergence criterion, conditioning access to EMU). These factors taken together paved the way for monetary union, the ultimate form of central bank cooperation.

This interpretation of the European monetary unification process is consistent with the arguments advanced by Borio and Toniolo in chapter 1, namely that the intensity of central bank cooperation crucially depends on domestic politics and the state of international relations. At the same time, Lamfalussy reminds us that favorable domestic and international conditions – and, therefore, effective central bank cooperation itself – can never be taken for granted. In his view, the delicate balance that favored the establishment of the ECB and the launch of the euro in the 1990s seemed to have become rather less secure only a few years later, for mainly three reasons: the weakening of monetary policy restraint; the unsatisfactory performance of the eurozone economy up to 2005; and, finally, the slow progress in necessary supply side reforms in the early years of the twenty-first century.

These considerations seem particularly relevant at a time when closer monetary cooperation is high on the international agenda, particularly, but not exclusively, in the Arabian peninsula and in South-East Asia.

Having reviewed past experiences, one may feel tempted to take a little gamble and speculate about the future of central bank cooperation. Beth Simmons ventures into the notoriously tricky field of "futurology," never leaving the solid ground provided by a thorough analysis of the political and economic determinants of central bank cooperation yesterday and today. In chapter 5, she looks in particular at the extent to which central bankers across the world today agree on theory and on goals, and evaluates whether the broader economic and political environment facilitates or impedes cooperation. Simmons notes a marked convergence in the values central bankers share, in their long-term horizons and even in their academic backgrounds, conditions that may be conducive to high levels of cooperation in the future. Reviewing the different forms of central bank cooperation, Simmons predicts that the "easiest" form – information sharing – will become increasingly routine. Cooperation in support of global financial stability, she finds, poses a more difficult cooperative dilemma because of the ever-present tension between efficiency and inclusiveness. In the area of exchange rate and monetary policy coordination, Simmons notes that the consensus on the effectiveness of exchange market interventions has withered, but that this does not preclude a new consensus from emerging in the future. Much in line with Kapstein's findings in chapter 3, Simmons concludes that the main future challenges for central bank cooperation will be to deepen its legitimacy by embracing other cooperative forums – including elected officials – and to broaden its outreach by including emerging monetary and financial powers, such as China, in the cooperative management of international monetary conditions.

To conclude, Tommaso Padoa-Schioppa, former member of the Executive Board of the ECB, reflects on the merits of cooperation in an interdependent world (chapter 6). Isolationism, or "going it alone," he argues, is no realistic option in an integrated world economy. Nevertheless, this is, to a certain extent, the prescription of the popular "house in order" doctrine. This doctrine postulates that as long as each individual country gets its own fundamentals right (keeps its own house in order), the international economic and financial system as a whole will benefit automatically, and no large amount of formal cooperation will be required. Padoa-Schioppa holds the house in order precept up to the light and finds it to be a sound recommendation *per se*, but "a fallacy as an adequate rule to deal with the policy issues raised by economic interdependence." On the contrary, he argues that economic interdependence, which has grown at a galloping pace, and international policy cooperation should be regarded as an inseparable pair. Indeed, the house in order precept itself requires a fair degree of successful international coordination, as decent international relations and a functioning international financial system are prerequisites for keeping one's house in order in the first place. Padoa-Schioppa regards international policy cooperation as the best way to deal with the inexorable broadening and deepening of cross-border economic interdependence in a world that is still largely defined by political borders and in which nation-states preserve the largest share of public power. In a globalized world, Padoa-Schioppa concludes, "unlimited national autonomy does not exist any longer" and "sovereignty can in fact be regained – rather than lost – when delegating tasks to supranational forums and institutions."

What lessons are to be drawn from the history of 130 years of central bank cooperation? Today, international central bank cooperation is very active in a number of fields and at varying levels of intensity. This ranges from firsthand information exchange, to the development of common standards for banking supervision, to taking emergency action when required (as exemplified by the joint action of the main central banks in making liquidity available after the 9/11 terrorist attacks or at the height of the 2007–08 sub-prime crisis). It would seem no exaggeration to state that central banks – together with other monetary and financial authorities – continue to play a key role with regard to many crucially important aspects of the international monetary and financial system. Moreover, a broad consensus exists today as to the desirability of promoting consistent policies with regard to fiscal discipline, central bank independence, price stability, free currency convertibility, and capital mobility. This more or less global consensus – quite unique by itself in a longer-term perspective – would seem to make effective central bank cooperation a more viable proposition today than it has been in the past, when views on appropriate monetary and financial policies were repeatedly at loggerheads.

How, then, can international central bank cooperation meet the future demands of an interdependent world economy? A clear picture emerges from the different contributions to this volume: in order to cope with future challenges, central bank cooperation will have to become both wider and deeper. The expanding geography of cooperation is a theme common to all forms of international cooperation, be it political, economic, or, indeed, monetary. To take account of a shifting economic and financial power balance and to tie new global players, such as China and India, into the international financial architecture, central bank cooperation in the twenty-first century will have to become more inclusive. At the same time, and in the face of the challenges outlined above, central bank cooperation, in all likelihood, will have to become deeper, that is, more closely aligned with political and economic cooperative processes, thereby acquiring improved democratic legitimacy. The question arises as to whether these developments will prove to be compatible with the central, and at times bitterly fought, tenet of the 1980s and 1990s, namely the independence of central banks. Does seeking democratic legitimacy not open up new approaches to "politicizing" central bank cooperation, which might ultimately prove its undoing? Or will the prestige and independence of central banks and financial supervisors continue to be indispensable assets in resolving complex and intricate policy dilemmas in a fair and even-handed way? These are important questions the globalized world will have to grapple with over the decades to come.

1

One Hundred and Thirty Years of Central Bank Cooperation: A BIS Perspective

CLAUDIO BORIO AND GIANNI TONIOLO[1]

INTRODUCTION[2]

The idea that an "international bank" would facilitate central bank cooperation dates back to the late nineteenth century (Toniolo 2005: 20–23). It was officially revived in the immediate postwar period, particularly at the 1922 Genoa economic conference. In keeping with the vision of Governor Montagu Norman of the Bank of England, the Bank for International Settlements (BIS), established in 1930 to facilitate the transfer of German reparations, was also given the mission of promoting central bank cooperation.[3] Since July 1931, when the Hoover moratorium put an

[1] Claudio Borio, Head of Research and Policy Analysis, Bank for International Settlements. Gianni Toniolo, Research Professor of Economics and History, Duke University, Durham, NC.

[2] The authors would like to thank Gunter Baer, Piet Clement, Andrew Crockett, Marc Flandreau, Charles Freeland, Ryozo Himino, Miles Kahler, Alexandre Lamfalussy, John Lowen, Robert McCauley, Paul Van den Bergh, and an anonymous referee for their helpful comments. The views expressed by Claudio Borio are his own and not necessarily those of the BIS.

[3] Article 3 of the BIS Statutes.

end to reparations, central bank cooperation has been the main objective of the BIS.[4]

The 1935 BIS *Annual Report* asked: "Cooperation on what? With what objectives in view? How?"[5] With the insight of 130 years of history, this chapter tries to answer three questions: How did changing international monetary and financial conditions shape the targets and tools of central bank cooperation? What conditions determined its intensity? Did a structured organization, such as the BIS, make a difference?

This chapter will not discuss the *desirability* of cooperation. We focus primarily on the *process*, rather than the ultimate *outcomes* of cooperation, and we do so from a *positive* rather than *normative* perspective. In other words, while we fully recognize that cooperation based on the wrong "model" of how the economy works or on the wrong analysis of current and future conditions can have perverse effects, we do not make such assessments in the scope of our analysis. We are only interested in understanding what factors shape cooperation and in its immediate results. Thus, we consider cooperation *effective* simply to the extent that its *proximate* goals are achieved (e.g., supporting an exchange rate arrangement, reaching agreement on a set of prudential standards) and do not address the trickier question of whether those actions promote the ultimate goals (e.g., economic welfare more generally).[6] We define cooperation broadly to include both purposeful exchanges of information ("low-key" cooperation) and joint decisions and implementation ("high-profile" cooperation).[7]

---

[4] Article 3 of the current BIS Statutes, including also the ancillary missions of providing additional facilities for international financial operations and [acting] as trustee or agent in regard to international financial settlements.

[5] BIS, *5th Annual Report*, Basel, 13 May 1935, pp. 41–44.

[6] For example, central bank cooperation may have been effective in delaying the collapse of the Bretton Woods system, but whether the achievement of this proximate goal was, on balance, positive or negative for the world economy is a separate question – a question, in fact, about which a heated debate exists.

[7] In practice, exchange of information is critical and accounts for the lion's share of international cooperative efforts. The exchange is aimed at (a) developing a better

The chapter is divided into several sections. The first section outlines the main targets, tools, and determinants of central bank cooperation and their evolution over time. Against this backdrop, each of the subsequent sections broadly reflects a given set of conditions in the international monetary and financial arena. The second section deals with cooperation in the context of the pre-1914 "classical" gold standard. The third section traces developments from the wartime regime to the creation of the BIS. The fourth section covers the most uncooperative period in the history of the twentieth century (1931–45), marked by autarky, beggar-thy-neighbor policies, and open conflict. The fifth section is devoted to cooperation under the Bretton Woods system. The sixth section considers the years from about 1973 to the present, when the balance of the targets of cooperation shifted from monetary to financial stability. A final section summarizes the chapter's main findings and draws some general conclusions.

CENTRAL BANK COOPERATION OVER TIME: CHANGING TARGETS, TOOLS, AND INTENSITY

Central bank cooperation throughout history has ultimately been directed to ensuring monetary and financial stability. However, the conception of these objectives, the relationship between the two, the balance in their pursuit, and the tools used have evolved over time, reflecting changes in the monetary and financial environment as well as in the

---

understanding of different points of view (e.g., concerning the "model" of the economy, other constraints on decisions, preferences, intentions, etc.) and/or (b) developing a convergence of viewpoints on the link between policy actions and outcomes (e.g., about the model of the economy, prevailing and prospective economic conditions, etc.). This definition is broader than the one typically used in the international relations literature, where what is envisaged is some form of coordination of actions in a game theoretic context (see, for instance, Keohane's [1984] notion of "mutual adjustment," which is more akin to the concept of policy coordination in the economic literature [e.g., Bryant 1987]). Our definition is closer to Truman's (2003) and Cooper's (2005).

political and intellectual climate. Accordingly, *depending on the circumstances and the intellectual perspective of the time*, we define "monetary stability" as either stability in an aggregate price level (index) or in the relative price of two units of account, that is, the exchange rate between national currencies or between a given currency and gold. We define "financial stability," in a narrow sense, as the avoidance of widespread defaults, typically associated with either banking or sovereign debt crises.

We shall see that changes in the operational conception of monetary and financial stability against the background of an evolving monetary and financial environment have deeply affected the targets and instruments of central bank cooperation (Table 1.1). Broadly speaking, the first 100-odd years covered in the chapter were characterized by the belief that a fixed exchange rate system was a desirable goal that underpinned the pursuit of domestic objectives, notably price stability. Cooperation therefore focused either on supporting or, when it broke down, on restoring that system. International liquidity packages were a prominent instrument in this context. During the gold standard period, international cooperation aimed at financial stability was not easy to disentangle from cooperation in pursuit of monetary stability as conceived at the time, as banking or external debt crises could threaten convertibility that was seen to underpin both. Without a prudential apparatus in place, international cooperation primarily took the form of liquidity assistance to support convertibility. By contrast, in the Bretton Woods period, financial repression tended to keep overt financial instability in check, obviating the need for international cooperation in this area. After 1973, with floating exchange rates and fully fiat money regimes, the pursuit of domestic price stability came to be increasingly regarded as a task that individual central banks could and should perform outside of international cooperation (except as far as the exchange of information was concerned). By contrast, as financial liberalization gathered momentum, cooperation was seen as crucial in promoting financial stability. In addition to international emergency liquidity packages aimed at emerging market

Table 1.1: *Regimes, targets, and tools of cooperation*

	Gold standard	Bretton Woods	Post-Bretton Woods
Regime Characteristics			
Monetary regime	– Gold convertibility as ultimate constraint (on countries and overall system)	– Fixed but adjustable exchange rates – Gold as (soft) constraint on overall system	– Unrestricted fiat money
Financial regime	– Liberalized financial markets – No (limited) prudential regulatory apparatus in place	– Financial repression (administrative controls)	– Progressive liberalization – Prudential regulation in place
Conceptions and Experience			
Monetary stability	– Identified with gold convertibility – Approximate price stability (until Great Depression)	– Increasingly identified with price stability – Seen as consistent with fixed exchange rates until late 1960s	– Identified with price stability – After the Great Inflation, global disinflation
Financial stability	– Financial instability can threaten convertibility – Financial instability not uncommon (especially at the periphery)	– Financial repression keeps overt financial instability in check	– Reemergence of financial instability

Targets of cooperation	– Maintaining gold convertibility	– Reestablishing conditions for current account convertibility – Sustaining fixed exchange rates	– Price stability seen as a domestic affair (except in Europe) – Financial stability gains ground
Tools of cooperation*	– Emergency liquidity lending	– Emergency liquidity lending – Gold Pool	– (Sporadic) foreign exchange intervention – Emergency liquidity lending (to EMEs**) – Developing codes and standards (banking, payment, and settlement systems) – Strengthening market information

* Other than exchanges of information ("low-key" cooperation).
** Emerging market economies.

countries in distress, the major innovation was the joint development and acceptance of codes and standards aimed at strengthening the global financial infrastructure through so-called "soft laws", especially in the prudential regulatory field.

Throughout the past 130-odd years, international financial cooperation was first and foremost the government's business. Central banks played a larger or smaller role according to their room for maneuver in the international arena. As the chapter focuses on cooperation among central banks rather than overall financial diplomacy, it is useful to try to pin down what factors influenced the degree of involvement of central banks in the overall game of financial cooperation (or lack thereof).

One can think of the intensity of central bank cooperation as varying over time according to three main factors: (1) the overall conditions in international relations; (2) the prestige enjoyed by central banks with the public at large, which also affects their institutional relationship with the political authorities (i.e., the allocation of tasks in monetary policymaking, including provisions for central bank independence); and (3) the technical nature of the problems requiring cooperation. Table 1.2 provides our subjective assessment of the varying strength of each of these three factors, resulting in an overall ranking by subperiods of the intensity of central bank cooperation, as described in the main sections of the chapter.

International Relations

Needless to say, international financial diplomacy was always dictated and largely run by governments as part of their foreign policy. Over the period covered in this chapter, the state of international relations varied enormously from war (1914–18 and 1939–45), to competitive nationalism (1873–1913), to confrontational unilateralism (1918–39), to various degrees of cooperative multilateralism within the so-called Western world

Table 1.2: *Intensity of Central Bank Cooperation*

Period	International relations	Prestige and independence of central banks	Technicality of issues requiring cooperation	Overall intensity of cooperation (total score/3)
	(1)	(2)	(3)	(4)
1870s–1913	2	2	3	2.33
1920s	1	3	4	2.67
1930s	0	1	1	0.67
1950s	4*	2	2	2.67
1959–73	3*	3	4	3.33
1973–mid-1980s	3*	2	4	3.00
Mid-1980s–2005	3	4	4	3.67

Note: All rankings on a scale of 0–4.
* "Western world" only.

(1945–2000). In most cases, central bank diplomacy closely mirrored governments' foreign policy, central bank governors being, after all, high-ranking civil servants. In the few instances when central bankers exercised a degree of autonomy in the international arena – as in the case of the European Economic Community (EEC) Governors in the 1960s – they were still strongly conditioned by the overall state of international relations. The notion, sometimes expressed at the BIS meetings, that the governors in Basel could be free from political "interference" was to a large extent an illusion.

Prestige and Independence of Central Banks

Central banks were never terribly popular with the public at large. Knowledge of their arcane tasks was limited even among the most educated members of the public. Similarly, "banks" have been quite unpopular with ordinary citizens ever since the Middle Ages. In this context, however, the prestige of central bankers varied considerably over time, depending on how well they seemed to deliver monetary and financial stability. The overall standing of central banks with public opinion affected their relationship with governments and therefore the latter's willingness to allow central bankers discretional powers in financial diplomacy.

Technicalities Involved in Cooperation

Naturally, the more technical the issue calling for cooperation (and the more special the central bank expertise), the greater the scope for central bank cooperation. Other things equal, these conditions tend to channel international cooperation through central banks by leveraging their expertise. They can also provide central banks with a greater degree of discretion in pursuit of that cooperation. Accordingly, central banks played a larger role when cooperation required keeping the exchange rate within the gold points, engineering complex currency swaps, and agreeing on supervisory standards.

Table 1.2 contains our own subjective appreciation (on a 0–4 scale) of the weight of the three above-mentioned factors in explaining the overall intensity of central bank cooperation over seven relevant subperiods into which the time spans covered in the chapter can be conveniently divided.

Nationalism strongly affected international relations before 1914; the scars of the war and of the peace treaty strained them further in the 1920s. Tension was increased by the Great Depression, making the 1930s the most confrontational peacetime decade. By contrast, "consensual American hegemony" (Maier 1988) made the 1950s possibly the decade of smoother international relations within the Western world. As American leadership lost ground from the 1960s onward, international relations became less harmonious; nevertheless, cooperation remained at a much more intense level than at any time before 1939. The chapter also deals with the peculiar type of international cooperation that existed among the allied powers during World War I and, in an implicit way, even among enemy central banks during the Second World War.

Before 1914, central banks were relatively little known to the public and quite strongly dependent on governments as far as their international operations were concerned (e.g., emergency lending to a foreign central bank was a highly sensitive political matter). In the 1920s, central banks gained power and prestige, as well as a higher degree of independence, owing to their role in the restoration of gold convertibility. With the Great Depression central banks everywhere lost prestige, as public opinion associated "bankers and financiers" at large with the debacle. Responsibility for monetary policy was shifted to the treasuries; in some cases, central banks became little more than dignified government departments (the German Reichsbank representing an extreme case in point). To be sure, in the 1930s many central banks were given new regulatory and supervisory responsibilities (Allen 1938). But these did not have a significant impact on international cooperation until half a century later. With their contribution to postwar reconstruction, in the 1950s European central banks slowly began to refurbish their public image. By the 1960s they had regained prestige and, in several cases, a degree of *de facto* autonomy from their respective governments. While key decisions in support of Bretton Woods required government direction and approval, the fact that central banks and governments generally agreed on the objective to be pursued – maintaining the system afloat – made the degree of independence less relevant. After the loss of prestige associated with the Great Inflation phase, starting in the mid-1980s central banks slowly regained a high standing, as their efforts to bring inflation under control bore fruit. From the 1990s, this was progressively enshrined in greater and more formal central bank independence. If, paradoxically, this autonomy and focus on domestic price stability at times proved inconsistent with efforts to implement international cooperation on exchange rates, it was valuable in the international cooperative efforts undertaken in the field of prudential regulation.

As for the degree of technicality involved in the matters requiring cooperation, Norman believed that central banks were the sole repository of the sophisticated techniques required to manage the international gold standard (Toniolo 2005: 163). Thus, contrary to textbook assumptions, at the day-to-day operational level, the actual running of the pre-1914 system did not rest on adherence to simple mechanical rules. The arcane subtleties of managing exchange rates within the gold points, nurturing market expectations, maintaining a high level of reserves as required by politicians and public opinion alike, and sterilizing gold inflows were all the exclusive domain of central bankers. International cooperation to keep the system viable could only rest on their technical expertise. An even higher degree of technical sophistication was probably required in the 1920s, when the reinstatement of the gold standard was the main task of cooperation. In the 1950s, cooperation for multilateral settlements called for a payments network and a clearinghouse technology developed at the BIS, but required little of the typical financial and monetary expertise of central banks. After 1958, with current account convertibility and the demand for financial engineering to prop up the dollar and the pound, the technical expertise of central banks again proved invaluable, for instance, in coordinating currency swaps and in the management of two separate gold markets. International cooperation in prudential regulation and the development of "soft laws" that marked the period from the mid-1970s onward was also characterized by a high degree of technical content, which central banks derived from their intimate knowledge of national banking systems, on which international convergence of prudential standards and rules could be based.

An unweighted average of the scores given to the three factors affecting central bank cooperation yields an overall ranking of the seven subperiods according to the intensity of cooperation, which reached its highest points in the years from 1958 onward and its lowest in the 1930s.

We next describe in some detail central bank cooperation from the mid-1870s to the present.

COOPERATION UNDER THE CLASSICAL GOLD STANDARD

With the Reichsbank's commitment to convert its notes into gold in 1876, the yellow metal became the unchallenged monetary standard of the developed "core" of the world economy. For the following forty-odd years, until the outbreak of World War I in 1914, the "classical gold standard" provided the background for a relatively efficient and stable system of international payments, in an epoch of rapidly expanding commodity trade, record-high labor migration, and free and growing capital mobility, often called the "first globalization."

Under the classical gold standard, convertibility was seen as the single anchor that underpinned both monetary and financial stability. On the one hand, gold convertibility was identified with monetary stability and thought to deliver stable prices, at last over medium- to long-term horizons.[8] On the other hand, the convertibility constraint would give way or threaten to do so at times of financial instability. Thus, in the context of liberalized financial markets with few or no prudential regulatory constraints, a single tool, the regulation of the supply of liquidity and of its price by central banks, was seen as underpinning the pursuit of both objectives.

Economic historians disagree on the extent of central bank emergency cooperation during the classical gold standard and on its usefulness for the viability of the system (e.g., Eichengreen 1992, 1995; Gallarotti 1995; Flandreau 1997). They do agree, however, that whatever cooperation did occur was carried out on a strict bilateral basis and was undoubtedly less intense than in the years following 1914.

The fact that central bank cooperation was limited and bilateral is partly explained by the strongly nationalist character of international

---

[8] The ultimate goal, however, was seen as convertibility rather price stability *per se*, itself subordinate to convertibility (e.g., Goodhart 1992). It was only subsequently, mainly following the Great Depression, that the objective of price stability came properly into its own in the policy world (e.g., De Kock 1974).

27

relations (which, for instance, made governments reluctant to lose gold reserves in favor of would-be enemy countries) and by the fact that international financial relations were more the domain of governments than of central banks, which were privately owned, if tightly supervised, institutions.

Managing the gold standard was a fairly complex technical matter, but international cooperation was not considered of paramount importance for the stability of the system.[9] If there was an understanding of the gold standard as an international public good, it underpinned emergency cooperation only: there was little grasp, except by some practitioners and non-mainstream economists, of the usefulness of day-to-day cooperation in technical matters such as payments technology. On the other hand, the economic environment made maintaining convertibility easier before 1914 than at later times. The balance of payments adjusted smoothly to domestic monetary policy thanks to labor and product market flexibility. Unrestricted international capital mobility produced the expected stabilizing flows and London's financial hegemony gave it some *de facto* coordinating powers. More important still, the perceived political costs of maintaining gold convertibility were relatively small for three main reasons. First, the system delivered (or was believed to deliver) price stability and growth. Second, given flexible markets, the output and employment trade-offs entailed by the commitment to the gold standard were relatively contained and therefore socially acceptable. Finally, suffrage limitations and the weakness of workers' organizations made it politically affordable for governments to guarantee gold convertibility, a priority for the upper and middle classes, even at the cost of some unemployment (Eichengreen 1992, 1996).

---

[9] There is, of course, considerable debate about what exactly those rules were and how closely they were followed. See, in particular, Bloomfield (1959) and, for a broader discussion, the articles in Eichengreen (1985).

Even among core countries, however, the classical gold standard did not assure continuous domestic financial stability and this in turn led to instances when cooperation did take place. Occasionally, contagious banking crises did occur (e.g., Kindleberger 1996). In the most severe instances – for example, in 1890 and 1907 – they resulted in emergency lending among banks of issue. In 1890, the drain on the reserves of the Bank of England seemed to be putting the gold standard at risk and the central banks of France and Russia stepped in by offering London a gold swap large enough to reverse market expectations about the adequacy of the Bank of England's gold reserves (Clapham 1944; De Cecco 1974). In 1906 the Bank of France purchased an extremely large amount of sterling-denominated bills to avoid a sharp increase in the London bank rate in response to a gold outflow from England to the United States. Again, in 1907, both the Bank of France and the Reichsbank allowed their reserves to decline, moving gold to London to finance England's transfer of gold to the United States (Eichengreen 1992). Even though their relevance is played down by some scholars (Flandreau 1997), these episodes indicate that some central bank cooperation took place when the survival of the fixed rate system was at stake.

This reluctance to cooperate except in circumstances when the gold standard was threatened also explains why cooperation to address instability at the periphery was even rarer. In contrast to the experience of core countries, at the periphery the gold standard did not deliver stability (Bordo and Flandreau 2001), and banking and exchange rate crises were not infrequent (Bordo et al. 2001).

To sum up: under the gold standard, cooperation took place only in emergencies and on a bilateral basis. The political and intellectual legitimacy of the gold standard, the relatively minor adjustment costs, and the character of nineteenth-century democracy all provided incentives for pursuing exchange rate stability by simple domestic adherence to the "rules of the game."

It must be added that international relations based on power politics stressed the need for a high level of metal reserves (except in London), inducing central banks of surplus countries to sterilize gold inflows – an uncooperative behavior that increased the adjustment cost of those in deficit. The observation that asymmetric adjustment was unnecessarily costly and a threat to international monetary stability drove proposals for more systematic forms of central bank cooperation.

In 1892 Julius Wolff, a professor at the University of Breslau, submitted a project at the Brussels international monetary conference for the creation of an international currency, to be used for emergency lending to central banks, backed by gold reserves contributed by the central banks themselves, and issued by a joint institution based in a neutral country. Similar suggestions, including the creation of an international central bank located in Berne, Switzerland, were made by several others. But it was Luigi Luzzatti who gave these ideas more precise shape and wider publicity. He observed that the US financial problems of 1907 had created an international liquidity crisis (a "monetary famine" as he called it) from which the main central banks had tried to protect their respective markets, scrambling for gold through competitive interest rate increases and other means. A "monetary war" of this kind was – according to Luzzatti – both detrimental and unnecessary: "peace" could be achieved through "cordial cooperation" in supplying gold to illiquid central banks. He argued that lending among monetary authorities should become the norm, rather than being occasional and emergency-driven. Central banks – Luzzatti argued – lent to each other out of their long-term self-interest, but politics could get in the way of a clear vision of economic self-interest. Hence the need for an international body, to be set up in normal circumstances, in order to provide for emergencies in a technical, apolitical way.[10] Among

---

[10] "There is no absolute remedy for financial crises – Luzzatti wrote – that are the consequence of human weakness, greed and imperfect forecasting. (. . .) What I simply ask for are agreements among experts capable of eliminating from inevitable crises

the several favorable reactions to Luzzatti's ideas was that of George B. Cortelyou, the US Treasury secretary, who announced his intention of convening a European conference of central banks to better specify and implement Luzzatti's proposals (Toniolo 2005: 20–22).

COOPERATION IN WAR, MONETARY STABILIZATIONS, AND THE CREATION OF THE BIS

The First World War led to the abandonment of the gold standard and the imposition of exchange controls. Once the war was over, countries sought at varying paces to reestablish the previous order, sometimes after having experienced traumatic bouts of inflation.

From the perspective of the broad objectives and instruments of cooperation, the period did not represent a major break with the past. True, the experience with high inflation in some countries and with large excess gold reserves in the United States helped to develop notions of monetary stability more closely identified with domestic price stability than with convertibility.[11] But the objective of convertibility remained paramount. And in the absence of a well-established regulatory framework, both monetary and financial stability were primarily pursued through a similar set of instruments, namely the provision of liquidity, domestically and internationally.

What did change, and markedly, was the global constellation of economic and political constraints. In particular, the German reparations problem loomed large throughout the period. In contrast to the classical

---

those elements that are due to poor organization of the banks of issue and treasuries or to the lack of agreements for mutual self-interested gold lending." See Luzzatti, L. (11 December 1907), article in the *Neue Freie Presse*. See also Istituto Veneto di Scienze, Lettere e Arti, Venice, Archivio Luigi Luzzatti, b. 154, fasc. III, sez. B.

[11] See, for instance, Laidler 1999 for an interesting discussion of the monetary policy debates in the United States at the time. See also De Kock (1974) for a discussion of the evolving notion of monetary stability.

gold standard phase, the prospect of a potential default in a core country profoundly shaped the evolution of events, the forms of cooperation, and their success or failure. It was also the factor that, surprisingly perhaps, would be at the root of the creation of an institutionalized vehicle of cooperation for central banks, the Bank for International Settlements (BIS).

In what follows, we consider sequentially the forms of central bank cooperation during the wartime period, those during the subsequent years, and the specific factors leading to the establishment of the BIS.

Wartime

One might think that World War I made central bank cooperation both unnecessary and infeasible. After all, in the summer of 1914 central banks all over Europe suspended gold payments, putting an end to the classical gold standard. A fiat money monetary regime was adopted by all belligerent countries and most neutrals. In financing military expenditure, each country found its own mix of tax, debt, and printing press. The more or less extensive use of the printing press depended on social and economic conditions specific to each country. Against this backdrop, one would think that no cooperation among central banks was necessary and that no incentive existed for it.

In fact, the opposite is true: total war made financial cooperation unavoidable. Cooperation largely took the form of interallied lending, but did not stop there. As public opinion – friendly, enemy, and neutral – took the rate of exchange as a good predictor of military success and failure, exchange rate pegging policies became part of the military effort. Thus, a strong incentive existed for interallied cooperation in the foreign exchange markets. It was during the war that central banks established standing bilateral agreements for the first time. The Governors of the central banks of England and France even set up a direct telegraph line between their respective offices to provide swift, regular communication.

Governor Benjamin Strong of the New York Fed spent a long time in Europe in order to promote formal links between his bank, London, and Paris, while the Bank of Italy sent a permanent representative to New York (Toniolo 2005: 16–17).

As soon as the wartime conditions ceased, however, so did the incentives to maintain allied financial solidarity and the cooperation that had gone with it.

Toward the New Gold Standard

There was a broad consensus after the war on the desirability of a return to gold convertibility. But its practical implementation was difficult. A return to the prewar gold parity would have spelled macroeconomic disaster for any continental European country, given the intervening inflation. At the same time, the distributional implications involved in choosing a new parity were politically explosive. Government assistance in the transition from a wartime to a peacetime economy was hardly consistent with the fiscal and monetary policies needed to convince the markets of a credible gold standard commitment. Internationally, the problems of debts and reparations had to be solved in order to recreate a stable system of international payments.

In principle, therefore, cooperation looked attractive in the postwar conditions; indeed, more lip service was paid to central bank cooperation than had been the case before 1914. In 1921, Norman issued a *manifesto* outlining four principles of central banking: independence from national governments; separation from commercial banks; banking supervision; and cooperation. He saw the latter as "confidential interchange of information and opinion," the conduct of foreign banking operations through the central bank of the country concerned, and the mutual extension of such facilities as "the custody of gold, monies and securities and the discount of approved bills of exchange" (Sayers 1976). At the 1922 Genoa conference, central banking was the subject of profound debates by economic experts, academics, and central and private bankers. A resolution was passed containing the first official international recognition of the desirability of formal cooperation among central banks.

In spite of the obvious incentives to cooperate, strained international relations stood in the way. The war and its settlement had left in their wake a long list of unresolved issues, old and new conflicts of interest – not least among allies – incomprehension, new nationalisms and old ethnic rivalries, and deeply rooted desires for revenge. As observed by Eichengreen (1992), "so long as governments were at loggerheads, it was unlikely that national central banks could successfully collaborate."

Nevertheless, in the 1920s cooperation among central banks was more explicit than it had been before 1914 for three main reasons. First, in many countries, the central bank's prestige had been enhanced by the contribution made to the war effort, while at the same time the prospect of a return to gold convertibility gave back to central banks the aura of technical wizardry they had enjoyed before 1914. Second, the backing of the community of central banks, in the form of syndicated hard-currency loans, was the seal of approval, awaited by the markets, of the sustainability of a country's pledge to convertibility. Finally, contrary to pre-1914, cooperation was tirelessly preached and promoted (understandably primarily *pro domo sua*) by the heads of the two leading central banks: Montagu Norman of the Bank of England and Benjamin Strong of the Federal Reserve Bank of New York.

The Creation of the BIS

The BIS, as the organization for central bank cooperation, owes its existence to German reparations. In the late 1920s a short window of opportunity existed to try to provide a stable solution to a problem that had poisoned international relations since 1919. The conferences of Paris, The Hague, and Baden Baden, which gave birth to the BIS, are a good example of how economic cooperation may develop out of partly converging interests when the international political environment is not poisoned by unbridgeable divisions.

The main driving force behind the creation of an "international bank," as part of a treaty on reparations, was the so-called commercialization of the reparation payments, whereby part of the German debt would be issued in the form of long-term bonds to be subscribed by international private banks and financial houses. Governments were keen on receiving lump sums up front rather than payments over a very long period of time, while private bankers saw a major business opportunity in underwriting and managing the operation. The German government, for its part, considered it essential that a mechanism be found for a good portion of the reparation payments to be reinvested in Germany.[12]

Given that obligations of sovereign states are notoriously difficult to enforce, the creation of an international organization such as the BIS was seen as potentially useful in improving the chances of future payments enforcement (Simmons 1993). It could do so, for instance, by overcoming information asymmetries about economic and policy conditions that might affect the regular flow of payments and by linking the fulfillment of the debtor's obligations to various incentives, such as the reinvestment in Germany of part of the proceeds from payments of interest and principal. At the same time, such an international institution, as the bondholder's trustee, could facilitate collective creditors' actions in case of default. More generally, central bank cooperation was also seen as conducive to a more stable international monetary environment, which would facilitate the fulfillment of both lenders' and borrowers' contractual obligations.

It is against this background of converging interests that central bankers, led by Montagu Norman, also made the BIS an instrument of their technical cooperation and independence.

---

[12] A large literature exists on the origins of the BIS; for recent contributions, see Simmons (1993), Baffi (2002), and Toniolo (2005: 33–60).

Claudio Borio and Gianni Toniolo

THE FAILURE OF COOPERATION (1931–45)

In the summer of 1930 when the BIS began to operate, the Great Depression was rapidly approaching. Soon afterward, a severe contraction in output and prices came to be intertwined with a succession of major banking crises, of which the failure of Creditanstalt in Austria was just the first, as well as sovereign defaults. The gold standard progressively disintegrated and countries retreated into autarky. In the meantime, international relations suffered continuous blows and became increasingly strained until the time when they would be consigned only to the language of arms during World War II.

Before central bank cooperation was to progressively atrophy, although never quite disappear, in the early 1930s, its main objectives and tools remained those developed during the gold standard era, that is, the provision of liquidity, domestically or internationally, in the attempt to prop up the system. Admittedly, the widespread banking crises led to the establishment of elaborate domestic regulatory and supervisory frameworks, with central banks often in charge (Allen 1938). But in contrast to what would occur later in the century, they did not give rise to international cooperative efforts, given the inimical conditions of the time. And with the final abandonment of the gold standard, monetary stability became more firmly identified with price stability. This meant that, for the first time, monetary and financial stability became clearly distinct goals, both conceptually and operationally.

For our purposes, when considering central bank cooperation in the new context of the BIS, the period can best be divided into three parts: the Great Depression, autarky, and war.

The Great Depression (1931–33)

The international lending to Austria, Germany, and Hungary in 1931 was the first multilateral international action undertaken in response to a financial crisis. Fear of contagion and of a German default on public and private debt provided the rationale for the scheme, which, however, failed. Among the reasons for the failure, scholars cite poor understanding of the situation and political conditionality, as well as the inadequate timing and size of the loans (e.g., Kindleberger 1987). Central banks acted both individually and through the BIS, their recently created cooperative agent.

The creation of the BIS had somehow produced new expectations about collective action by central banks: when Spain contemplated the convertibility of the peseta, it approached Basel, rather than London and Paris individually, for advice and a possible loan. Likewise, as soon as Creditanstalt's predicaments became known, the BIS was involved in studying the Austrian situation and played a role of its own in the syndicated central bank loan that followed. It also advised on, and participated in, lending to Germany. Thus, the new multilateral player was drawn into the game in its own right.

Autarky (1933–39)

There are four main reasons why, in the 1930s, central bank cooperation at the BIS was reduced to research and exchange of information: strained political and economic international relations; a destructured international monetary system; diminished central bank power and prestige; and political (and intellectual) disagreement on how to reform the system of international payments.

In spite of their division between gold standard and non-gold standard countries and of the fact that what little cooperation existed took place on a strictly bilateral basis, central bankers continued to appreciate the services provided by the BIS. They kept meeting regularly in Basel, and taking advantage of the Bank for settling payments and making gold transfers. Besides providing those services, the BIS stepped up the collection of statistics, its monetary research, and the training of central bank staff. Moreover, it elaborated and disseminated its own ideas about reforming the gold standard (it would not consider floating rates as a permanent option).

Can regular, personal intercourse and day-to-day technical cooperation be dismissed as irrelevant in the autarkic context of the 1930s? The answer depends on expectations. If one believes that international multilateral cooperation was hardly natural in the first part of the twentieth century, then even the minor exception to the rule provided by the BIS might be seen as a material development. This is particularly true if one takes a longer-term perspective. Effective institutions take time to develop. Had the BIS suffered the fate of other interwar international organizations, it would not have been available for central bankers after the war, when more favorable conditions for multilateral cooperation prevailed.

War (1939–45)

Oddly enough, one can plausibly speak of wartime low-key cooperation among BIS central banks of enemy countries. As they shared an interest in keeping the BIS alive, central banks cooperated, even against the wishes of their own governments, to create the conditions for the BIS to survive the war. Central banks believed that the expertise, networking, and assets of the BIS would turn out to be useful in the eventual reconstruction of the international monetary system, in which they hoped to play a substantial role. They all also tacitly agreed on the desirability, even in wartime, of an observation post on international monetary conditions, accessible to all, and of a place where informal, tenuous links might be maintained even among belligerents. This was, after all, the reason why both sides accepted the existence of neutral countries even in a context of total, unrestrained conflict.

In order to keep the BIS alive during the war, central banks maintained open communication lines among themselves through neutral emissaries – a form of central bank diplomacy often frowned upon by their respective governments. As a result, the BIS was the only international organization to stay active during the war, trying to adhere to a self-imposed neutrality code. This, however, did not prevent it from making considerable blunders (Toniolo 2005).

ENHANCED CENTRAL BANK COOPERATION (1950–73)

The BIS emerged from the war a small institution with apparently no or only a meager future ahead. Owing to a mix of misinformation and truly objectionable aspects of its wartime conduct, the Basel institution was strongly opposed by the American Treasury and frowned upon in influential British circles (Toniolo 2005). The United States fought hard at Bretton Woods for the liquidation of the old "International Bank," which they saw as compromised with the past, too European in outlook and, in any event, made irrelevant by the creation of the new twin institutions, the International Monetary Fund (IMF) and the World Bank. Central banks, with the support of Lord John Maynard Keynes and thanks to the complex legal setting put in place in 1929–30, succeeded in fending off the assault on the BIS but were themselves too busy with reconstruction to make much use of their cooperative tool in the immediate postwar years. Moreover, economic (including monetary) policy was by then in the hands of governments, with central banks in many countries confined to the role of high-profile departments of the treasury. Little central bank cooperation, therefore, took place in the second half of the 1940s. Nevertheless, the body of international civil servants based in Basel took care of settling the problems inherited from the war (of paramount importance was the restitution of looted gold), reviving the BIS's banking activities and strengthening its balance sheet, thus preparing for future central bank cooperation.

The monetary and financial environment in which the BIS would thereafter support central bank cooperation was profoundly different from anything seen since its inception. On the monetary side, Bretton Woods saw the establishment of a fixed but adjustable global exchange rate regime, with gold convertibility a tenuous constraint for a system that *de facto* evolved into a dollar standard. On the financial side, the system allowed for controls on foreign exchange transactions and on capital flows, so as to retain autonomy for domestic macroeconomic policies. Domestically, these controls were generally complemented by a complex web of regulations/constraints designed to reduce cost of funding for governments, to allocate credit, and to operate monetary policy. The overall objective was to combine progressive trade liberalization with stable exchange rates, so as to avoid the perceived "chaotic experience" of the interwar years, while at the same time allowing national policies to try to achieve full employment. Exchange rate parities were to be adjusted only in cases of fundamental disequilibrium.

In this environment, central bank cooperation largely focused, initially, on reestablishing the conditions for international convertibility of currencies and, subsequently, on supporting the system once it came under strain. Despite their loss of formal independence, thanks to their technical expertise and operational capabilities over time central banks regained a significant degree of influence, even though the ultimate policy decisions rested with treasuries. For the rest, in a context of domestic financial repression and constraints on external capital flows, financial stability concerns did not figure prominently on the policy agenda. The prudential framework put in place in the 1930s would continue to remain largely dormant for a while longer.

The discussion of the role of the BIS during this period is best conducted under three headings: its support for intra-European payments on the road to currency convertibility; the efforts to keep Bretton Woods afloat through coordinated international lending and the creation of a gold pool; and the initial steps taken to address emerging concerns about the rapid growth of the eurocurrency markets.

Technical Skills at the Service of Cooperation

It was to a large extent American aid, particularly the Marshall Plan, that created the incentives for postwar European cooperation. The Organisation for European Economic Co-operation (OEEC) was set up in Paris as a forum for discussion and coordination of the use of American grants and loans. Soon, however, its scope was broadened, as it became clear that one of the main postwar economic problems concerned the revival of Europe's international trade. Given the low level of European gold and dollar reserves, Europe's trade deficits with the United States could be financed only with American credit. This was the main economic purpose of the Marshall Plan. But intra-European trade also needed reviving. This meant the gradual dismantling of the myriad of barriers to trade erected from the early 1930s onward. As a precondition for freer trade, the intricate system of bilateral (basically barter) payment agreements had to be relaxed. Free convertibility of European currencies into each other and the dollar, while explicitly set as a policy target, was deemed to be premature.[13] A viable alternative seemed to be the creation of a managed system of intra-European settlements (basically an international clearinghouse).

The September 1949 devaluation of the pound and the realignment of the other main currencies were conducted in a coordinated fashion, reflecting the new postwar cooperative mood, and moved exchange rates closer to the purchasing power parity of European currencies. The stage was thus set for trade liberalization and a form of multilateral settlement. These were bold political moves for European governments to make, as long years of tight bureaucratic controls on trade and foreign exchange had created well-entrenched vested interests. The matter, therefore,

---

[13] Eichengreen (1993) believes that conditions for convertibility existed in the early 1950s – an opinion that was quietly shared in Basel at the time.

stood firmly in the hands of governments, whose representatives met at the OEEC. Central banks were required to provide the technical backing.

The European Payments Union (EPU), created in September 1950 by eighteen countries, was the cooperative tool for introducing intra-European multilateral settlements. Within the EPU, bilateral balances were automatically offset, so that each country had one single balance, debtor or creditor, toward the EPU rather than toward its individual trading partners. At the same time, the EPU extended credits to debtor countries, drawing from a fund created by surplus balances and by an initial allocation of dollars from the US Treasury.

The BIS was appointed agent for the EPU, in charge of managing multilateral settlements. The Bank had by then accumulated unrivaled experience in performing trustee and agent functions, a non-negligible part of its original mission. It had also established a system for cross-reporting by central banks of their own payment balances, which provided the technical basis for the EPU network. Thus, besides again acting as a well-established forum for confidential exchanges among central bankers from the EPU countries, the BIS made a significant technical contribution to the success of the scheme.

The EPU was one of the great success stories in international monetary cooperation. Its aim was fully realized with the introduction of current account convertibility for European currencies, at fixed dollar-gold parities, at the end of 1958. The reasons for this success reside mostly in the political climate of the decade, underpinned by the strong American stance in favor of multilateral Atlantic and European cooperation.

It is in this climate that, for the first time since 1930, the United States took a very positive view of the BIS. M. S. Szymczak, a Federal Reserve Board Governor, argued that the BIS was "likely to provide the most practicable way in which central bankers of the 'Atlantic community' could find regular occasions for informal discussions on matters that concern them as members of the community" (Toniolo 2005). The return of the

Americans to Basel considerably enhanced the prospects for cooperation at the institution.

Keeping Bretton Woods Afloat

With the introduction of current account currency convertibility at the beginning of 1959, the postwar international monetary system appeared to be set on a steady state based on fixed dollar exchange rates, a gold-dollar anchor, multilateral organizations intended both to regulate and to facilitate the operation of the system, and rules for parity adjustment.

Even before convertibility was formally introduced, experts believed that international monetary cooperation should be stepped up after its introduction. A report by the Federal Reserve Bank of New York argued that the "Paris set-up" (i.e., the OEEC) was created to deal with "an inconvertible world whereas Basel was an ideal set-up for a convertible world." In a letter to New York Fed President Allan Sproul, Szymczak wrote: "From the point of view of finance the arguments for its existence are not so cogent, but as a vehicle for providing monthly gatherings of central bank governors, and others, the arguments for it are overwhelming. The BIS is perhaps the most effective vehicle of cooperation amongst central banks in the world today."[14]

In the 1960s a large number of international monetary decisions originated at the "Basel Club." At the informal governors' meetings, matters were discussed and often decisions made (to be subsequently formalized at official meetings). The Gold Pool, the Sterling Group Arrangements, the IMF General Arrangements to Borrow (GAB), and the G10 multilateral surveillance exercise all originated at the Basel Club, which also played a role in helping to shape the reform of the international monetary system. The BIS supported an increasing number of official and

---

[14] Letter from Szymczak to Allan Sproul, 11 September 1950, quoted in Toniolo (2005: 320).

semiofficial "groups," sometimes made up of both government and central bank officials, through secretariat services and analytical background work. Since the matters addressed by these groups often overlapped, as did participation, Basel also provided informal coordination among them. Thus, the Basel Club came to be an active locus of financial diplomacy.

According to Bank of Italy Governor Guido Carli, in the 1960s the BIS played the dual role of decision-maker and executive organ. Decisions were made "by the group who met on the afternoon and evening of the day before the Board official meeting." The operative side consisted in executing those decisions, subject to government approval, for instance, in the case of the support to the pound and the Gold Pool (BIS 1980).

There are many reasons why the 1960s turned out to be years of intense central bank cooperation at the BIS. First, the very nature of the international monetary set-up (including the implicit political pact upon which it was based) required constant, almost day-by-day coordinated intervention on the currency and gold markets. Second, with the resumption of convertibility, the role and prestige of central banks was enhanced, not least because of the high skill content of monetary policymaking required by the new environment. Third, the decision-making processes at the larger multilateral institutions (the IMF and World Bank) were often more cumbersome. Finally, the BIS was host to the representatives of the countries that then mattered for international policymaking (soon nicknamed the G10), within a setting that provided confidentiality, technical support and, when needed, the backing of independent financial weaponry.

We now turn to a brief description of the main central bank cooperative efforts undertaken in the 1960s.

Support for the Dollar

Soon after the introduction of current account convertibility, the US government stepped up bilateral economic diplomacy aimed at persuading the governments of the European surplus countries to fulfill their responsibilities in the adjustment process. In particular, the Europeans were urged to avoid sterilization of dollar inflows, to liberalize imports and, most of all, to show their confidence in the system by steering clear of gold conversion. It soon appeared, however, that there was a limit to what bilateral diplomacy could achieve. The September 1960 annual meeting of the IMF registered concern about the dollar's exchange rate. Kennedy's election as US President, two months later, did little to reassure markets. It is in this context that the United States "rediscovered" the BIS, thirty years after its short-lived enthusiasm about the "International Bank." In January 1961, Alfred Hayes, President of the Federal Reserve Bank of New York, attended the governors' meeting in Basel for the first time.

In the following months (and years), both sides of the Atlantic came to terms with the notion that no drastic measures for a structural adjustment of the US balance of payments would be politically acceptable. Ruling out a "permanent solution" to the dollar-gold convertibility problem, all parties concerned felt it imperative to gain time and allow the system to remain viable for as long as possible. Gaining time basically meant exercising imagination on how best to "recycle" European surpluses by various forms of lending to the United States. To this end, Basel became the focal point for operational international coordinated action in support of the stability of exchange rates. The Federal Reserve Bank of New York participated regularly in the BIS monthly meetings, highlighting, as Coombs put it, "a shift to a low-key, cooperative search for the right answers" that shaped "the course of international financial cooperation for the [following] decade" (Coombs 1976). From the BIS perspective, Gilbert saw a "spirit of trust and cooperation" being established through the "expertise, frankness and concern for the problems and opinions of other countries" of people like Roosa and Coombs (Gilbert 1980).

The Gold Pool

For dollar-gold convertibility to be credible, it was essential that gold traded at the London free market close to the official price at which the

United States was committed to convert dollars into gold on demand from central banks. When in late 1960 the free market price of gold shot up by over 15 percent above the official price, it was first suggested at the BIS governors' meetings that a scheme should be created by central banks to buy and sell gold in the market in order to keep the free and official prices close to each other. The suggestion was at first dismissed, but the BIS began to monitor the London gold market closely.

In the autumn of 1961, as concerns about the free market gold price increased, the US secretary of the Treasury revived with the UK chancellor the idea of joint central bank operations on the London gold market. Discussions on the Gold Pool scheme were first conducted between the two governments but when the continental Europeans had to be brought on board, the Americans were easily convinced by the British to turn to Basel's multilateral venue. The BIS governors agreed to give the Gold Pool a try. Europe's central banks together matched a US contribution to a pool of gold made available for sales on the London gold market. The Bank of England acted as the Gold Pool's operative branch, with its operations being reviewed on the occasion of the BIS Board meetings. It is perhaps noteworthy that the BIS commanded sufficient communality of purpose and mutual trust for the scheme to be agreed there and then, without a formal written agreement.

As the market calmed, interventions were discontinued. At the same time, central banks agreed to continue to abstain from buying gold in the free market on an individual basis; the task was left to the Gold Pool itself, which would thus act also as a purchasing syndicate. The running of the Gold Pool settled into a routine pattern. The Bank of England reported on a monthly basis to a group of experts from the participating central banks, who met at the BIS at regular intervals. The BIS also provided secretariat services to the Gold Pool, feeding the group of experts with more complete and reliable statistical data on world gold production and consumption than had been previously available.

The Gold Pool is a clear example of multilateral cooperation facilitated by the existence of the BIS, which played a crucial role in both creating and supervising it. Until about 1965 the very existence of the Gold Pool contributed to keeping the free price of gold close to the official one. In fact, the Pool bought considerable amounts of gold, which was allocated *pro quota* to participating central banks. After 1965, however, sales far outweighed purchases. Participating central banks accumulated losses on their joint gold operations that they eventually felt unwilling to sustain. In 1967 France withdrew from the Gold Pool. In March 1968 the Gold Pool central banks announced that they would no longer supply gold to the free market but would only buy and sell the metal at the official price among themselves (Toniolo 2005: 421).

The Sterling Group Arrangements

Throughout the 1960s, the weakness of the pound sterling, the junior reserve currency in the system, remained an almost constant threat to exchange rate stability. As Gilbert put it: "Whenever sterling might be devalued, confidence in the dollar price of gold could be expected to evaporate and a large rise in the market demand for gold, as well as in central-bank conversions of dollars for gold at the US Treasury, could be anticipated" (Gilbert 1980: 135).

In 1961, following the deutsche mark (DM) revaluation, and again in 1963, the pound was hit by heavy sales. On both occasions it was supported by international lending arranged on a bilateral basis. When the pound again came under fire in 1964, the Bank of England sounded out the BIS governors at a Basel meeting about a joint support package. Speed and absence of conditionality suggested looking to Basel for assistance rather than going to the IMF (Toniolo 2005: 390). A $3 billion facility was granted by eight central banks, under the auspices of the BIS.[15]

---

[15] As noted by Hirsch (1965: 103), quoted in James (1996), "In twenty-four hours the central banks created more international liquidity with fewer questions asked than the

In 1966, a first Sterling Group Arrangement was finalized. It consisted of a line of credit opened to London by nine central banks and the BIS. The latter acted as principal for the group. The novelty of the arrangement was that it was not made in response to an emergency but rather created a permanent stabilizing buffer for sterling, justified by its role as reserve currency. On this occasion, the coordinating role of the BIS was again particularly in evidence.

After the 1967 devaluation of the pound, the Bank of England worked directly with the BIS to prepare the blueprint for a second Sterling Group Arrangement aimed at keeping the pound at the new fixed parity. In June 1968, a $2 billion "safety net facility" was finalized between the Bank of England and the BIS acting on behalf of twelve central banks. The facility consisted of foreign-currency swaps made available by the BIS to the Bank of England for a three-year period.

These are just the most relevant cases of multilateral central bank cooperation arranged at or through the BIS in the 1960s and aimed at maintaining the system of fixed exchange rates envisaged at Bretton Woods for as long as possible. After 1968, however, these efforts looked increasingly doomed to failure; the United States began a policy of "benign neglect" of the dollar and multilateral cooperation to prop up the system lost momentum.

The Emergence of the Eurocurrency Market

During the 1960s, European central bankers began to be concerned about the rapid growth of the so-called eurocurrency markets – largely dollar-denominated deposits held by banks outside of the United States, not least in London. At this time, the concerns focused primarily on the monetary policy implications of these markets, including the possible loss of monetary control and the fueling of speculative pressures on exchange

most expansionist Triffinite would ever suggest for the IMF." The episode is described in detail in Coombs (1976).

rates. The market was the clearest sign of how increased mobility of capital flows could potentially add to strains on the Bretton Woods system. There were, however, also budding questions about its impact on banking stability, given its largely unregulated nature – an interest that would become much more important after the end of the Bretton Woods era.

Central banks thus began to improve the statistical information about this hitherto largely unknown phenomenon by pooling the information available to individual countries at the BIS. In 1964, central banks presented to the G10 deputies a first report on "The Eurocurrency Market and the International Monetary System." At the time, central banks felt satisfied that the eurodollar threatened neither macro nor banking stability and only required closer monitoring, as "anything that grows by 25–40 per-cent per annum" would call for (Toniolo 2005: 459). In the following years, they quietly also intervened in the market to try to keep interest rates paid on eurodollar and domestic-currency deposits within a limited range. From the early 1970s, however, concerns about the eurocurrency market were frequently voiced in the press. Central banks refocused their interest on the issue and in April 1971 established the Standing Committee on the Euro-Currency Market. At the time, they also announced an agreement not to deposit their reserves in the market (McCauley 2005).

POST-BRETTON WOODS (1973–2005): FROM MONETARY TO FINANCIAL STABILITY

The collapse of Bretton Woods deeply affected central bank cooperation and, therefore, the life of the BIS. Floating rates and rapidly increasing international capital mobility influenced the objectives of cooperation, its forms and instruments, as well as its functional and geographical scope.

The objectives of cooperation shifted away from monetary stability toward financial stability. To be sure, neither central banks nor the BIS abandoned their involvement in foreign exchange matters. In particular, they played a significant role in the journey toward a single currency in Europe and a more peripheral one in the few instances of high-profile coordinated foreign exchange intervention. Exchanges of information on international and domestic monetary issues continued to take place and even intensified at the governors' meetings and other gatherings of experts in Basel. But the balance of BIS activities shifted toward safeguards against financial instability. This evolution gathered momentum with the passing of time, both reflecting and entailing a significant shift in the forms and instruments of cooperation. By the end of the century, the BIS had become one of the main players shaping the so-called new international financial architecture (Crockett 2002; White 2000).

The BIS continued to perform its core function of facilitator of low-key exchanges of information and views among central banks. But its decision-oriented activities shifted away from operational or "practical fire-fighting" (Baer 1999) to the design and implementation of policies. In this area, new high-level committees, notably the Basel Committee on Banking Supervision (BCBS) and the Committee on Payment and Settlement Systems (CPSS), played a major role. The process through which these codes and standards were developed and implemented represented an innovation on the previous instruments of international cooperation in the financial field. This is because these codes and standards were not the outcome of internationally legally binding agreements ("hard law") but were voluntarily implemented in national law and regulation, through a mixture of peer pressure and market forces, following informal international agreements among participants ("soft law")[16] (Giovanoli 2000; Crockett 2002; Giannini 2002).

---

[16] The definition of "soft law" used here is close to, but somewhat more specific than, the one sometimes used in international law. There, "soft law" sometimes has the general connotation of recommendations, guidelines, or principles that are not sufficiently specific to have legally binding force. Those recommendations, however, can be and often are issued as part of legally binding international agreements, such as treaties. The term here highlights the fact that the international agreement itself is not legally binding on the parties reaching it. On this, see, in particular, Hillgenberg (1999). An example

These developments also inevitably led the BIS to broaden its functional and geographical scope. Functionally, while owned by and working for central banks, the BIS gradually began to provide services for supervisory and regulatory authorities more generally. Geographically, the codes and standards elaborated by the Committees were adopted well beyond their member countries. And beginning in the early 1990s, the institution embarked on a major "outreach" effort designed to involve in its activities an increasing number of countries, implying significant changes in its governance structure. This marked the transformation of the BIS from what had generally been regarded as a European institution into a global one.

Why the Shift? The Evolving Backdrop to Cooperation

As in previous periods, the origins of the evolution in central bank cooperation can be traced back to the changes that took place in the international monetary and financial environment.

Bretton Woods had been a system designed from first principles by governments and largely run by governments. It was governments that ultimately sanctioned exchange rate parities and decided on the broad contours of adjustment processes. For their part, central banks were entrusted with the day-by-day management of international liquidity and acted as the main government consultants on international monetary issues.

The new "system" that emerged in the 1970s was one in which exchange rates, liquidity, and adjustment became largely determined by decentralized financial markets, with governments playing a more indirect role. Exchange rates among the main currency areas were left to float; the financing of external positions was predominantly driven by

of a "hard law" approach would, for instance, be the creation of a World Financial Authority, as advocated by Eatwell and Taylor (2000).

private capital flows; and adjustments were induced by either the threat or the reality of a market reaction. Needless to say, this evolution from a government-led to a market-led system (Padoa-Schioppa and Sacco-manni 1994) did not take place overnight. In fact, it had started well before the breakdown of Bretton Woods, in part contributing to its demise. But by the mid- to late 1990s it was largely complete. The underlying force driving the change was financial liberalization, both within and across national borders, together with the quickening pace of financial innova-tion, supported by technological advances in the elaboration and trans-mission of information. The end result was the "second globalization" wave of the century.[17]

The new global system, while unique, shared a number of character-istics with its predecessors. With the gold standard it had in common the freedom for financial capital to move unimpaired within and across national jurisdictions. From Bretton Woods it had inherited the gov-ernments' ambition to pursue autonomous macroeconomic objectives based on the management of national currencies. Unlike Bretton Woods, though, it had dropped even the pretense of an external anchor in the form of gold. The floating of exchange rates among the main currency areas was the most tangible sign of the system's mixed antecedents. It reflected the wish to regain autonomy in the management of the domes-tic economy, and the growing difficulties in maintaining fixed rates in a world of increasing capital mobility. Efforts to fix rates were limited to regions, notably Europe, or left to countries' unilateral decisions, notably in the developing world.

The forms of cooperation that developed were the offspring of the new challenges that policymakers faced in this unfamiliar environment and of the mindsets with which they approached them. Cooperation in

---

[17] For comparisons between the two globalization waves, see, for instance, Bordo, Eichen-green, and Irwin (1999), James (2001), and, especially for the real side of the economy, Feenstra (1998) and O'Rourke and Williamson (1999).

macroeconomic, and hence monetary, issues followed divergent paths at the global and regional levels. By contrast, financial cooperation inexorably gained ground, evolving from the purely technical to the political and from the core of industrialized countries to the global economy.

Monetary Cooperation

Domestically, the emergence of stagflation in the early 1970s shook policymakers' long-held beliefs about the workings of the economy and cast doubt on their ability to reconcile full employment with price stability. It also resurfaced long-standing differences of perspective between key countries – notably the United States, on the one hand, and Germany, on the other – whose historical memories had been deeply scarred by two contrasting defining moments in the interwar period, namely the Great Depression and hyperinflation, respectively. Internationally, a central question for much of the period remained how to address US balance of payments deficits while maintaining world non-inflationary growth: the United States would typically seek to foist expansion on reluctant partners abroad and other countries would expect an equally reluctant United States to retrench, notably by cutting its budget deficits in the 1980s.

Macroeconomic cooperation efforts, for which the informal grouping of the G5/G7 took increasing responsibility, waxed and waned in the light of the evolving political, economic, and intellectual backdrop (Volcker and Gyohten 1992; James 1996; Truman 2003). A high-profile example was the Bonn summit of 1978. This, however, was soon followed by disillusionment with the real growth results and with the subsequent flare up of inflation. After a lull, by the mid-1980s high-profile multilateral cooperation efforts had largely become limited to coordinated intervention to address perceived large-scale misalignments in the dollar, as exemplified by the Plaza (1985) and Louvre (1987) Accords: macroeconomic policy coordination took a back seat as central banks became increasingly reluctant to sacrifice monetary orthodoxy on the altar of global cooperation. As under the classical gold standard, policymakers became increasingly convinced that the best way of maintaining economic stability was to keep "one's own house in order." Faith in the ability to influence exchange rates through intervention failed to elicit a consensus sufficient to underpin anything other than sporadic actions (e.g., Galati and Melick 2002; Saccomanni 2002; Cooper 2005a). The long battle against the Great Inflation, finally won in the 1990s, remained essentially a domestic affair, if in various ways shaped by global conditions.

By contrast, macroeconomic cooperation was intensified at the regional level, notably in the case of the European Monetary System. The establishment of economic and monetary union in 1999 crowned a long period of closer monetary and exchange rate cooperation in the area. The project yielded undoubted economic benefits, not least shielding the area from the episodic financial turbulences in global markets. But its success was above all testimony to the importance of a strong political consensus in this field: from its inception, the project had been first of all political, and only secondarily economic. Moreover, it was underpinned by the willingness to accept German leadership in the fight against inflation (e.g., Giovannini 1988). By the end of the period, embryonic signs of closer regional monetary cooperation could be seen elsewhere, including in the Gulf countries and Asia, in perspective, Latin America.

Financial Cooperation

Cooperation in the financial sphere, by contrast, had a more linear evolution. The trigger was the increasing frequency and severity of episodes of financial instability. These emerged particularly in the wake of the liberalization of financial systems and capital flows, echoing developments that had already been seen under the gold standard and during the interwar period (Goodhart and Delargy 1998; Bordo et al. 2001; Bordo and Flandreau 2001). These episodes varied in breadth and intensity, variously affecting individual institutions, whole banking systems, and countries' external debt.

Learning how to operate in a liberalized and more competitive environment, how to price and manage risks after so many years of financial repression, would inevitably be a long process, for the authorities and market participants alike. Initially, it was the unexpected rapid rise in inflation and efforts to bring it down that caused the major problems. Subsequently, it was booms and busts in credit and asset prices, even in the context of low inflation (BIS 1997; Borio and Lowe 2002; Borio and White 2003). Especially in emerging market countries, problems were exacerbated by the interaction between volatile global capital flows and macroeconomic or structural deficiencies (e.g., Goldstein and Turner 1996; G10 1997).

Obviously, not all episodes of financial instability could act as a trigger for cooperation. As long as such instability remained a domestic affair, there was no need. Purely domestic instability played a role only insofar as it raised the authorities' awareness that the challenge was a shared one. But in an increasingly globalized economy, in which financial markets knew no borders, instability could not entirely be contained within national boundaries. If the eurodollar markets had epitomized this internationalization as far back as in the 1960s, their subsequent rapid growth during the period in the wake of the recycling of oil surpluses now took center stage. Even the failure of a single, rather small institution, heavily involved in foreign exchange transactions, could easily spread instability abroad, as shown by the collapse of Bankhaus Herstatt in 1974. The financial difficulties of a sovereign or a banking system could cause major losses to foreign lenders and investors. And, arguably more than before, problems at the periphery could easily be transmitted to the core, owing to the greater economic weight of the countries involved. The major banking crisis threatened by the sovereign debt crisis of Mexico in 1982 represented a watershed in this domain. Moreover, in a highly competitive international environment, unilateral action by regulators in one country risked putting their firms at a competitive disadvantage. This was all the more so now that other restrictions on financial activity were being, or had been, dismantled; hence the pressure from the regulated firms to ensure a "level playing field."

Against this background, cooperation followed two trajectories that by the end of the 1990s had fully converged. On the one hand, following the failure of individual financial institutions in the mid-1970s, supervisory authorities and central banks began the long journey to strengthen prudential regulation and the payment and settlement system infrastructure. On the other hand, starting with Mexico's default in 1982, policymakers also made strenuous, if not very successful, efforts to address emerging market countries' debt crises. Here, while the central banks played an important technical supporting role, the main decisions were made by national treasuries and coordinated by the IMF. Following the Asian crisis of 1997, these two strands met in the stepped-up concerted attempt to strengthen the "international financial architecture" (Camdessus 1998). The root cause was the recognition that deficiencies in the financial infrastructure of individual countries could have a first order effect on financial instability, both domestically and internationally (e.g., G10 1997). This heralded a paradigm shift in policymakers' and academic thinking – one which, paradoxically, was rediscovering lessons already learned at the time of the gold standard: the macroeconomy and the financial sector were inextricably intertwined.[18]

Cooperation at the BIS

The BIS adapted to this new environment, which implied a shift in the forms of cooperation. The room for global macroeconomic cooperation was somewhat reduced by central banks' focus on domestic price stability

---

[18] Contrary to the prevailing macroeconomic approach, it would no longer be possible to evaluate the soundness of macroeconomic policies or the sustainability of external positions without making a thorough assessment of the strength of the financial sector and of global financial market conditions.

and by the concern of some of them that cooperation might undermine this stability when it called for expansionary policies at home to correct global imbalances. Moves to strengthen central banks' independence to increase their credibility in pursuing price stability limited this room further (e.g., Simmons 1996). At the same time, negotiations on tough policy questions took place elsewhere or on a bilateral basis, with the involvement of governments. Even so, the BIS did function as a place where central banks exchanged views, improved mutual understanding of issues of common interest, and influenced the solutions reached. At a regional level, the BIS built on its tradition in support of European integration. Above all, a world of increasingly seamless capital markets, in which international banking and finance played such a pivotal role, was also one which naturally placed central banks, and the BIS, in a prominent position (see also Kahler 2000). This was so by virtue of their knowledge of payment systems and market functioning, their closeness to the banking sector, and their long-standing responsibilities for financial stability, often complemented by banking supervisory functions. In this area, their independence actually facilitated joint initiatives; arguably, it provided a degree of insulation from the political process that helped to keep decisions at a more technical level. Let us consider each area in turn.

Monetary Cooperation

In relation to global exchange rate cooperation, the role of the BIS was one of indirect support. Exchange rates were discussed in the regular meetings, especially by the Gold and Foreign Exchange Committee, at the technical level. And the BIS provided secretariat support for the G7 Working Group on Foreign Exchange Intervention that produced the Jurgensen Report (1983), which defined the policy consensus of the time on the issue. While concluding that intervention could be useful under certain circumstances in the short run, the report stressed the importance of complementary macroeconomic policies for longer-lasting effects (Volcker and Gyohten 1992; Truman 2003). This conclusion was confirmed in a subsequent G7 statement and set the basis for further coordinated policy actions in this area, up to the present day.

The BIS maintained its support for closer monetary cooperation in Europe, resuming a thread that had started with the EPU and had already seen some significant further developments beginning in the 1960s. For it was in 1964 that the Committee of Governors of the Central Banks of the Member States of the European Economic Community had been established. Importantly, contrary to a proposal by the European Commission, the Committee would regularly meet in Basel and not in Brussels, and would not operate under the Commission's leadership – a way for the governors to underline their wish to retain independent room for maneuver. Likewise, the mandate of the Committee, watered down relative to the initial proposals, was "to hold consultations concerning the general principles and broad lines of policies of the central banks" and to "exchange information at regular intervals about the most important measures that fall within the competence of the central banks." Over time, however, the Committee also took over more operational tasks, starting in 1970 with the setting up of a system to provide short-term financing to address temporary balance of payments deficits and continuing with the operation of the "snake" one year later (Baer 1994).

In the period following the breakdown of Bretton Woods, the BIS's support for the journey toward closer monetary arrangements in Europe took various forms. The BIS continued to provide secretariat services to the Committee of Governors of the EEC central banks (Baer 1994) and to host regular meetings of officials who discussed regional and global monetary issues. Notably, the BIS acted as a facilitator for the work of the Delors Committee, whose 1989 Report set the roadmap for European Monetary Union (EMU), laying out concrete stages to achieve the objective and the general contours of the final goal, taking into account the lessons from the less successful Werner Report of

1970 (Baer 1994; Lamfalussy 2005).[19] The new Report also set the basis for the Statute of the European System of Central Banks, subsequently approved almost without change. Operationally, the BIS provided the technical infrastructure for the European exchange rate arrangements, starting in 1973 with the agency function for the European Monetary Cooperation Fund. And it also acted as a clearing agent for the "private ecu," a claim issued by banks mimicking the composition of the official ecu basket, the fulcrum of the exchange rate mechanism adopted in 1979.

Did the BIS also make a material contribution to the global fight against inflation? Here, the assessment is necessarily more speculative. Operationally, the fight against inflation was not founded on policy coordination. At the same time, it is possible that the regular and frank discussions among governors and senior officials that took place in Basel may have helped to develop a common understanding of the problem, to consolidate the determination to address it in difficult conditions, and to elaborate adequate solutions.

Financial Cooperation

The BIS's role in cooperation in the financial sphere involved both crisis management and crisis prevention. The crisis management role echoed its activities during 1931. Crisis prevention aimed at strengthening three core elements of the financial system, namely institutions, payment and settlement systems, and market functioning. These two strands evolved in complex ways, sometimes quite independently, at other times crossing each other's path as a result of common catalytic events, normally in response to crises. For these reasons, in what follows, rather than proceeding strictly chronologically, we discuss each aspect in turn.

---

[19] Governors served on the Committee in a personal capacity alongside three external experts, including Alexandre Lamfalussy, then BIS General Manager. The two independent rapporteurs were Tommaso Padoa-Schioppa and Gunter Baer, the latter from the BIS.

The operational aspects of crisis management largely took the form of bridge financing to countries experiencing financial difficulties, generally intended to prefinance disbursements by the IMF. The financing was granted with the backing and guarantee of a range of central banks, often comprising the G10. The BIS rarely took on credit risks. The catalyst for this type of operation was the Mexican crisis of 1982. The crisis had largely caught policymakers by surprise (but see later paragraphs). The BIS could thus exploit its comparative advantage in speedy execution, based on the mutual trust among governors honed by the regular meetings, and its fully functional operating infrastructure (Volcker and Gyohten 1992), not least as the conditions for an IMF stabilization loan were not yet in place (Cooper 2005a). The Mexican bridging loan was just the first of a long list of similar operations, several to help contain the shockwaves from the Mexican crisis,[20] and others in subsequent episodes, including Mexico and Argentina in 1995 at the time of the Tequila crisis, and Thailand in 1997 during the Asian crisis. Special disbursement procedures introduced by the IMF in the late 1990s seemed to remove the need for BIS prefinancing. Nevertheless, it was felt that multilateral support packages of this kind could on occasion reduce the risk of a financial crisis in one country spreading elsewhere. This was the case with the last (and largest) BIS-coordinated package, granted to Brazil in 1998 to supplement, rather than prefinance, IMF lending, with the intention of boosting market confidence. The BIS applied no policy conditionality to this type of lending and remained reluctant to tie up its resources for long (e.g., BIS 1984).

Following the failure of Bankhaus Herstatt and Franklin National Bank of New York in rapid succession in June and October 1974, in December that year the G10 Governors established the BCBS, at the time known as the Committee on Banking Regulations and Supervisory

---

[20] The Mexican debt crisis led to the rescheduling of two-thirds of the outstanding debt of twenty-five developing countries (Lamfalussy 2000).

Practices. The Committee brought together for the first time central banks and banking supervisory authorities (in those cases where supervision was not performed by central banks). The initial motivation for establishing it was to exchange information on the condition of internationally active banks, since at the time these were not providing consolidated statements of their activities (Kapstein 1994).[21] Unsurprisingly, the proposal came from the Bank of England, with London playing host to hundreds of foreign banks operating in the most active segment of the euromarket. No one could have imagined at the time, though, that the Committee would, over the years, become the core body influencing banking supervisory standards worldwide.

The Committee's evolution was marked by several milestones. Reflecting its original purpose, it started with a low-key agreement allocating cross-border supervisory responsibilities among member authorities ("the Concordat") in 1975, closely followed by the principle of home-country consolidated supervision.[22] But it rapidly extended its activity to developing good practice guidelines and then standards in all areas of banking regulation and supervision. The first landmark agreement was the development of minimum capital standards in 1988 (Basel I), designed to raise banks' cushions against failure and to adapt them to the growing off-balance sheet exposures. In some respects, the agreement was a distant child of the Mexican debt crisis, since the US Congress's insistence on tighter capital standards for US banks as a *quid pro quo* for granting higher resources to the IMF and its concern with avoiding a loss in US banks' international competitiveness played a catalytic role (Kapstein 1991). A second landmark agreement was the Core Principles for Effective Banking Supervision in 1997. In this case, the catalyst was

---

[21] In fact, the press communiqué announcing the establishment of the Committee in February 1975, at the time of its first meeting, simply stated that its objective was "to assist the governors in their continuing work of surveillance and exchange of information."

[22] The Concordat was subsequently revised and tightened twice, in 1983 and 1991, following the failures of Banco Ambrosiano and BCCI, respectively.

the Mexican crisis of 1995 and the contagion it caused, which highlighted the need to strengthen banking systems in emerging market countries. The Core Principles were designed as a model for banking supervision regardless of the specifics of individual banking systems. In subsequent years, the principles were adopted by supervisors across the world. A third landmark was the revision of minimum capital standards in 2004, known as Basel II. This was in part motivated by the need to adapt the previous, admittedly coarse, standards to advances in risk management techniques, which had encouraged regulatory arbitrage. Beyond individual measures, though, what makes the Basel Committee important is that its processes set an example for international cooperation efforts of other regulatory authorities in the financial field (Zaring 1998; see also following paragraphs).

The intellectual, if distant, origins of the CPSS also go back to the disruptions caused to foreign exchange settlements by the failure of Bankhaus Herstatt. The episode raised awareness of the critical, if underestimated, role of wholesale payment and settlement systems in securing financial stability. In contrast to the gold standard period, when concerns with payment systems had largely pertained to disruptive shifts between bank deposits and cash, now they focused entirely on the credit and liquidity risks incurred in the process of executing transactions (Borio and Van den Bergh 1993). The reason was the unprecedented surge in gross payment and settlement flows associated with the quantum leap in financial activity, a distinguishing feature of the second globalization wave of finance compared with the first. As guardians of domestic payment systems, as active participants and as suppliers of a risk-free settlement medium, central banks were in an ideal position to take the lead in joint action.

The forerunner of the CPSS was the Group of Experts on Payment Systems, established in 1980. But it was not until 1990 that standard setting work started in earnest, as the CPSS was established following a report setting principles for wholesale net settlement systems (the "Lamfalussy

Report"). Thereafter, the CPSS continued its activities, analyzing issues of common concern, setting standards, and encouraging the adoption of risk mitigation techniques by the private sector (BIS 1994; Borio 1995). The latest such example was the establishment of Continuous Linked Settlement (CLS) in 2003, a private sector scheme aimed at reducing the settlement risk in foreign exchange transactions – the risk originally highlighted by Herstatt's failure some thirty years previously (Galati 2002).

Following the end of Bretton Woods, the concerns of the Euro-Currency Standing Committee gradually shifted from monetary issues toward financial instability and its focus shifted from the euromarkets *per se* to market functioning more generally. In the mid-1970s the Committee improved the coverage of its international banking statistics to cast light on the rising exposure of banks to the developing world. The statistics started being published in 1974, and in 1978 were complemented by information on the exposures' maturity structure. These figures revealed the extent of the massive growth in countries' indebtedness and its increasingly short-term character, which was sowing the seeds of the subsequent crisis. By 1978, the BIS *Annual Report* was drawing attention to the risks involved. In the meantime, behind-the-scenes efforts were being made by the BIS General Manager at the time, Alexandre Lamfalussy, with the agreement of the G10 Governors, to encourage banks to exercise greater prudence in their lending, but to little effect.[23] Once the Mexican crisis did erupt, the Committee further upgraded the coverage of the statistics. Enhancements were again made in the wake of the Asian crisis of 1997 (Wooldridge 2002) and have continued to the present day.

In addition, the Euro-Currency Standing Committee took the lead in the study of market functioning generally, with specific attention to the implications of financial innovations. The first study in this domain was the "Cross Report" in 1982, a key reference at the time for the

---

[23] These efforts, based on a checklist of questions drawn up by Arthur Burns, Chairman of the Fed at the time, are discussed in detail in Lamfalussy (2000).

understanding of derivatives markets. Several subsequent studies laid the basis for the development of statistics for over-the-counter derivatives as well as the foreign exchange markets. Improving the flow of information to the markets so as to contribute to their smooth functioning has been a *Leitmotiv* of the Committee since its inception. This has included, *inter alia*, work aimed at improving the disclosure of official foreign exchange reserves in 1999, conducted jointly with the IMF and subsequently incorporated into the SDDS (Special Data Dissemination Standard). Over time, the Committee systematized its monitoring of global markets with a view to identifying potential vulnerabilities. Partly to reflect this shift, in 2000 it was renamed the Committee on the Global Financial System (CGFS).

With the BIS-hosted Committees active across a range of areas relevant to the strengthening of financial systems, it was not surprising that, following the 1997 Asian crisis, they became more closely drawn into efforts to shape the new international financial architecture. Two developments epitomize this change. First, when in 1999 the G7 established the Financial Stability Forum (FSF) to help coordinate and catalyze initiatives, the BIS was represented on it in various forms. The FSF brought together senior representatives of central banks, supervisory authorities, and finance ministries alongside international regulatory bodies and international financial institutions. All three Committees – BCBS, CPSS, and CGFS – as well as the BIS had separate seats at the table; in addition, the BIS hosted the FSF's secretariat and gave the body its first Chairman, Andrew Crockett, at the time BIS General Manager (albeit serving on the FSF in a personal capacity). Second, the core principles issued by the BCBS and the CPSS became part of the set of twelve codes and standards seen as critical for the new architecture.

From the viewpoint of the instruments of cooperation, probably the most interesting aspect of the workings of the BIS-based Committees, pioneered in the financial regulatory field by the Basel Committee, has been the reliance on "soft law." Setting standards through non-binding agreements reached by national authorities, implemented largely through peer-group pressure within national jurisdictions, possibly after adjustments to the local law, and with the support of market forces, has become the norm for most of the standards underpinning the new architecture. Arguably, "soft law" is particularly well suited to financial matters, where it can provide a balance between quality, speed, flexibility, and efficiency, on the one hand, and ownership and accountability, on the other. This balance is necessary for the subsequent acceptance and implementation of the standards. Financial arrangements are highly technical, evolve quickly, and differ considerably across countries, reflecting different historical experiences, cultures, and legal traditions. Working together, national experts are in a good position to ensure the quality of the regulatory framework. Moreover, accountability of the experts to the national political institutions and implementation through peer-group pressure can foster close ownership.

While "soft law" has allowed a solid body of codes and standards to be put in place, as the importance and geographical reach of the task have grown, some questions have begun to emerge. There have been calls for greater inclusiveness. Notably, the Basel Committee process was initially designed for internationally active banks, not necessarily for setting standards with a global reach. In addition, the process has become more politicized, as national legislatures have taken a keener interest in its outcomes, and sometimes even raised issues about the degree of accountability.[24] The Basel Committee has been adjusting to the new

---

[24] The issue of the "accountability" and "democratic deficit" of international financial institutions has risen to prominence in the wake of the second globalization wave; given space limitations, it is not possible to do justice to it in this short essay. For a detailed discussion of these issues, see, in particular, Keohane and Nye (2001) and Kahler (2004). Within this broader debate, a specific question has been whether "soft law" processes such as those typified by the Basel Committee, based on networks of subgovernment agencies, are more or less accountable than those enshrined in "hard law" processes such as those that underlie the operation of the World Trade Organization (WTO) or IMF. Those who see legitimacy arising from the operation of governments, as the

environment, especially by intensifying and broadening its dialogue with regulatory authorities beyond member countries as well as with the industry and by greatly increasing the transparency of the process. The merits of the "soft law" approach in the financial area have been highlighted by the recent move within the European Union to adopt a framework for regulatory standard setting that in some respects resembles the one used by the Basel Committee (the so-called Lamfalussy approach), with a clearer distinction between primary and secondary legislation and a more intense and broader consultative process than in the past (Lamfalussy 2001).

A Broadening Geographical and Institutional Reach

The increasing breadth of the activities performed by the BIS during this historical phase naturally went hand in hand with a functional and geographical widening of its client base.

Functionally, the shift in focus toward financial stability meant that the BIS provided an increasing range of services to non-central bank

---

supreme representatives of sovereign nation-states in the international arena, tend to argue that "hard law" processes are more accountable, and regard with some suspicion the room for maneuver afforded to the agencies (e.g., Keohane and Nye 2001; and, in particular, Alston 1997; Picciotto 1997). By contrast, those who favor a more "disaggregated" notion of the state and sovereignty and allow for the legitimate direct operation of transnational networks at the subgovernment level in the international arena argue that the latter can afford some advantages also from the perspective of accountability (Slaughter 1997, 2004). In the specific case of central banks, their delegated "independence" in the domestic context naturally extends to their international operations. While this independence is largely intended to insulate their monetary policy functions (e.g., Cukierman 1992; Berger, de Haan, and Eijffinger 2001), similar arguments have been put forward also for financial supervisory functions and hence supervisory authorities more generally (e.g., Quintyn and Taylor 2003). This raises interesting questions about the meaning and substance of accountability in these situations, about the balance between autonomy and accountability, and about the trade-offs that might arise between "effectiveness" and "politicization" (see, for instance, De Gregorio et al. 1999, who argue for reduced oversight of the IMF by national governments, by analogy with national central banks).

supervisory authorities. The Basel Committee was just the first case in point. Accordingly, partly in order to better reflect the shift of supervisory responsibilities away from central banks in some key jurisdictions, in 2004 the Basel Committee began to report directly to a body bringing together the governors and heads of banking supervision of member countries. In addition, in 1999 the BIS set up the Financial Stability Institute, which has largely concentrated on disseminating best practice and providing training services to supervisory authorities. And in 1998 and 2002, respectively, the BIS began to host, although without providing secretariat services, the International Association of Insurance Supervisors (IAIS) and the International Association of Deposit Insurers (IADI).[25]

Geographically, the changes were even more extensive, as the BIS came under growing pressure to become more global. On the "push" side, the establishment of the European Central Bank (ECB) meant that part of the activities, including purely banking ones, previously centered in Basel moved to Frankfurt. On the "pull" side, the growing weight of emerging market countries in the world economy acted as a powerful magnet for an institution whose policy setting functions were already extending their geographical reach. The challenge the institution faced

---

[25] The cooperative efforts aimed at preventing systemic strains associated with computer failures at the turn of the century are another example of the broadening range of BIS services. In 1998, the Basel Committee, the CPSS, the IOSCO (International Organization of Securities Commissions), and the IAIS (International Association of Insurance Supervisors) set up the Joint Year 2000 Council in order to ensure high-level attention to the year 2000 challenge and promote a coordinated, consistent approach across the financial sector regulatory community. The secretariat of the Council was provided by the BIS. While its activities were principally directed to financial market authorities, the Council also worked closely with other groups, such as the G7 finance ministers, the United Nations, the World Bank, the IMF, the European Commission, the OECD (Organisation for Economic Co-operation and Development), the FSF, the G10 Governors, and the Global 2000 Coordination Group (the latter representing globally active financial firms that undertook to stimulate the year 2000 readiness of market participants around the world).

was how to become more global while at the same time retaining that "clublike" atmosphere so much treasured by its founders. The strategy followed included changes in the composition of the Board of Directors,[26] extension of membership, broader participation in its various activities, a rebalancing of the analytical work toward the emerging regions of the world, and greater physical proximity through the opening of representative offices. By the end of the period, the range of central banks participating in BIS meetings had been greatly expanded, the number of shareholding central banks had risen from thirty-two in the early 1990s to fifty-five, and the BIS had opened representative offices for Asia and the Pacific in Hong Kong SAR (in 1998) and for the Americas in Mexico City (in 2002). Partly echoing its technical services in support of European monetary integration, in 2003 the BIS started to provide assistance to joint financial efforts by central banks in Asia. This took the form of managing ABF1 (Asian Bond Fund 1, 2003) and acting as administrator for ABF2 (2005), a dollar and a local-currency bond fund, respectively, set up by EMEAP (Executives' Meeting of East Asia and Pacific central banks) to encourage the development of bond markets in the region (Ma and Remolona 2005).

CONCLUSIONS

This chapter has investigated three main issues: How have changes in the international monetary and financial system shaped the objectives and tools of central bank cooperation? Under what conditions could central bank cooperation develop? Did the existence of the BIS make any difference in promoting central bank cooperation? It is now possible to pull together and summarize the partial answers hinted at in the various parts of the chapter.

---

[26] The US Federal Reserve, the Bank of Japan, and the Bank of Canada joined the Board of Directors in 1994.

Targets, Tools, and Intensity of Central Bank Cooperation

While the tasks of cooperation have consistently been the pursuit of international monetary and financial stability, the definition of these tasks, their relative importance, and mutual interaction have evolved alongside the global monetary and financial regimes, international relations, and developments in economic thinking.

Under the gold standard, monetary and financial stability were perceived as largely coincident for practical purposes. Monetary stability was broadly identified with gold convertibility. And financial instability could and did threaten gold convertibility. In a financial environment characterized by open financial markets and the absence of a framework for prudential regulation, authorities responded to monetary and financial instability by bilateral emergency liquidity assistance. The pursuit of a generalized reintroduction of the gold standard in the 1920s induced the first attempts at multilateral central bank cooperation. The creation of the BIS also responded to the perceived need for an institutional and permanent approach to central bank cooperation. The BIS received its baptism of fire during the international financial crisis of 1931, when the battle was fought, and lost, with the old weapons of international emergency lending. It was then, however, that experts at the BIS realized the limitations of the instrument, given the complex links between Central Europe's underlying banking problems, liquidity crises, and exchange rate stability.

In the following years of uncertainty about the international monetary system and generalized administrative controls on capital movements, the monetary and financial stability objectives of cooperation ceased to have any practical meaning of immediate relevance. Central bank cooperation at the BIS continued only in the form of low-key exchanges of information and the provision of mutual technical services.

Under Bretton Woods, cooperation was also focused on convertibility of domestic currencies at fixed exchange rates, as under the gold standard. But its relationship to monetary and financial stability objectives markedly changed. On the one hand, monetary stability was more firmly identified with domestic price stability. This would be easily achieved, it was believed, as long as domestic demand was not pushed too hard beyond full employment. Fixed exchange rates were seen as a means of avoiding the chaotic beggar-thy-neighbor policies of the 1930s and of supporting the orderly reduction of trade barriers and global trade expansion. Financial repression, both domestic and international, provided a check on overt financial instability, so that securing financial stability was not a major policy objective. Toward the end of the period, though, the rapid growth of the eurocurrency market – both a reaction to financial repression and the herald of the arrival of a new era of international capital mobility – began to raise financial stability issues separate from those of monetary stability.

In the post-Bretton Woods years, the aims of central bank cooperation progressively shifted from monetary to financial stability, and new tools were introduced. The experience of the Great Inflation of the 1970s convinced central banks that domestic monetary stability, their overriding responsibility, could be pursued primarily by domestic policy. After some disappointing attempts in the 1970s, cooperation on exchange rates became largely subordinated to the pursuit of that objective. At the European level, cooperation in pursuit of the stability of the European Monetary System, created in 1978, rested on accepting the leadership of Germany in bringing inflation down. At the global level, cooperation on monetary issues became less feasible once the more inflation-conscious countries or currency areas saw it as not entirely consistent with domestic price stability.

At the same time, financial liberalization allowed the reemergence of overt financial instability. It became increasingly clear that such instability could no longer be fought with *ex post* emergency lending only. To be sure, emergency liquidity lending to countries in financial distress was stepped up, echoing similar actions during the gold standard period. But now an elaborate prudential regulatory apparatus was in place, set up following the widespread banking crises of the Great Depression, and central banks in most countries enjoyed supervisory powers over the banking system. Between the 1930s and the 1960s, regulatory powers had largely been used as a complement to financial repression policies. In the new context of international capital mobility, prudential regulation became a crucial element in the pursuit of financial stability, within the ambitious aim of creating a new international financial architecture. Central banks led international cooperative efforts to strengthen prudential frameworks, helping to prevent an international race to the bottom in deregulation.

In the evolving framework of international monetary and financial regimes, economic conditions and consensus on priorities and policy tools, the effectiveness of central banks' specific contribution to multilateral cooperation also depended on a broader set of conditions, some of which were directly related to central banks themselves. In particular, we have seen how central bank cooperation was more intense in periods when international relations were friendlier and oriented to multilateral rather than bilateral cooperation, when the reputation and independence of central banks was high, and when the issues requiring a cooperative approach were such that the technical expertise of central banks would make a difference.

Did the "International Bank" Make a Difference?

Did the BIS make a difference? Or would an equally active cooperation have taken place in its absence?

There is no obvious way of proving a case one way or the other. Economists, divided on the pros and cons of cooperation itself, are rather mute on the merits of its institutionalization. By contrast, those political scientists in the institutionalist tradition are naturally predisposed to assigning a positive coordinating role to international institutions (for instance, Keohane 1984).

We believe the case for the BIS to be fairly well grounded: the institution appears to have made a material difference, at least when conditions allowed.

There are good *a priori* reasons to believe that an institutionalized and permanent mechanism for cooperation enjoys a number of advantages over *ad hoc* cooperative tools. First, it provides a kind of "neutral territory" for cooperation to take place, largely thanks to an independent secretariat, which can allay concerns about national biases. Second, it guarantees a continuity and depth that would be harder to achieve through looser, *ad hoc* arrangements. Third, through regular meetings at all levels in a familiar setting, it creates an environment particularly well suited to the development of a mutual understanding, to learning from each other's experience, to building consensus and to breeding close and long-lasting personal relationships. Finally, through these channels and the presence of a functioning infrastructure, it can make it easier to take speedy decisions at times of need. It is the sometimes uneventful series of meetings in more tranquil times that lays the basis for more effective action-oriented cooperation when such is required.

From a more empirical perspective, one can point to the governors' revealed preferences. For seventy-five years they made time in their busy schedules for regular and frequent visits to Basel; they also placed their senior staff in the various Committees based at the BIS and insisted on assiduous participation. And they went a long way toward preserving its viability and very existence, at times against the indifference or even the opposition of their own governments. It is likely that they believed the BIS to be a facilitating tool for cooperation.

Beyond *a priori* reasoning and the governors' revealed preference, in the absence of a clear counterfactual, it is hard to find uncontroversial evidence for the usefulness of the BIS in promoting multilateral cooperation. It is, however, possible to point to a number of instances consistent with the notion that it did make a difference. Here are just a few of them.

As soon as it was established, the BIS received a request for support in a stabilization scheme for the peseta, breaking with the previous practice of organizing such support packages on a bilateral basis. As soon as the EPU was created, the BIS turned out to be ideally placed to provide the needed international clearinghouse services. It is also telling that the secretariat of the European Communities (EC) Governors was not located in Brussels but in Basel, despite political pressures to the contrary. It was certainly not by chance that cooperation among prudential supervisors started in Basel, acting as a model for regulatory authorities in the securities and insurance industries. Likewise, the ease with which emergency liquidity assistance was put together at the time of the Mexican crisis would be difficult to imagine in the absence of an institutionalized cooperative mechanism (Volcker and Gyohten 1992).

The Mexican crisis also highlights one of the idiosyncratic advantages of the BIS: that of being set up as a bank. As such, it was able to provide a number of services to member central banks (gold swaps, shipments and custody, deposits and short-term loans in various currencies, reciprocal settlements, etc.) and to pay for the meetings, statistics, reports, support staff, and secretariat without requiring appropriation from its members, a feature that contributed to the independence of the institution. Moreover, the availability of financial resources on a swift commercial basis allowed the BIS to provide international lending either alone or, more frequently, as a member or leader of a consortium of central banks. If the BIS's resources were never of a magnitude that could make a major quantitative difference to international lending, its participation was seen as the seal of approval by a reputable financial institution appreciated by markets and private lenders.

One should perhaps also point to the resilience of the BIS, its ability not only to survive but to reinvent itself at various junctures. Created to facilitate the transfer of German reparations, when these ended in 1931 the BIS found a natural role as the locus for central bank cooperation for the stability of the gold standard. When gold lost its glitter after 1936, the BIS refined a system of international settlements to adjust it to the increasing regulations restricting currency convertibility. This showed its worth again in the 1950s, when the EPU was established. As an institution designed for a fixed exchange rate environment, the BIS seemed to be destined to policy irrelevance after the end of Bretton Woods only to prove its usefulness in support for the European journey toward monetary union and, above all, in a new role centered on financial stability and prudential regulation. In the process, the BIS extended its provision of cooperative services beyond the central banking community to include non-central bank supervisory authorities – a step that should stand it in good stead in future, given the incipient trend in shifting supervisory responsibilities away from central banks.[27] And when the establishment of EMU and broader geopolitical shifts risked limiting the global relevance of its activities, the BIS responded by expanding its membership, by involving a much broader set of central banks in its activities and by establishing *in loco* offices in Asia and the Americas. This capacity to respond to unexpected events has been the key to the institution's continued relevance.

We are obviously not arguing that cooperation among central banks would not have taken place without the BIS. Central bank cooperation predates the birth of the Institution. However, while scholars disagree about the extent of such cooperation before 1930, they do agree that it was mostly *ad hoc* and always bilateral. This is why personalities like Governor Montagu Norman of the Bank of England, and others before

---

[27] Consistent with this shift, in its own analytical work the BIS has been highlighting the tight nexus between monetary and financial stability as well as the importance of paying due attention to the systemic (macroprudential) orientation of prudential frameworks, thereby highlighting the complementary role that monetary and prudential authorities can play and the need for cooperation between the two (e.g., Crockett 2001b; Borio and White 2003; BIS 2005).

him, had long advocated the creation of an "international bank." Our conclusion from looking back at seventy-five years of history is simply that the presence of the BIS has facilitated and deepened cooperation, ensuring a degree of continuity and effectiveness that would otherwise have been harder to attain.

2

Almost a Century of Central Bank Cooperation

RICHARD N. COOPER[1]

The Bank for International Settlements (BIS) was created in 1930 primarily to administer the Young Plan, including reparations loan repayments from Germany. But the first objective of the BIS, as defined in its Statutes, is to "promote the cooperation of central banks" – to provide a meeting place for central bankers to exchange information, discuss common problems, agree on shared aims, set common standards, and possibly even provide mutual support. This objective must be viewed against the background of the 1920s, when there had been episodic, typically bilateral cooperation among central banks. Indeed, episodes of such cooperation can be found in the pre-1914 period, for example, a gold loan by the Bank of France to the Bank of England during the Baring crisis of 1890, or the discounting of English bills by the Bank of France in 1906, 1907, 1909, and 1910, thereby relieving pressure on the gold reserves of the Bank of England (Bloomfield 1959: 56). Examples can be found from even earlier, including the Latin and Scandinavian currency unions (Schloss 1958: 7–24).

---

[1] Harvard University. The author is indebted to Edwin Truman for detailed comments on an earlier version of this chapter.

With the post-1918 breakup of the Austrian, Ottoman, and Russian empires, many new countries were created that needed central banks and economic stabilization. The League of Nations had a program to assist the new states in setting up their financial systems and stabilizing their economies. An early interwar example of cooperation was the loan in 1923 from the Bank of England to the National Bank of Austria in anticipation of proceeds from a League of Nations stabilization loan. Similar loans were made later to Bulgaria, Estonia, Hungary, Poland, and Romania, among others, usually by the Bank of England, of which Montagu Norman was Governor. Gradually a network of loans, succeeded by lines of credit, developed between central banks, often with conditions imposed (Einzig 1930: chap. 2; Clarke 1967).

A second purpose of interwar cooperation was to prevent a scramble for gold, as new and old central banks alike attempted to establish the basis for restoring gold convertibility. An understanding was reached that central banks would not acquire gold in London, even newly mined South African gold, without the concurrence of the Bank of England (Einzig 1930: 18). However, these various arrangements, though often effective, were too vague and reliant on infrequent personal contacts to be systematic. Hence the need, it was argued, for regularizing and institutionalizing contacts among central bankers, in a place such as the BIS.

One of the most celebrated channels of central bank cooperation during the 1920s was the close friendship and frequent contact between Benjamin Strong, Governor of the Federal Reserve Bank of New York from 1914 to 1928, and Montagu Norman of the Bank of England. The Federal Reserve had been created only in 1913, and in the 1920s its twelve regional banks were still shaping their roles, their relationships with one another, and their relationships to the Board of Governors in Washington. New York, however, was clearly the preeminent market for foreign exchange in the United States, and its Federal Reserve Bank had the most frequent contact with financial developments in Europe and elsewhere. Britain returned to gold convertibility of the pound in 1925, at the prewar parity, and then struggled to maintain convertibility during the next six years. Sympathetic to the Bank of England's problem, Strong leaned toward providing such help as he could through the Federal Reserve from 1925 to 1927. Concretely, the New York Fed (with the approval of the Board and the secretary of the Treasury) opened a line of credit of $200 million in early 1925 to help backstop Britain's return to gold convertibility in April. The credit was never drawn.

A celebrated and notorious example of central bank cooperation occurred in the fall of 1927, when, following a meeting between Benjamin Strong, Montagu Norman, Charles Rist of the Bank of France, and Hjalmar Schacht of the German Reichsbank, the Federal Reserve lowered the discount rate from 4 to 3.5 percent. The Federal Reserve Bank of Chicago held out at 4 percent until ordered to lower its rate by the Board. This allegedly was to help Britain, in particular, to avoid raising interest rates in an already depressed economy, following gold convertibility resumption in 1925. Later, Adolph Miller, former member of the Federal Reserve Board, suggested that the subsequent course of events would have been very different had this reduction not occurred, and hinted that the stock market boom and subsequent crash of 1929 might have been avoided. This episode will be discussed in the final section of this chapter.

The opposite of cooperation – hostile action – can also be found. In one example, Schacht (1956: 221–22) reports an obviously coordinated withdrawal of French banking funds from Berlin, which occurred during a tense period of negotiation on the Young Plan in 1929.

WHAT DO WE MEAN BY "COOPERATION"?

What are the possible ways in which central banks might cooperate? Mutual financial support and coordinated actions in monetary policy

have already been mentioned, but they certainly do not exhaust important avenues of cooperation. One might broadly distinguish six types of
cooperation, in roughly increasing order of intensity.

The first is simply to exchange information, providing basic facts for
each major national market on outstanding credits, new borrowings,
central bank regulations, and the like. Economists usually assume full
information is available, particularly when it is published. But collecting
that information in usable form is itself a chore, and such activity can be
eased if central banks provide it directly to one another.

The second, a natural extension of the first, is to standardize concepts
and fill gaps in information. Some central banks may collect information that others do not but would find useful. Some forms of credit, for
example, from outside each country, may escape the national statistical-
gathering net but be identified when information is exchanged and subsequently fill the existing gaps.

A third is to exchange views on how the world works and on objectives of central bank policy. Since central banks have at least some similar
responsibilities in all countries, and since in open economies the actions
of central banks in large financial markets can strongly influence the conditions in other financial markets, large or small, having some knowledge
about the views of the senior officials of the large central banks provides
useful information about economic and psychological relationships in
those markets. This exchange of worldviews can also yield useful information about how central banks are likely to respond under different
contingencies.

A fourth is to share information on the economic outlook – that is,
not on facts, but on perceived short- and medium-run prospects. Since
those responsible may assess the same contemporary facts differently,
such an exchange can be helpful in several ways by emphasizing some
facts more than others or providing alternative interpretations, and thus
act as a corrective (or reinforcement) to one's own interpretation of the

outlook. It may also provide some advance guidance as to how other central banks may act in the near future, even without actual discussion of future actions.

A fifth is to standardize concepts and even regulations, adjusting as necessary the information that is collected, so that the data collected by different central banks can be directly compared, even added up, and so that it is as complete as it must be to perform central bank functions. Some standardization may be directed at increasing convenience and/or reducing costs, for example, the standard weight and fineness of gold to be acceptable by central banks operating under a gold standard.

The sixth channel of cooperation, the most demanding and what many people think of as the sole form of cooperation, is commonly agreed actions. This in turn can be subdivided in various ways. Central banks could agree to give one another advance notice of upcoming actions. They could require prior approval of actions occurring in the markets of other countries. They might agree on generic rules of behavior, including proscriptions, for example, on how foreign exchange reserves are to be held. They might agree on mutual financial support, either episodic or in the form of a framework for providing support, as under the European Monetary System of the late twentieth century. And they might coordinate their actions, for example, in the form of intervention in foreign exchange markets or even movements in discount rates or changes in regulations.

Examples of all these kinds of cooperation can be found in the history of the last seventy-five years. Indeed some of them are discussed directly in the *5th Annual Report* (for the year ending 31 March 1935) of the BIS, which explicitly discusses central bank cooperation in the BIS context. The BIS makes clear, however, that despite their cooperation each central bank fully retains freedom of action to respond to each situation as judgment dictates. That is, its *Annual Report* downplays the sixth channel mentioned earlier, joint action, except regarding rules of behavior and actions in the markets of others.

WHAT ARE CENTRAL BANKS?

If our topic is cooperation among central banks, we need not only to understand what cooperation is but also to clarify what exactly we mean by central banks. Most central banks evolved out of private institutions, which at some point were endowed with special statutory powers, such as a monopoly on the issue of banknotes, and perhaps also special responsibilities, such as with respect to short-term financing of the government. Gradually they were transformed into public institutions, through government appointment of governors and perhaps other senior officials, and eventually often through outright nationalization. This process started in the 1930s (for example, with the Reserve Bank of New Zealand; the Bank of France in 1936, when Prime Minister Léon Blum assumed appointment of virtually all the regents; and the Bank of Canada in 1938), but was greatly accelerated by the financing and other requirements of the Second World War and its immediate aftermath. The Bank of England was nationalized in 1946, the Reserve Bank of India in 1948.

From the beginning, the Federal Reserve System of the United States had a peculiar status. Although created by federal legislation in 1913, it is technically owned by its member banks, which appoint 72 of its 108 regional bank directors, who in turn select the regional bank presidents (subject to approval by the Board of Governors in Washington), who in turn participate in framing monetary policy. The seven governors are appointed by the president of the United States, subject to confirmation by the Senate, for fourteen-year non-renewable terms, with the chairman appointed for a renewable four-year term (for instance, Alan Greenspan, 1987–2006). Originally the secretary of the Treasury and the comptroller of the currency, both public officials, sat as *ex officio* members of the Board of Governors, but that provision was eliminated in 1934. The Federal Reserve thus remains a curious hybrid, a privately owned, quasi-public institution, whose sole function is central banking (including bank regulation and supervision).

Richard N. Cooper

Central banks have long valued their independence and, when not literally independent of government, their operating autonomy. Immediately before and during the Second World War most central banks became the agents of their governments, in particular of ministers of finance, *de facto* if not literally nationalized until later. They regained their autonomy of action only gradually (the Federal Reserve in the celebrated "accord" of 1951, when the Fed ceased to support the government bond market), with many central banks achieving statutory independence only in the 1990s.

Even then, important ambiguities sometimes remain, for example, with respect to the setting of exchange rate policy and the management of exchange rates. Whether decisions are made by governments or by central banks is not always clear, nor who runs exchange risk, although execution is almost invariably the task of central banks. Thus "central bank cooperation," or lack of it, often reflects the decisions of governments, not of central banks themselves. This ambiguity was concretely acknowledged when central bank governors were invited to join the Group of Ten in 1962 and the informal G5 ministers of finance meetings starting in 1973, and their representatives also attended many meetings of the deputy finance ministers. Even during the 1920s, when the ethos of central bankers was to keep governments at a respectable distance and the Federal Reserve Bank of New York took the lead in cooperating with European central banks, Federal Reserve Bank of New York Governor Benjamin Strong regularly reported his intentions to the Board of Governors and to secretary of Treasury Andrew W. Mellon (who at that time sat with the Board), and thus had their actual or tacit approval in his various proposals and actions.

CENTRAL BANK COOPERATION SINCE 1930

As noted earlier, an explicit purpose of the BIS was to encourage cooperation among central banks. It could hardly have begun at a less auspicious time. The convening function was exercised at once, as governors of the equity-holding central banks gathered once a year, and their representatives gathered almost monthly from the opening of the BIS in April 1930. As the first few of their annual reports suggest, these gatherings did some useful coordination, for example, on the standard of gold bars to be acceptable by member central banks, and as a clearinghouse for information on the physical location of monetary gold, so that gold transactions among central banks could, if possible, avoid or reduce shipment costs from capital to capital. This also advanced the notion of foreign exchange clearing through the BIS, so central banks could engage in foreign exchange transactions without directly affecting local foreign exchange markets.

The BIS also convened or served as host to a number of conferences on technical issues of interest to central banks and provided (partly through such conferences, partly through private consultations) technical assistance to the newly created central banks of Central and Eastern Europe. But the rapid decline in economic activity and prices that we now call the Great Depression overwhelmed the capacity of central banks to cooperate closely beyond such technical matters. The *2nd Annual Report* proudly proclaimed that in May 1931 the BIS convened representatives from twenty-four central banks, including twenty governors – the largest number ever assembled. But it was not enough to contain the looming crisis. Before the departure of the British pound from gold convertibility in September 1931, however, the BIS both encouraged and participated in a series of short-term stabilization loans, starting with Yugoslavia and eventually including Hungary, Austria, the German Reichsbank, and Danzig. All in all, a total of 740 million Swiss francs had been lent in (ultimately futile) emergency loans to central banks, mostly during the international financial crisis of the summer of 1931, of which SFr 211 million was funds of the BIS itself (Schloss 1958: 81). But such transactions disappeared after September 1931. Events overwhelmed the limited capacity of central banks to cooperate; even loans to the Reichsbank at the height of the summer crisis, as well as the Hoover moratorium, were critically delayed by political sensitivities in France over the issue of reparations (Eichengreen 1992: 264–78). In any case, central bank support loans during this period often imposed conditions similar to those desired by private financial capital thus reinforcing rather than countering pressures from the market (Simmons 1994: 282).

The first three BIS annual reports contain a section called "central bank collaboration." This was dropped in the fourth report (1934), presumably because there was little such collaboration to report. The section was revived in the fifth report (1935), to enable an extensive discussion of the desirability of central bank collaboration under headings covering the why, what, and how (the entire passage is included in Schloss 1958: 63–71). Subsequent reports revert to "developments affecting central banking," the heading that first replaced central bank collaboration in the fourth report. The key *objectives* of central bank collaboration were stated to be: support for a stable monetary system based on gold and for a smooth business cycle that would contribute to greater equilibrium in the general level of economic activity. Note the absence of any reference to price stability, although some would interpret that to be implicit in a gold standard (see Cooper, 1982, for a contrary view).

Central bank cooperation did not cease in the 1930s, however. Britain remained the world's largest trading country and had only recently lost its position as premier capital market to the United States. When sterling left gold in 1931, many other currencies – about half the world's total – chose to leave with it, and many currencies remained pegged to sterling. This gave rise to the "sterling bloc," which during and after the Second World War evolved into the Sterling Area, a time when associated countries pegged their currencies to sterling (although the peg was occasionally changed). They bought and sold local currencies against sterling, and they held the bulk of their central bank reserves in sterling in London rather than in gold, dollars, or some other form. At first this arrangement was informal, describing practice, but it became more formal with the introduction of exchange controls by the United Kingdom (and others) in 1939. With limited exceptions, the entire Sterling Area formed a financial zone of free movement of currencies (especially sterling, the leading currency) with all members operating under similar exchange control regulations. The exchange controls continued after the Second World War, and so did the Sterling Area. In addition, some members of the Area had built up large sterling balances during and immediately after the war, in effect providing Britain with goods and services during the war on short-term credit, continually rolled over. By 1952 the Sterling Area was composed of Britain, its colonies, and many of its former colonies – such as Australia, Burma, Ceylon (now Sri Lanka), India, Ireland, New Zealand, Pakistan, and South Africa (but not Canada) – as well as other countries such as Iceland, Iraq, Jordan, and Libya (Bell 1956: 48). At various times other nations were also adherents. The nature and stringency of controls changed over time, but the Sterling Area gradually atrophied during the 1960s as member countries put increasing increments to reserves into forms other than sterling, and especially after May 1966 when Britain placed restrictions on capital flows to the developed members of the Area (Australia, Ireland, New Zealand, and South Africa). Sterling balances became a continuing source of concern overhanging sterling (more on this under the Concerted Support for Sterling and the French Franc section in this chapter), and the area disappeared in 1979, when Britain abolished exchange controls and moved to full currency convertibility. In the meantime, the scope for currency convertibility (in practice, use of sterling for payments outside the Sterling Area) was gradually extended, first through bilateral payments arrangements between Britain and non-member countries, then especially through Britain's membership in the European Payments Union, starting in 1950, since the entire Sterling Area participated in that arrangement through Britain.

The key decisions during this period were made by governments, often embodied in legislation. Central banks were the agents of government, whether formally independent or not, both in intervention in the foreign exchange markets and in administration of exchange controls. The point here is that the Sterling Area was a cooperative system, with the aim of protecting and ultimately strengthening the position of sterling in international markets while preserving a high degree of commercial and financial freedom within the Sterling Area.

THE EUROPEAN PAYMENTS UNION

Europe's trade and payments were heavily restricted into bilateral channels immediately after the Second World War. Several attempts were made both to liberalize and to multilateralize trade, especially within Europe, starting in 1947. They led in 1950 to the creation of the European Payments Union (EPU) by the Organisation for European Economic Co-operation (OEEC, predecessor to the OECD, the Organisation for Economic Co-operation and Development), which had been established to administer the European side of the Marshall Plan assistance from the United States. The EPU was initially endowed with $350 million of Marshall Plan funds. Policy was in the hands of the intergovernmental OEEC Council, but the BIS was the agent that kept the books and provided clearing facilities. A key feature of the EPU was its provision for unlimited intramonth credit among participating European central banks, netted and cleared at the end of each month with partial payments in gold or hard currency (mainly US dollars), with debtors paying less than creditors (initially mainly Belgium) received – hence the importance of the initial endowment in dollars. By the end of 1952, two-thirds of intra-European trade was free of restriction, while only 11 percent of imports from North America were restriction-free (Solomon 1977: 19). Intra-European trade was gradually liberalized (with occasional reversals, especially France in 1957–58) and the terms of EPU settlement gradually hardened until European currencies became convertible *de facto* for current account transactions in the last few days of 1958. Germany alone had also made its currency convertible for capital transactions. Formal acceptance of the commitment of convertibility under Article VIII of the IMF

Articles of Agreement waited until 1961. With convertibility, the EPU was terminated. As noted earlier, the entire Sterling Area was covered by British membership, as were the remaining colonial territories of other European countries. While the BIS played mainly a facilitating role, the EPU was a vehicle for central bank cooperation in the form of automatic short-term mutual credits (Tew 1970: chap. 12; Eichengreen 1993).

SUPPORTING THE POUND AND THE DOLLAR, 1960–73

Article VIII convertibility of the European currencies (the Japanese yen joined them in 1964) reflected not just recovery from the Second World War but rapid economic growth, significant improvements in productivity, and improved competitiveness, as reflected in export performance. France had gotten an additional boost from the devaluation of 1958. Indeed, Germany and the Netherlands revalued their currencies by 5 percent in 1961. According to Gilbert (1980: 104), the 5 percent was Chancellor Adenauer's compromise between the conflicting advice he received: 10 percent versus no change.

The United States lost $2.3 billion in gold in 1958, still seen as a welcome redistribution of monetary gold excessively concentrated in the United States by the late 1940s. Gold sales diminished in 1959 but rose again in 1960 to $2.1 billion. The US administration began to be concerned about the balance of payments position. At this time, also Robert Triffin of Yale put forward his famous dilemma: a growing world economy needed additional international reserves. During the 1950s these were predominantly provided by increased official holdings of US dollars that were convertible (by monetary authorities only) into gold, as well as by gold sales by the United States. But eventually the credibility of this gold convertibility had to come into question as official dollar holdings outstripped US gold holdings.

The United Kingdom had not experienced the robust productivity improvements of other Western European countries or Japan. It had

experienced more inflation than some, and still had large sterling liabilities held by Sterling Area countries that increasingly traded outside the
Area. In 1957, in the wake of the Suez crisis, Britain prohibited the use
of sterling in third country financing and tightened exchange controls in
other ways, just as Germany was abolishing controls on all international
transactions – thus giving birth to the eurodollar market, whereby British
banks accepted deposits in US dollars and re-lent them at short-term,
thereby continuing a long tradition of British financing of international
trade but now no longer in sterling.

Thus the 1960s, which saw the real birth of multilateral central bank
cooperation envisioned but stillborn in 1930, was characterized by a number of financial improvisations designed initially to protect the British
pound but secondarily also to protect US gold reserves: (1) the Gold
Pool, (2) a network of swap facilities among central banks, (3) concerted
central bank loans to the UK, and (4) management of the eurodollar
market, or at least certain aspects of it. Other innovations, such as the
General Arrangements to Borrow (GAB) by the International Monetary Fund (IMF), did not directly involve central banks, but they were
generally financial agents of governments (at that time only the Federal
Reserve Board, the German Bundesbank, and the Swiss National Bank
were genuinely independent of the executive branches of government –
although subject to legislation – and even then ambiguities remained with
respect to foreign exchange transactions). Moreover, from the beginning
central banks were represented in the Group of Ten (eleven, counting
Switzerland, which was not then a member of the IMF) set up to oversee
the GAB and international financial matters more generally.

The Gold Pool

In 1954 Britain reopened the London gold market, resuscitating one
of many commodity markets that had historically been located in that
city. Thus, new gold (mainly from South Africa, secondarily from the

Soviet Union) could be readily purchased by private parties. The price was determined by supply and demand. After 1958, however, the United States worried about the psychological implications of a London price of gold significantly above the official price of $35 per troy ounce. Such an event occurred in November 1960, and eight central banks agreed to sell gold into the market. The following year the "Gold Pool" among eight central banks (those of the United States, United Kingdom, Belgium, France, Germany, Italy, the Netherlands, and Switzerland) was formed to sell gold into the London market when the price threatened to rise above $35.20. The US share was 50 percent (59 percent after France withdrew in June 1967). It was understood that any gold sold by other central banks (for dollars) could be replenished by converting the newly acquired dollars into gold at the US Treasury, hopefully with a lag. This arrangement endured until March 1968 when the "two-tiered" gold market was introduced. The Pool purchased gold from the market through 1962–63, more than replenishing its sales in 1961. A crisis erupted in 1967–68 associated with the speculative crisis around the British pound, but following an acceleration of inflation in all the Group of Ten countries, in the United States from 1.2 percent in the consumer price index in 1964 to 3 percent in 1967 and 4.7 percent in 1968. The Gold Pool sold $400 million in the first ten months of 1967, mostly in October, and an additional $3 billion from November 1967 following the devaluation of sterling to March 1968 when Gold Pool sales ceased and the "two tier" system was adopted. A statement followed that the participating central banks would no longer sell gold to private parties and "no longer feel it necessary to buy from the market" in view of the prospective creation of special drawing rights (SDRs). Many other central banks indicated their acceptance of this agreement (which was requested). France did not formally accept it but adhered to it.

Between September 1967 and March 1968, US and UK gold reserves dropped by 18 percent with lesser declines by the other participants. The two-tier agreement was formally abandoned in November 1973 after the United States had ceased gold convertibility (in August 1971) for official holders of dollars, the official price of gold had been raised (in two steps, to $42.22 an ounce), and when the market gold price was around $100 an ounce. According to the IMF rules, central banks thereafter would be able to sell gold to the market but not buy it at a price above the official price (Solomon 1977: 114–24).

Central Bank Swaps

Another mechanism of central bank cooperation introduced during this period, like the Gold Pool aimed in part at protecting US gold reserves, was the network of "swaps" created around the US Federal Reserve, although later it extended also between pairs of other central banks. A swap line was an arrangement whereby each of two central banks deposited an equivalent amount of its currency in the other central bank, usable by the second central bank either for market intervention or (in the case of the Fed) to purchase dollars from the other central bank that might otherwise be converted into gold. The deposits were typically for three months, renewable, but it came to be understood that they should not be renewed for more than one year. The form was first suggested by Julien Koszul of the Bank of France, and the first swap of $50 million was opened with France in March 1962 (Coombs 1976: 74). It was renewed once but not drawn upon, so after six months it was placed on standby, in effect a line of credit, the form in which most swaps were subsequently kept. Arrangements were made to avoid gains or losses in the event of changes in exchange rate parities (such as then prevailed). Swap arrangements totaling $2 billion had been established between the Federal Reserve and eight other central banks by the end of 1962. By 1975 the total had grown to $20 billion with fourteen central banks and the BIS (Coombs 1976: 78). These arrangements continued to 2004, with maximum authorized foreign exchange holdings of $25 billion. In addition, the mechanism had been adopted by East Asian central banks already before the Chiang Mai initiative of 2000, whereby the central banks of China, Japan, and others agreed to bilateral swaps with other central banks of East and South-East Asia, typically acting as agents for their finance ministries.

The swaps were activated and used by Canada in 1962 and by Italy in 1963–64 (when the Bank of England and the German Bundesbank also provided credits), as well as by the United States on several occasions in the 1960s. Most of the activated swaps were quickly repaid as speculative sentiment reversed and the drawing central bank regained reserves, but on a few occasions they ran one year and by agreement with the US Treasury were repaid by selling foreign-currency-denominated "Roosa bonds" to the relevant central bank, or by a US drawing on the International Monetary Fund. The latter had been made technically feasible by the creation in 1961 of the GAB, whereby ten countries (plus Switzerland, not at that time a member of the IMF) agreed to lend to the IMF if necessary to enable a US drawing, or indeed for drawings by others if the IMF was short of usable funds. In the event, the GAB was first drawn to help sterling, then the French franc.

Concerted Support for Sterling and the French Franc

Britain was plagued throughout the 1960s with a weak balance of payments, inflation higher than that of the United States and some other European countries, and balances in sterling amounting to the equivalent of $5 to $6 billion left over from the Second World War. Sterling came under pressure following the revaluations of the German mark and Dutch guilder in early 1961, and eight European central banks provided short-term financial support to the Bank of England totaling $910 million, described by Gilbert (1980: 64) as the first concerted central bank support package. The remaining outstanding "Basel" credits were repaid by drawing on the IMF in July 1961. Charles A. Coombs, the official responsible for the international activities of the Federal Reserve Bank of New York and a major player in central bank cooperation during his fifteen-year tenure there (1960–75), describes these credits as "a major

Richard N. Cooper

breakthrough in postwar international finance . . . European central bank cooperation had not only saved sterling, but had also protected the dollar against heavy gold drains" (Coombs 1976: 37).

This pattern was to be repeated on several occasions. Indeed, there was almost continuous central bank help to the Bank of England through Basel arrangements during 1964–68. The announcement and use of a new support package typically reversed the speculative pressures, permitting some repayment. The remaining outstanding credits would be repaid by drawing on the IMF, which occurred in late 1964, May 1965, December 1967, and June 1968 (Tew 1970: chap. 15). Eventually eleven central banks were involved, including those of Canada, Japan, and the United States. The newly created GAB was first activated in 1965 to support IMF loans to Britain rather than the United States. Federal Reserve swap lines were increased in stages from $500 million to $2 billion in March 1968, when the two-tiered gold arrangements were introduced, and several such increases were included in the announced support packages. Despite this support, sterling was devalued in November 1967 (Cairncross and Eichengreen 2003). Indeed, Bank of England Governor Leslie K. O'Brien used a monthly BIS meeting to canvas his central bank counterparts on the acceptability of a sterling devaluation and received assurances that so long as it did not exceed 15 percent, other European countries would not follow, as they had in 1949 (Gilbert 1980: 69). The parity of sterling was changed from $2.80 to $2.40, a devaluation of 14.3 percent from the perspective of Britain's competitors if British export prices were unchanged in sterling, but 16.7 percent when seen from the perspective of British importers, who could expect to see the prices of imported goods rise by that amount if they did not change in foreign currency.

In addition to these support packages, two "Basel Group Arrangements" were offered to the Bank of England, one in June 1966 for up to $1 billion, the other in August 1968 for up to $2 billion, to provide special support in the event of overseas holders of sterling balances drawing down those balances significantly. The second arrangement required the Bank of England to reach agreement with major official holders of sterling to draw down their balances only in case of balance of payments need (i.e., to avoid cashing in sterling for other reserve assets) (Tew 1970: chap. 15; Gilbert 1980: 68, 71). A third support package was assembled when sterling ran into trouble again in 1976.

Altogether, Britain had outstanding debt associated with successive rescue operations totaling $8 billion at the end of 1968, of which more than half had been repaid by mid-1970 (Tew 1970: 270). Canada also received support from several central banks during early 1968.

During the period of sterling difficulties the French franc had seemed to be in fine shape. Thanks to the devaluation of 1958 and the more conservative policies under de Gaulle's Fifth Republic, France ran payments surpluses. It was during this period that President de Gaulle raised questions about the desirability of the prevailing international monetary arrangements and expressed displeasure at the "exorbitant privilege" of the United States arising from the dollar's use as a reserve currency. In various ways France added to the strains on the system, by conspicuously converting recently acquired dollars into gold and, for example, by withdrawing from the Gold Pool in 1967 and circulating rumors that other central banks would soon do so (Solomon 1977: 114). During May 1968, however, France experienced widespread student protests, reinforced by widespread strikes. Police had to be called out in force, and financial markets turned skittish about the French franc. France drew on central bank support from the Federal Reserve, other members of the European Community, and the BIS, totaling $1.4 billion. The speculative movement subsided but resumed again in 1969 in connection with on-again, off-again speculation on a revaluation of the German mark. Again central bank support was provided to France by the United States, Belgium, Germany, Italy, the Netherlands, and the BIS. The franc was devalued by 11 percent during August 1969, a period of temporary quiet.

Richard N. Cooper

Management of Eurodollars

As noted above, the London-based eurodollar market had come into being in 1957 when Britain placed restrictions on the use of sterling for third country financing. By the mid-1960s it had become sufficiently significant that seasonal movements of funds into and out of the eurodollar market, particularly around accounts reporting days at the end of each quarter for "window dressing," affected the movement of official foreign exchange reserves significantly. Moreover, movements out of eurodollars at such window-dressing dates sharply increased short-term eurodollar interest rates, which in turn could draw funds from New York and worsen the US payments deficit as it was then officially reckoned (the so-called liquidity deficit; the United States ran a current account surplus throughout the 1960s). Led by the Swiss National Bank, agreement was reached in Basel to avoid these private withdrawals by encouraging repurchase agreements with a central bank, whereby the central bank would purchase dollars for local currency before the window-dressing date, to be automatically reversed after the date in question; or to offset them via placement by central banks of their newly acquired dollars in the eurodollar market before the window-dressing date, to be reversed afterward. Such operations at the end of 1967, including placements by the BIS, amounted to $1.4 billion (Coombs 1976: 196–98, 200).

Later, a different problem arose with the eurodollar market. A number of central banks had developed the practice of placing some of their dollar reserves in the eurodollar market. These funds were of course subsequently re-lent by the accepting banks. Such re-lending created a source of dollars not directly related to the US payments deficit, providing a kind of multiplier on US-originated dollars. When in the early 1970s speculation against the dollar resulted in large reserve accruals by other central banks, these accruals were augmented by this "carousel" effect. Agreement was accordingly reached in March 1971 that G10 central banks would henceforward not place their dollar reserves in the eurodollar market, but rather would hold them directly in the United States (Solomon 1977: 177). This agreement did not apply to other central banks, so the practice continued, albeit on a smaller scale.

The emergence of the eurodollar market, outside the national monetary system of any country, created the need to acquire information and track its evolution, simply in the interest of understanding what was happening. This role fell to the BIS, which was requested by the G10 in 1964 to collect and collate information on international claims and liabilities of the leading banks in those countries, in the context of available financing for payments deficits and an early attempt at "multilateral surveillance" (Solomon 1977: 68). Thus began a process of regular monitoring of cross-national international banking claims, which by 2004 covered thirty-eight countries. Regular discussion of the eurocurrency market, with an attempt both to define and to quantify it, began in the *34th Annual Report* (1964). The BIS played an analogous role for world demand and supply of gold, and in the 1990s began to track cross-border transactions in derivatives.

DEPRECIATIONS OF THE DOLLAR

Market pressures shifted from the pound and the franc to the dollar in the early 1970s, resulting in August 1971 in suspension of the gold convertibility of the dollar for foreign monetary authorities. In December 1971 the dollar was devalued relative to other leading currencies, most with respect to the Japanese yen, and the notional price of monetary gold was raised. From June 1970 to March 1973 currency parities were gradually abandoned, starting with the Canadian dollar in May 1970, and with that abandonment went fixed exchange rates among the major currencies. While central banks were involved as supporting actors, these dramatic developments were more directly in the hands of finance ministries, and thus fall outside the focus of this chapter.

Richard N. Cooper

In some circles, the monthly and later bimonthly BIS meeting of central bankers was considered a "cabal" where policies were determined away from the glare of publicity and even against the interests of national economies. In fact, as Coombs reports, "at the Basel meetings little if anything in the way of coordination of national monetary policy was ever accomplished. Each governor reported his problems but rarely forecast policy recommendations" (1976: 198). Indeed, after the inauguration of the Nixon administration in the United States in January 1969, when Paul Volcker became the senior US Treasury official responsible for international financial policy, according to Coombs the role of the Federal Reserve in international matters was drastically curtailed, and the "action center . . . at Basel fell into disuse" (1976: xii). It later revived, and indeed in 1996, nine additional central banks were invited to join the BIS (Brazil, China, Hong Kong, India, Republic of Korea, Mexico, Russia, Saudi Arabia, and Singapore). By 2004 the membership had grown to fifty-five central banks, and private shareholders had been bought out. Of the fifty-five members, thirty-three (and thirteen of seventeen directors) were European, so the BIS remained a heavily European institution (it was still performing certain trustee functions related to German payments on the Dawes and Young loans, of 1924 and 1929 respectively, and was expected to do so until 2010, nearly a century after the Dawes loan was made).

There was one respect in which the "cabal" proved vitally useful. In September 1971, after suspension of gold convertibility and the imposition of an import surcharge by the United States on dutiable imports, but before the December Smithsonian agreement on the currency realignments, Arthur Burns, Chairman of the Federal Reserve Board, requested Jelle Zijlstra, Governor of the central bank of the Netherlands and Chairman of the BIS Board of Governors, to quietly canvas his European counterparts as to what change in currency values would be acceptable. Zijlstra produced a report on the desirable change in the US current account and the exchange rate changes required to bring it about, including a modest "devaluation" of the dollar against gold, that is, a rise in the dollar price of gold (France considered such a step necessary for a negotiated deal). US officials felt that the numbers were too small, but it provided a concrete basis for the negotiations that took place later in the fall (Solomon 1977: 196, 202).

During the turbulent decade of the 1970s most economic cooperation, when it occurred, was driven by governments, by ministers of finance, or even by foreign ministers and heads of government, institutionalized from 1975 by the annual G5 economic summit meetings, which continued for three decades thereafter. After the dollar crisis of the early 1970s, major currencies floated against one another (except within the European Monetary System), and the world economy experienced two major increases in oil prices, followed by recessions and an acceleration of inflation. People wanted to know what was happening and what their governments were going to do about it – not conditions conducive to quiet cooperation among central banks. In any case, governors of central banks were involved and had participated in meetings of the G5 (later G7) finance ministers and their deputies, and, along with government officials, in Working Party Three of the Economic Policy Committee of the OECD since its beginnings in 1961. Thus central bank staffs were engaged in preparations for the international discussions of monetary, financial, and exchange rate policies, and about reform of the international monetary system, even if ministries of finance called the tune.

To combat inflation more effectively and more persuasively, the Federal Reserve under Paul Volcker's new chairmanship underwent a major change in operating procedures during the fall of 1979, a shift from targeting short-term interest rates to targeting some measure of the quantity of money. Volcker had worked in the Treasury Department in the early 1960s and again during the first Nixon administration. He subsequently served as President of the Federal Reserve Bank of New York for four years before being appointed Fed Chairman in 1979, in part

Richard N. Cooper

because of his international connections and the respect he commanded abroad as well as in the United States. Before being implemented, the proposed change in policy was vetted with Otmar Emminger, President of the German Bundesbank, and with other central bankers assembled in Belgrade for the annual IMF and World Bank meetings, partly to alert them to the pending change (which had not yet been agreed within the Federal Reserve) and partly to get their reactions and implicit approval for it (Volcker and Gyohten 1992: 168).

THE 1982 DEBT CRISIS

The resulting sharp increase in short-term interest rates signaled the Fed was really serious about combating inflation, but it also produced an unexpectedly deep recession, despite which interest rates were held up well into the recession, coming down only in July 1982. Warnings of pending debt problems in some developing countries had already surfaced; many had borrowed heavily in foreign currency during the two oil shocks, at floating interest rates. Now they experienced first rising and then high interest rates even while demand for their exports declined as the United States and other major markets slipped into recession. Normally, interest payments would be expected to decline under these conditions, but in this case the decline did not come until the second half of 1982.

Mexico was in the final year of its president's six-year, non-renewable term, typically a year of high government spending to facilitate the election of the chosen candidate of the PRI, the ruling party. Mexico's reserves were put under great strain, and the Bank of Mexico, with Fed complicity, engaged in overnight window dressing of its reserves around reporting dates. The hope was to get through the presidential election so that the newly elected, economically literate President Miguel de la Madrid could install an IMF-approved stabilization program that would provide the basis for continued foreign lending to Mexico, something the haughty and economically illiterate outgoing President Lopez Portillo refused to contemplate.

The Fed's $700 million swap facility with the Bank of Mexico was activated after the election in July but before the president's inauguration in December. The crisis erupted in August as Mexico nearly exhausted its reserves, and a support package of $1.85 billion was assembled, half from the United States, half from Japan and various European central banks. Volcker comments on this emergency loan as follows: "It was a remarkable example of international financial cooperation . . . The agreements really rested on mutual trust among financial officials and perhaps most particularly among central bankers. By virtue of experience, tenure, and training, they are almost uniquely able to deal with each other on a basis of close understanding and frankness . . . We didn't have to spend a lot of time explaining to each other the nature of the emergency" (Volcker and Gyohten 1992: 201). This emergency arose from the threats to national banking systems whose leading banks had engaged heavily, excessively as it turned out, in lending to developing countries, as well as the threat of financial collapse in Mexico and other Latin American countries.

Volcker is too kind to add that the financial officials in the first Reagan administration were strongly inclined to a hands-off approach to exchange rate and financial issues, on the supposition that the "market knows best," and even when it doesn't, government intervention is likely to make things worse. The lead in dealing with the 1982 debt crisis was taken by the Federal Reserve, operating through the BIS on the basis of Mexico's commitment to go to the IMF after the inauguration, out of its concern for the functioning of the financial system, and the US Treasury found itself playing catchup at first, although later it resumed its lead role, with the Baker Plan of 1986 and the Brady Plan of 1989. The role of central banks receded also as the financial prospects of the commercial banks improved.

Richard N. Cooper

PLAZA AND LOUVRE

The US dollar appreciated sharply from early 1980 to early 1985, from 1.7 to 3.4 DM per dollar, and by lesser amounts with respect to the Japanese yen. By 1985 the weak competitive position of American manufacturing led to strong protectionist pressures in Congress. Newly installed secretary of Treasury James Baker took the lead in January 1985 to change the US policy of non-intervention and got the G5 finance ministers and central bank governors to issue the so-called Plaza agreement in September 1985, to the effect that the dollar was too strong and that they stood "ready to cooperate more closely to encourage [appreciation of other currencies] when to do so would be helpful." Against the background of a stated US policy toward non-intervention in foreign exchange markets during the first Reagan administration, this communiqué – the first issued by G5 ministers and governors although they had been meeting together for more than a decade – carried a strong message to financial markets. It was backed up by a concerted sale of dollars in foreign exchange markets in Tokyo, Frankfurt, London, and New York. Indeed, concerted intervention had begun on a smaller scale in January 1985, before the dollar reached its peak.

The dollar fell continuously following the Plaza agreement and throughout 1986, to the point that Japan began to worry about the implications of a strong yen for the Japanese economy. US-Japanese conversations occurred between finance ministries, and the Bank of Japan began to buy dollars. Following a G6 (G5 plus Canada) meeting in the Louvre in February 1987, ministers and governors announced that "further substantial exchange rate shifts among their currencies could damage growth and adjustment prospects" with the suggestion in some quarters, never officially confirmed, that a target exchange rate zone had been established. Again, concerted exchange market intervention occurred, this time buying dollars on a substantial scale to stabilize the rates. Altogether during the period early 1985 to early 1991 there were seventeen episodes of concerted intervention in exchange markets, mainly dollar purchases in 1987 and dollar sales in late 1988–90 (Dominguez and Frankel 1993: 16).

Exchange market intervention by major central banks was less common during the 1990s than it had been in the late 1980s, but several notable concerted interventions occurred, sometimes on a larger scale and with attendant public announcement, especially to strengthen the dollar against the yen in August 1993 and again in August 1995, and against the German mark in the summer of 1992 and again in May 1995. Steps were taken also to strengthen the yen against the dollar in early 1992, early 1995, and in June 1998, and the mark against the dollar in early 1990 and July 1991. The newly established European Central Bank (ECB) also intervened in support of the euro in September 2000, in collaboration with the US Treasury and the Federal Reserve, the Bank of Japan, and other central banks (Dominguez 2003a: 230–40).

Most of these interventions were sterilized in the first instance, often automatically, to neutralize their effects on domestic monetary conditions, although over time the impacts of the interventions were sometimes allowed to affect the money supply; and ministries of finance were typically implicated in the decisions. Even in the case of the ECB, embarrassingly independent of the political process, the European Council of Finance Ministers (Ecofin) was consulted before intervention (Dominguez 2003a: 233).

As noted earlier, it was virtually unknown for monetary policy as such to be coordinated, at least across the Atlantic. Monetary policies were occasionally discussed in the OECD's Working Party Three, and arguably sometimes led to subsequent action, for example in March 1971, when Europeans eased and the Federal Reserve tightened in the presence of large short-term outflows from the United States (Solomon 1977: 178). A clear exception occurred in March 1986 when the dollar was still depreciating following the Plaza agreement. Fed Chairman Volcker was concerned about a runaway decline and was therefore hesitant to lower US interest rates even though weakening domestic economic conditions

Richard N. Cooper

would support such a move, and the Reagan administration had made known its desire for lower rates. Several Reagan appointees to the Federal Reserve Board outvoted Volcker and his supporters on whether to lower the discount rate, in what has become known as the "palace coup."

As the full implications of this revolt began to sink in, two of the governors offered later in the day to reverse their votes before a public announcement of the change was made. Volcker in turn pledged to support a lower rate if he could persuade the Bundesbank and the Bank of Japan to lower their rates at the same time, thus neutralizing any effect on the dollar exchange rate. This he succeeded in doing. Indeed he had talked with his counterparts in January about the possible need for a concerted reduction in interest rates, so they were prepared for his request. A second reduction in the US discount rate, coordinated with the Bank of Japan, took place in April. Monetary authorities together also took prompt action to avoid possible financial crisis and recession following the stock market crash of October 1987 (Funibashi 1989; Volcker and Gyohten 1992: 272–74, 285).

EUROPEAN MONETARY COOPERATION

There is a long and complex history of attempts at monetary cooperation in Europe, following the EPU. Indeed, such cooperation was envisioned, in general terms, in the 1957 Treaty of Rome, and a committee of the governors of central banks of the European Community was established in 1964, which typically met in Basel on the occasion of the BIS meetings. Here is not the place for a detailed review of that history, which can be found in Apel (2002) or Gros and Thygesen (1998). Suffice it to say that technical and political issues were commingled in these discussions and that central banks were generally under instruction from their political masters, although the former – and especially the German Bundesbank – had a strong if not always determining voice in the discussions and negotiations. Sometimes they even ignored political decisions, as in the case of the European Monetary Cooperation Fund (EMCF) of 1973, to be sure with the acquiescence of the political masters, who were conscious of unresolved differences in emphasis and priorities among themselves and chose not to resolve them, at least for a time.

Consultations on a wide range of technical issues occurred almost continuously over the years, as Europe moved successively through the European Monetary Agreement (EMA) and the Werner Plan to the EMCF, the European Monetary System (EMS), the Delors Plan/Maastricht Treaty, the European Monetary Institute, eventually to an economic and monetary union and the creation of the ECB and the European System of Central Banks in 1998. Central banks were involved in almost all these discussions, the major exception being the EMS, which was planned from the chancellery of Helmut Schmidt with the presumably deliberate exclusion of the Bundesbank, although the latter institution was engaged in detailed planning and execution once the main outlines were drawn.

Beyond standardizing, compiling, exchanging, and assessing information, central bank cooperation was especially required, over the years, on two fronts: market intervention and short-run financial support. Under the Bretton Woods system as embodied in the IMF Articles of Agreement, countries were enjoined to have currencies convertible for current account transactions, to declare par values in terms of the gold dollar of 1944, and to keep market exchange rates within 1 percent of par value. This implied a maximum range of flexibility between any two European currencies of 4 percent, which was deemed too high, so Europeans early on agreed to narrow this possible range to 3 percent. Following the Smithsonian agreement of 1971, when currency bands by consensus were widened to ± 2.25 percent (permitting a 9 percent maximum swing for two non-dollar currencies), the six members of the European Community, later joined by others, agreed in April 1972 to halve their intervention limits leading to a "snake in the [dollar] tunnel." The "tunnel" disappeared with the generalized move to floating exchange rates in March 1973, but the European "snake" remained, with constantly changing membership (for example, France withdrew in 1974, rejoined in 1975, withdrew again in 1976). Intervention limits and the conventions for deciding them was a continuing issue, as was intramarginal intervention (which several central banks preferred, both to limit exchange rate movements and to keep markets uncertain about where exchange rates would move next within the allowable band), which was viewed as a necessarily cooperative venture, at least in terms of prior notice and exchange of information between the two central banks directly involved.

The second issue was short-term credits among European central banks to support their exchange rate commitments. These arose out of swap arrangements agreed at various times during the 1960s, which were systematized in principle in 1973 in the EMCF, but in fact remained under the management of the central banks. They were further systematized and enlarged in late 1978, in preparation for the launch of EMS in January 1979. To support market intervention at the boundaries of the band, creditor central banks were obliged to extend unlimited credits (defined as very short-term credit) to debtor central banks, to be repaid forty-five days after the end of the month of intervention (up from thirty days under the "snake"). Beyond that, if the outstanding debt could not be settled, creditor central banks would extend "short-term credit" to debtor central banks up to a specified ceiling for three months, renewable for three months. Thus some form of central bank credit was available for up to eight months. Beyond that, governments would assume responsibility for extending any further credits, subject to such conditions as might be determined by Ecofin. Even after their enlargement in 1978, these short-term credit facilities were limited, roughly the size of IMF quotas of those participating in the EMS.

The settlement of very short-term credits could be made up to 50 percent by drawing on gold and foreign exchange (largely dollar) reserves that were mobilized through the EMCF. Twenty percent of such reserves were notionally "deposited" in the EMCF as ecu, the synthetic European currency unit. This arrangement had the effect of enabling some gold reserves, whose market price was now way above the official price, and was used for these notional deposits, to be used once again for official international settlements. The Bundesbank, however, was uneasy about all this potential credit, and on request acquired assurances from the German government that if EMS commitments ever conflicted with the objective of price stability, the former would be sacrificed. That is, the Bundesbank would be relieved of its obligation to support currencies that it considered to be in fundamental disequilibrium.

In the event, inter-European central bank credits were little used during the 1980s, partly because the national central banks had ample reserves, partly because exchange rates within the EMS were adjusted more often, roughly once a year, than perhaps had been envisioned in 1978.

This situation changed in the early 1990s, after the Maastricht Treaty had been negotiated and signed. Europe experienced a full-fledged monetary crisis in September 1992, which led Britain and Italy to leave the exchange rate mechanism (ERM; Britain had joined in 1990). Several countries also altered their currency parities (central rates), and the crisis led in 1993 to the enlargement of the permissible exchange rate band to ±15 percent, in effect preserving the ERM in name only. During the crisis, however, extensive credits were extended, reported to have been $30 billion by the Bundesbank on behalf of the British pound and the Italian lira before it ceased support, and a total of $27 billion in support of the French franc, which survived the crisis with no change in central rate (Dominguez and Frankel 1993: 46).

The ultimate form of central bank cooperation was achieved in 1998 when the ECB was created with sole authority over monetary policy among its eleven members, and with the creation of a new common currency, the euro, in January 1999. National currencies were finally withdrawn in early 2002, national central banks continued, largely as operating branches of the European System of Central Banks (ESCB), and key decisions were made collectively. Some ambiguity remains about exchange rates, since policy toward exchange rates is currently reserved for governments, but management of exchange rates, closely related to monetary policy, is the responsibility of the ECB.

COOPERATION IN OTHER REGIONS

Central bank swap or buyback arrangements have been agreed among central banks in East Asia, mostly specified in foreign exchange rather than domestic currency (the exception is that between China and Japan, which is technically the Bank of Japan's only swap agreement in Asia; the others are carried by the Ministry of Finance, with the Bank of Japan as agent). The central bank of China entered into such arrangements with Hong Kong and Malaysia in 1996 and with Indonesia, the Philippines, and Thailand in 1997.

A network of swaps was formalized in the Chiang Mai initiative of 2000, although the arrangements remained bilateral, and by 2005 they had attained a face value of $39.5 billion, although none had actually been drawn. In 2005, an agreement in principle was made to double the amount and to increase to 20 percent (up from 10 percent) the amounts that could be drawn without an IMF program.

By 2004 the Executives' Meeting of East Asia and Pacific central banks (EMEAP) had eleven members: Australia, Japan, Republic of Korea, New Zealand, China, Hong Kong SAR, Indonesia, Malaysia, the Philippines, Singapore, and Thailand. In June 2003 they created the first Asian Bond Fund, and in December 2004 a second such fund whereby central banks agreed to put some portion of their reserves, up to $2 billion, into regional bonds (Zhang Zhixiang, personal communication). The BIS acted as agent for the bond funds.

COOPERATION IN REGULATION

Starting as early as 1974, central banks began to be concerned about the possibly unhealthy implications for the international financial system of unrestrained and unregulated competition among the leading commercial banks of the world, and they began to frame a series of prudential regulations with regard to which central banks bore ultimate responsibility for banks operating out of their home jurisdictions in currencies other than their home currency, adequacy of bank capital, and so forth. By 2004, the BIS had sponsored standing committees on bank supervision, payments and settlement systems, and the global financial system (formerly eurocurrencies). This important area of central bank cooperation will be covered in chapter 3 by Ethan Kapstein.

EVALUATION

As the foregoing account suggests, there has been extensive cooperation among central banks, mostly, but not only, European central banks, especially since the 1960s but starting well before that and into the present. Has it been a good thing? This may seem like a churlish question, but some economists these days question everything that public institutions do, especially when they try to do it together. It is sometimes seen as a conspiracy of elite technocrats against the true interests of the people. "Moral hazard" is frequently cited as an undesirable consequence of central bank cooperation, even of central banks acting alone. Attempts to influence exchange rates are tampering with otherwise efficient market forces.

Most of these criticisms are misplaced. One consequence of central bank cooperation has been much improved collection, standardization, and compilation of financial statistics, and even skeptics of public action usually agree that transparency of information is necessary for a well-functioning financial market. At the purely theoretical level, it can be

107

shown that cooperative solutions to policy choices in interdependent systems can lead to superior outcomes to non-cooperative choices in the same environment. For example, an attempt by monetary authorities to pursue tight monetary conditions to combat actual or threatening inflation, under floating exchange rates, can lead to unnecessary contraction of world output, since competing central banks try to get the advantages of an appreciating currency, which of course cannot be obtained by all countries in the system at the same time (Cooper 1985). With n currencies there are only $n - 1$ independent exchange rates, hence a degree of freedom for the system as a whole (the average degree of monetary ease) can be used to an advantage but requires a convention that at least one country is passive in foreign exchange markets and targets world monetary conditions. Or it requires a formal rule for intervention or active cooperation.

In contrast, however, Rogoff (1985) has shown that in a world of full information, perfect (stochastic) foresight, and wage setting with a one-period lag, central bank cooperation may lead to higher than expected and actual inflation because of the loss of the disciplinary effect on monetary policy of a depreciating currency. Rogoff concedes, however, that cooperation is superior to its absence in combating shocks to the system, and concludes that what would be desirable would be to find a credible regime for limiting inflation. Interestingly enough, Paul Einzig, in explaining the rationale for central bank cooperation in the BIS in 1930, also expressed concern that cooperative arrangements might lead to excessive credit creation and higher inflation, but judged the potential benefits of cooperation to outweigh the potential costs (his book went to press in December 1929!).

These models are probably largely irrelevant to the experience of the past half-century, since as we have noted there was little cooperation in framing monetary policy *per se*. Indeed, Maisel reported that during his seven years on the Federal Reserve Board (1965–72) there were only 8 out of more than 100 monetary policy actions in which he noted any influence of international considerations, usually affecting the timing of Fed actions (1973: 221–24). Thus, in five instances the Fed moved sooner than it might have on domestic grounds alone in tightening policy to inhibit US reserve losses. In three instances tightening was delayed out of concern for pressures, respectively, on the pound, the French franc, and the Italian lira. Only one of the eight, in December 1965 concerning sterling, was controversial within the Federal Open Market Committee (FOMC).

Cooper and Little (2000), on reviewing the minutes of the FOMC over a much longer period, find that international factors were frequently mentioned but were rarely decisive in determining policy. Nonetheless, a statistical test involving a Fed reaction function showed that dollar purchases by the Fed in foreign exchange markets were associated with a subsequent tightening of the federal funds rate, although dollar sales did not seem to influence US monetary policy (Cooper and Little 2000: 93).

Two episodes have been mentioned where, it is claimed, central bank engagement in international cooperation contributed to disastrous results: Federal Reserve help for the British pound in 1927 and the Louvre Accord to help inhibit Japanese currency appreciation in 1987–88. Neither claim will stand up to close scrutiny. Detailed examination of the first case, outlined early in this chapter, such as was undertaken by Chandler (1958: 438ff), reveals that the situation was much more complicated than some later portrayals, that the Fed decision on a reduction in the discount rate was taken overwhelmingly for domestic reasons (partly seasonal), and that even the international element as discussed by the Federal Reserve Board involved largely domestic conditions (Eichengreen 1992: 212–14). That is, an anticipated rise in the discount rate of the Bank of England, possibly leading to increases in continental Europe, would depress British and European demand for US products, particularly agricultural products, during the fall harvest season. The reduction in the US rate, justified by the Board to itself on domestic grounds, had the additional advantage of forestalling a rise in European rates and a reduction in demand for US exports but also eased pressure on sterling. The later debate was complicated by the somewhat arbitrary way in which the Board forced a reduction in Chicago's rate, over the objections of the Chicago President and directors (at that time each Federal Reserve Bank had its own discount rate, but of course as a national financial market evolved this became untenable over time; 1927 was a transition year, but New York feared funds would be pulled from New York and elsewhere to Chicago if the latter's rate was higher). This was an early example where international considerations – a prospective fall in European demand for US agricultural products – influenced US monetary policy. Help for sterling, however, did not lead US policy in a direction different from domestic considerations.

It is sometimes claimed that the financial and real estate bubble in Japan in the late 1980s was caused by US pressure, reflected in the Louvre agreement and elsewhere, for Japan to maintain a more stimulative monetary and, especially, fiscal policy than it would have done on domestic grounds alone (e.g., Siebert 2003). A close reading of the record, however, such as that provided by Funibashi (1989), suggests that close to the opposite may be the case: the ruling LDP party of Japan wanted stimulative policy for domestic, partly electoral, reasons. The powerful Ministry of Finance resisted stimulative fiscal policy, which shifted the pressure to the Bank of Japan and monetary policy. Japanese officials were also concerned about undue appreciation of the yen, which would damage the export sector. Again, that pointed toward a stimulative monetary policy. Secretary of Treasury Baker on several occasions called for more Japanese fiscal action, and the Japanese weakly complied. But they found it convenient domestically to rely more on monetary policy and to shift the responsibility to US *gaiatsu* for actions that they wanted to take on domestic grounds, partly to overcome the resistance of the domestic mandarins in the finance ministry.

There has been much controversy over the efficacy of official exchange market intervention under floating exchange rates with high capital mobility. Indeed the G7-commissioned Jurgensen Report of 1983 concluded that sterilized intervention, that is, market intervention that did not affect the domestic money supply, was at best small and transitory during the period 1973–81, and these results conformed to the views of many economists and some government officials, especially in the early Reagan administration. If that is the case, cooperation in exchange market intervention is pointless. However, Dominguez and Frankel (1993), using daily official intervention by the Federal Reserve, the Bundesbank, and the Swiss National Bank during the 1980s, find that such intervention can have a significant effect on market exchange rates, particularly when it is coordinated among central banks and when it is unexpected. Dominguez (2003a), adding information from the Bank of Japan, reaches a similar conclusion for the 1990s, calling into question the largely theoretical reasoning of economists, with some support from empirical work using much coarser data on intervention. Perhaps the reason is to be found in the fragility of expectations that often prevails in foreign exchange markets, with market participants unclear on what the key determinants of exchange rates should be during the next week, quarter, or even years. As Charles A. Coombs, the New York Fed official responsible for exchange market intervention for fifteen years, put it after three years of floating: "By its very nature, the foreign exchange market is a nervous, high risk, ultra-sensitive mechanism, primarily geared to short term developments. Of the tens of billions [now over a trillion] of dollars in daily transactions cleared through the market, only a fraction derive from such fundamental factors as foreign trade and long term investment. On a day-to-day basis, the market is instead dominated by short-term capital movements in search of quick profits" (1976: xiii). Under these circumstances, some guidance from central banks about what officials consider an appropriate rate, or more often a clearly inappropriate rate, can help focus market expectations.

In summary, central bank cooperation has grown extensively, if fitfully and sporadically, since the birth of the BIS and the inauguration of monthly meetings of central bankers in 1930. In Europe of the euro, it has reached the acme of full coordination of policy. Elsewhere, it remains sporadic but with a much more solid infrastructure of meetings, personal contacts (made easier by jet aircraft and reliable transoceanic telephone), and comparable, consolidated information than was available seventy-five years ago.

3

Architects of Stability? International Cooperation among Financial Supervisors

ETHAN B. KAPSTEIN[1]

Speaking in May 1998, in the shadow of an Asian financial crisis that was spreading globally, International Monetary Fund Managing Director Michel Camdessus announced that "the leaders of the world want to embark on the design of a new (financial) architecture." Reflecting the position that industrial world governments would formally adopt at their forthcoming G8 summit in England, he asserted that the new architecture must be built atop several cornerstones, including a commitment to financial sector openness, good governance, and greater economic transparency. In addition, he suggested that international financial markets required the continuing elaboration of multilateral standards, codes, and best practices if future crises were to be avoided (Camdessus 1998).

It did not take long for skeptics of this G8 proposal to rear their heads; after all, grandiose phrases like "new financial architecture" naturally

[1] Ethan B. Kapstein is Paul Dubrule Professor of Sustainable Development, INSEAD, and Visiting Fellow, Center for Global Development, Washington, DC. He wishes to thank Akshaya Kamath, Mahesh Narayanaswamy, and Lawrence Teh for their research assistance; Charles Goodhart and Ingo Walter for extremely useful comments; and Claudio Borio and William White – and their colleagues at the Bank for International Settlements – for warm hospitality and stimulating discussions on the topics developed in this chapter.

provoked them. In a speech before the World Affairs Council, for example, Berkeley professor and former US Treasury official J. Bradford DeLong stated that "there is no world-wide political consensus" with respect to the systemic risks facing the global economy and that, as a consequence, "dreams of a rebuilt, reformed, and renewed international financial architecture will remain nothing but dreams" (DeLong 1999).

Beyond these skeptics lurked the critics who – whether coming from the left or the right of the political spectrum – curiously shared the conspiratorial view that the new international financial architecture represented nothing more than another underhanded attempt by governments and international organizations to bail out reckless banks at taxpayer expense. Finance ministers were once again failing to confront the problem of moral hazard in a world with lenders of last resort, and far from strengthening global finance, the new international architecture would only make it more crisis-prone (Langley 2002).

The purpose of this chapter is to provide a balanced assessment of international cooperation among financial regulators, with specific reference to banking supervision. While recognizing the undeniable – and even unexpected – achievement of these regulators in crafting a more robust financial system, we will also try to show that it remains a work in progress in significant respects, given the financial risk environment that now exists.

Briefly, we argue that the contemporary risk environment has an almost paradoxical quality to it, in that risk has become both more consolidated and more atomized at the same time. On the one hand, large and complex financial institutions, which may have become both "too big to fail" and "too hard to regulate," increasingly dominate the banking landscape; on the other, these same institutions have worked diligently to shift at least a portion of their risks onto other firms and households via the instruments and markets that exist for such purposes. It is the integrity of the international supervisory architecture in the face of this risk environment that we put into question.

The chapter addresses these issues in the following sections. First, we briefly discuss the relationship between financial stability and international cooperation among financial supervisors, stressing that stabilization has been only one objective and that competitive concerns – specifically private sector pressures to "level the playing field" – have also loomed large. Second, we seek to explain how financial supervisors managed to overcome numerous political barriers during the 1970s and 1980s to achieve greater international cooperation, in the process laying the cornerstones for the regulatory architecture that exists today; here we focus on the events leading up to the Basel Accord of 1988. Third, we examine the role of the Mexican and Asian financial crises of the 1990s in catalyzing demands for a new financial architecture, and particularly in highlighting the need to extend the G10 supervisory structure to emerging market economies, with specific emphasis on the globalization of the Basel Core Principles for an effective banking supervision. Fourth, we address the major changes that have taken place in the financial risk environment in recent years, highlighting banking consolidation and asset securitization. This analysis leads us to ask whether the new financial architecture, and in particular the Basel II Framework that constitutes one of its regulatory anchors, is well suited to the changing risk environment that agents now face.

The chapter concludes with some thoughts regarding the further institutional reforms that might be required in light of this new risk environment, including closer cooperation not just among financial supervisors within and across nations, but perhaps with elected officials as well – innovations that could prove particularly difficult to put into practice, given the highly "technocratic" and silolike regime for supervision of financial markets that currently exists in most countries whose central banks are members of the Bank for International Settlements (BIS). Former US Treasury secretary Robert Rubin put the sentiments expressed in this chapter succinctly when he wrote: "Our politics may not be well suited to coping with the new risks of the global economy" (Rubin 2003: 6).

If that is the case, the question arises as to whether the politics of financial supervision can be reformed in a way that continues to promote the benefits of globalization while minimizing its costs, particularly during periods of crisis.

FINANCIAL STABILITY AND INTERNATIONAL REGULATORY COOPERATION

From a public interest perspective, the rationale for government-led financial supervision rests upon the fundamental assumption that the collapse of one or more financial intermediaries could ripple throughout the economy, producing social losses that are greater than the private losses. As Robert Litan of the Brookings Institution has explained: "Historically, perhaps the overriding reason for regulating financial institutions and markets has been the desire to avoid systemic risk – the possibility of a contagious spread of losses across financial institutions that threatens to harm the real economy" (Herring and Litan 1995: 50).

Given the increasing diversity of intermediaries that are now providing households and firms with financial services, many central banks have, in recent years, developed a capacity to monitor the health of their nation's overall financial system, expanding their oversight and supervisory responsibilities well beyond commercial banks and payments systems. That broad function, in which systemic risks and interdependencies among financial agents are assessed, is aimed at trying to maintain domestic financial stability, and associated with it is a complex array of regulatory and supervisory arrangements with other government agencies – banking and securities regulators, treasury departments, and so forth – in the hope of ensuring cooperation among them should a crisis occur.

Has international cooperation among financial supervisors been motivated by similar concerns with systemic risk and financial stability? After all, one could posit that, in a global economy, the risks of international contagion have greatly increased, and thus the need for collective action with respect to governing the financial system. Reflecting this view, Stanley Fischer once wrote that "the occurrence of major banking failures . . . has been a matter of great import for anyone concerned with the stability and prosperity of the world economy." He suggested that the Asian financial crisis, for example, was primarily caused by weakness in the banking sector, due to "bad lending practices and inadequate supervision and regulation" (Fischer 1998). This made the task of international cooperation among supervisors critically important from the financial stability standpoint.

Yet as seductive as that view appears, a shared concern with financial stability in light of heightened interdependence has *not* been the sole motivation behind international cooperation. After all, if interdependence alone were the decisive factor, we would probably witness much more cooperation on such issues as climate change and fisheries management. The differences that we observe across issue areas with respect to levels and types of international cooperation lead us to suspect that other factors beyond mere degrees of interdependence are at work in driving this policy project. In this chapter we focus on just one of those factors: the role of the private sector in providing the decisive impetus for international cooperation among banking supervisors.

Just as students of domestic regulatory policy have found it useful to incorporate a public choice or private interest perspective in their work in order to understand public policy outcomes, we too will highlight the utility of that approach when it comes to international cooperation. As Edward Kane writes of the public choice perspective, it "views regulation more realistically as the outcome of efforts of interest groups, politicians, and bureaucrats to direct the coercive powers of government to generating personal benefits . . ." (Kane 2001: 88). He suggests that we can usefully think of the financial sector and its associated regulators as making up a "financial-service production team," though this image leads us to conclude (incorrectly in my view) that the team has a single, shared objective, akin to "winning." Perhaps a better way to conceptualize financial intermediaries and financial regulators is as an old couple who stay married for a variety of reasons, despite all the tensions in their relationship.

Our particular focus is on the pressures that have been placed upon regulators by private institutions that seek to achieve a "level playing field" for their global business activities. Bankers have expressed the view that relatively high national regulatory standards, say with respect to capital adequacy, have placed them at a competitive disadvantage in the global marketplace as compared to banks coming from jurisdictions with relatively low standards. These "low-standard banks" could charge smaller fees for their loans and services and, through greater leverage, still provide a satisfactory return on equity to their shareholders. In a global economy, these banks could win market share at the expense of high-standard banks in competitive markets like wholesale banking. This could lead to a "race to the bottom," with regulations weakening everywhere. As a consequence, financial stability and a level playing field appear to be intimately related in the eyes of financial supervisors. *International cooperation among financial supervisors may therefore be defined as a multilateral effort to reconcile diverse demands for both a more level and a more stable environment for global finance.*

This is not to argue that stabilizing and leveling are identical, although even supervisors sometimes seem to treat these two objectives as if they were one and the same thing. After all, one could easily imagine a more stable financial environment that tips the playing field against certain nations or types of intermediaries, for example, by making regulatory compliance very expensive and thus possible for only the largest and most profitable banks; in fact, some critics make this precise point about banking codes and standards, arguing that they are designed in part by the best capitalized firms as an instrument for eliminating their weaker competitors (Schneider 2001). Conversely, one could imagine a level playing field that was not terribly stable, say through the blanket elimination of onerous banking regulations and the acceptance of "free banking" globally.

This suggests that supervisors (and firms) from different countries could have very different ideas concerning what constitutes financial stability and competitive equity, reflecting their particular national circumstances; as Kane puts it, states might end up placing very different "net regulatory burdens" on financial intermediaries. Further, to the extent that financial regulators are influenced by locally based financial interests, shaping the domestic environment in such a way as to ensure the competitiveness of their national champions, they will also be led to adopt policies that may conflict with those of their foreign supervisory colleagues. In addition, significant differences in legal and accounting regimes, and in allowable banking practices, could doom cooperative efforts among supervisors, even given a shared interest in "financial stability." Overall, then, the promise of international cooperation among financial supervisors would seem limited at best, even if one assumed that such cooperation was desirable or beneficial from a social welfare standpoint – an assumption that, admittedly, remains widely debated among scholars if not regulators, given the public choice perspective that is widely influential in this field of research (Oatley and Nabors 1998; Kane 2001; Holthausen and Ronde 2004).

So how does cooperation in international financial supervision arise? In previous work I argued that cooperation in this issue area could be conceptualized as the product of power and purpose; specifically, the combination of US (and to a lesser extent British) financial market power with the shared or convergent purpose of bank supervisors to provide their home markets with greater financial stability while also addressing the competitive concerns of their domestic firms (Kapstein 1994). Let us discuss each of these elements, power and purpose, in turn.

Power is important to international cooperation because in its absence collective agreements may be harder to achieve as each state pursues its own domestic agenda. Even when actors share interests, they may fail to cooperate and pursue strategies that leave all parties worse off. The prisoner's dilemma game is the oft-used (and much abused) model of these sorts of perverse interactions.

But most of these game-theoretic models assume that the players are perfectly symmetric with respect to their capacities to strategize and to shape outcomes. In the world economy, however, actors are not symmetric in these respects, and particularly in their ability to generate desired outcomes, be it in trade or in finance. Because of its market power, the United States, for example, has a greater capacity to influence global finance than do many smaller states. Still, that power is hardly unlimited for several reasons.

First, despite "globalization," domestic banking systems and regulatory regimes around the world remain remarkably national. Canada, for example, basically denies foreign banks the right to acquire domestic financial institutions, and in Italy foreign entry has also been strictly curtailed (a policy that is only now changing). In both France and Germany, which are relatively "open" to foreign banks (at least in theory), the available data suggest that they have captured only a tiny fraction of either domestic loans or deposits. As a consequence, domestic financial institutions continue to control their home markets, at least in the industrial world.

This local domination, of course, not only reflects preferential regulatory arrangements, but also exists for good, institutional reasons. Once households and firms establish close relationships with particular banks, there must be extremely strong reasons for them to leave those banks for a competitor. Recognizing this, domestic banks continue to invest heavily in "bricks and mortar," despite the presence of the Internet and electronic banking and the financial revolutions they have long promised. In finance, physical presence still seems to matter for market share.

Second, to the extent that the United States does not wish to act as the *sole* lender of last resort to the entire world, but instead prefers to lead

Table 3.1: *Foreign exposure of US banks, 1982 and 2000 (in billions of 1996 US dollars)*

Total foreign exposure of US banks, 1982 and 2000	1982	2000
Cross-border claims (excluding derivatives)	531	382
Derivative exposure	**0**	**82**
Subtotal	531	464
Local country claims including derivative exposure	**119**	**318**
All foreign exposure	650	782
Ratio of banks' total foreign exposure to capital	6	2
Percentage of total foreign exposure in emerging markets	39	23
Percentage of total foreign exposure, money center banks	58	80
Percentage of cross-border claims on private sector	28	43

Source: Congressional Budget Office based on year-end data from Federal Financial Institutions Examination Council, *Country Exposure Lending Survey*, Statistical Release E.16 (1982 and 2000).

Adapted from: Congressional Budget Office, *U.S. Banks' Exposure to Foreign Financial Losses*, May 2002.

others in a rescue attempt – as revealed, for example, during the major financial crises of the 1980s and 1990s – it must seek cooperation with other governments and their central banks. That desire for international cooperation, in turn, must usually come at a price in terms of respecting the preferences of other states, restraining Washington's behavior – at least when it comes to financial supervision – in important respects (Rubin 2003).

Third, US financial institutions are often deeply intertwined with the firms, households, banks, and governments of foreign nations, making it difficult to articulate policies – even if a regulator desired to do so – that will obviously benefit one at the expense of the others (see Table 3.1 on the foreign exposure of US banks). In short, while the United States may possess something akin to hegemonic power in financial markets, it is at best a *constrained hegemony* that we are describing.

Yet the exercise of even constrained hegemonic power must be directed toward some political purpose, and what that purpose has been with respect to finance (not to mention many other issue areas) remains a topic of considerable debate, at least among academics. As already noted, some analysts have emphasized the interest of supervisors in providing collective, public interest goods like financial stability – for example, by providing lender-of-last-resort services – based on the assumption that they are rewarded by their political systems for delivering that good; or, more to the point, condemned for failing to do so. As Sir Andrew Large of the Bank of England has written: "If financial instability occurs, costs to society may be high. Damage to our reputation could be potentially high too" (Large 2005: 4).

In contrast, other authors, building on regulatory capture models of the "public choice" variety, have argued that financial supervisors act mainly at the behest of private interests, without regard to any broader public or collective interest (Oatley and Nabors 1998). In this model, the main interest of regulators is to advance private preferences, using state and market power for that purpose. Instead of stability, supervisors seek to make the world safe for their banks by influencing the regulatory environment.

As we will see in what follows, these approaches are not necessarily incompatible, to the extent that the concerns of public officials and peak business interests may converge around particular solutions to given policy problems; the Basel capital adequacy schemes offer a case in point. Thus, the question of whether the United States has used its hegemonic power to promote global financial stability, or instead to promote the narrow, regulatory (or deregulatory) interests of its major financial institutions, like Citicorp and Goldman Sachs, could pose a false and unnecessarily stark choice. The answer might be both, to the extent that supervisors actually believe in the Wall Street equivalent of "what's good for General Motors is good for the United States."

Clearly, it is impossible to speak meaningfully of financial agreements like the Basel capital adequacy schemes, and associated demands by banks and other institutions for a "level playing field," without making reference to private sector preferences and interests. But adherence to a strict capture model may obscure our analysis of financial supervision rather than illuminate it. As Sam Peltzman reminds us, regulators are bureaucrats who attempt to resolve conflicting public and private sector interests in such a way as to maintain and enhance their positional power within their domestic political structures. Financial supervisors, for example, may be legitimately concerned with maintaining a safe and sound financial system, but they may also have been forced by narrow interest groups to adopt policies that are at odds with that objective; prohibitions on interstate banking in the United States, for instance, were hardly stability enhancing. The success of financial supervisors in maintaining or increasing their positional power within their domestic political systems will be a function of their ability to solve complex regulatory problems, given the various interests at stake; and judging from the relative growth of central bank authority in the field of financial supervision and financial stability over the past two decades, it appears that they have been reasonably successful (Peltzman 1976).

Our basic model of international cooperation among financial supervisors, then, is one that takes inspiration from Peltzman, as well as from Robert Putnam's concept of diplomacy as a "two-level game," in which negotiators must interact and strike multilateral deals not only with each other but also with their domestic constituencies; negotiators are thus "Janus-faced," looking out at other states and inward at their domestic polities (Putnam 1988). The globalization of financial markets has generated both higher levels of competition among financial intermediaries and greater risks of international spillovers from domestic banking crises, given the interdependencies that now exist (see Table 3.2 on the exposure of UK banks to foreign banks); and to the extent that more competition leads to higher levels of financial risk-taking, a possible relationship between these two phenomena. As a consequence of

Table 3.2: *Exposure of UK banks to non-UK banks, 2001 (in billions of pounds sterling)*

EU	135
Swiss	16
US	37
Japanese	10
Other	7
Total	205
UK Tier 1 capital	89
Total exposure / Tier 1 capital	2.3

Source: Patricia Jackson, "International Financial Regulation and Stability," 2002.

these developments, regulators have responded to widespread demands for both a *more level* and a *more stable* playing field for international finance.

Private actors have called for more leveling (although all actors really want the field tipped to *their* advantage) because of the possibility that regulatory arbitrage could provide certain firms with a competitive advantage. Public sector actors have sought stability because of the economic and political costs associated with financial crises; crises that could, for instance, turn governments (or at least financial regulators!) out of office. It is the ongoing effort to satisfy these twin demands for leveling and for stabilizing that lies at the heart of international cooperation among financial supervisors.

How, then, have these twin objectives of greater financial stability and a level playing field been advanced at the international level? In seeking to answer that question, we need to return to the early 1970s following the collapse of the Bretton Woods system. Then, as during the late 1990s, financial supervisors recognized the need for a new architecture, and the model they built, which combined a commitment to necessary liquidity provision with common, minimum regulations on financial institutions – and in particular, higher capital levels – continues to play a significant role in shaping the terms of international cooperation today.

BASEL POLITICS

While the demand for a "new international financial architecture" is normally associated with the Asian crisis of 1997–98, at least from a regulatory perspective many of that structure's significant multilateral building blocks – like the Basel Committee on Banking Supervision and several of its associated codes, standards, and best practices, like the Basel Concordat and the 1988 Basel Capital Adequacy Accord – had already been in place for many years prior to that shock. Indeed, the international community has expressed a shared and near constant concern with global financial stability since the collapse of the Bretton Woods system in the early 1970s, coupled with the oil shocks of 1973–74. These events created systemic and seemingly rampant financial instability, as flexible exchange rates replaced fixed ones, interest and inflation rates diverged sharply across countries, and the "old economy" sectors of the "advanced" industrial nations – steel, automobiles, textiles, and other manufactures – began to implode, leaving only unemployment and a demand for government intervention in their wake. As a consequence of these developments, would-be financial architects devoted much of the 1970s to devising ways to prop up the post-Bretton Woods monetary system, which lacked the firm anchors that gold or the dollar peg had once provided.

Financial intermediaries, and especially banks, were also uncertain about how to operate in this new environment, and several of them – including some relatively big US institutions (at least big for that time, as they would be considered much smaller today) whose names we only dimly remember, like Franklin National, First Chicago, Continental Illinois, and Republic Bank – failed in their process of adjustment. Many of these failures were the result of bad and excessive bets by bank managers, particularly with respect to currency movements and the future direction of real estate and energy prices. But with increasing financial integration across borders, the effects of these collapses were not so neatly contained by national banking authorities.

The cooperation that was achieved in the 1970s and 1980s in the face of these macroeconomic and institutional challenges, notably under the aegis of the Basel Committee but in other multilateral groupings as well, took many observers by surprise. If we return to June 1974, when the G10 central bankers gathered in Basel for one of their regular meetings at the BIS, the health of the international financial system was poor, and the prospects for international cooperation to revive it seemed negligible. Financial markets were reeling under the strain of the oil price shock, the collapse of Bankhaus Herstatt, and the implosion of Franklin National. In Britain, a number of "fringe" banks had fallen, requiring a Bank of England lifeboat operation. Financial intermediation in the euromarkets was grinding to a halt as banks sought to reduce their risk profiles, and many banks were being squeezed out of the interbank lending market altogether, threatening credit availability worldwide.

The question of how central bankers ought to respond to this financial instability was the topic of the day. And vociferous disagreements were expressed around the table. The United States argued that central bankers should send an explicit signal that they were prepared to provide lender-of-last-resort services to banks operating in the euromarkets. The Germans refused to make such an explicit statement for several reasons. First, they said that they had no mandate to announce such a policy. Second, they thought that banks that had failed due to managerial incompetence ought to be allowed to collapse and not be bailed out. Finally, they said that any blanket assurances would create severe moral hazard problems for the financial community. The meeting thus broke up without a G10 agreement, suggesting the limits of models of international cooperation among financial supervisors that parsimoniously emphasize only collective concerns with stability.

But the central bankers were not let off the hook by their domestic financial intermediaries. As word spread of the disagreement, small banks started to be shut out of the interbank markets, leading them to place strong political pressure on their financial supervisors. Influenced by these domestic actors for a stronger statement, the central bankers returned in September for another gathering. This time, their views converged and they were able to make a formal announcement about their market intentions: "The governors," they said, "had an exchange of views on the problem of lender of last resort in the euromarket. They recognized that it would not be practical to lay down in advance detailed rules and procedures for the provision of temporary liquidity. But they were satisfied that means are available for that purpose and will be used if and when necessary" (BIS press communiqué of 10 September 1974). With this statement, central bankers had seemingly indicated their willingness to intervene in the financial markets in the event of an international crisis.

Having given this assurance, the central bankers now expressed concern that international banking was inadequately supervised, particularly in light of the moral hazard problems that these new lender-of-last-resort assurances might engender. As a consequence, in the autumn of 1974 the Bank of England began to conceptualize the formation of a G10 group of bank supervisors. This idea was approved at the December 1974 meeting of the central bankers, when the Standing Committee on Banking Regulations and Supervisory Practices, or the Basel Committee, was established. This Committee held its first meeting in February 1975.

At this time, the objectives of the Basel Committee were appropriately modest. The central bank governors emphasized that the Committee's objective "should *not* be to make far-fetched attempts to harmonize the twelve countries' individual systems of supervision, but should be to enable its members to learn from each other and to apply the knowledge so acquired to improving their own systems of supervision, so indirectly enhancing the likelihood of overall stability in the international banking system" (cited in Kapstein 1994: 45; emphasis added). Thus, the Basel Committee was charged with the tasks of education about bank supervision; information sharing about banking practices; the establishment of an "early warning system" – how often that idea has been repeated by financial supervisors ever since! – to detect problems within international banks; research on international bank supervision; and finally, policy coordination in supervising international and consortium banks. In sum, as the first head of the Basel Committee, George Blunden once stated: "There is agreement that the basic aim of international cooperation in this field is to ensure that no foreign banking establishment escapes supervision." It is probably fair to say that the level and scope of regulatory harmonization that this cooperative process has subsequently induced was unimaginable when the Committee first began to meet.

The supervisory arrangement for international banks that emerged out of the Basel process was not based on multilateral surveillance but rather on the cornerstone of home country control; that is, the idea that every financial institution should have a "home supervisor," and that, as Blunden suggested, no institution should escape supervision. This philosophy of home country control was built on the principle that national central banks and national financial supervisors must take primary responsibility for the international operations of their domestic financial institutions. Looking at the evolution of international financial supervision, from the time of the first Basel Concordat of 1975 to the present day, the increasing influence of domestic financial authorities becomes apparent, a trend that is now spreading far beyond G10 borders (ironically, their influence may be growing at a time when the presence of many domestic banks is receding, particularly in the emerging market economies; this situation is creating new supervisory headaches of its own, as we discuss in a later section). It is notable in this context that despite having a single central bank, and despite the influence of EU directives on Europe's financial landscape, the members of the eurozone still retain national financial supervisors, though this structure may be adapted to changing market circumstances in coming years, a process that would likely be catalyzed by a Europe-wide banking crisis.

As a first step toward home country control, in 1978 the Basel Committee recommended that international bank supervision be carried out on the basis of a set of consolidated financial statements. While consolidated banking statements were the norm in the United States and a few other countries, it was not the case in much of Europe, and Germany even placed strict limits on the ability of its supervisors to collect information about the foreign activities of their banks. By the early 1980s, however, consolidated reporting was widespread, providing the accounting framework on which home country control could be built.

But ongoing events in the financial markets would demonstrate that the Basel Committee had much work to do in institutionalizing this regulatory concept. The collapse of Banco Ambrosiano – the "Pope's bank" – in 1982 had painfully demonstrated the many holes that remained in this nascent supervisory architecture. Who was responsible for providing the lender-of-last-resort function when the subsidiary of a bank collapsed? Was it the home or the host authority? What information were home and host supervisors expected to share across borders; indeed, what were they permitted by law to share? Today, as European and US banks assume a major presence in the financial markets of developing and transition economies, these questions about the appropriate dividing line between supervisory and liquidity functions remain a crucial topic. Still, at that time the trend toward home country control of consolidated financial institutions would continue, pushed on by the shadow of the largest crisis the global economy had faced since the end of the Second World War: the debt crisis that erupted in August 1982.

Essentially, the debt crisis represented a twofold risk to the international payments system. First, it threatened to stifle financial and investment flows between the industrial and developing worlds, choking the world economy. Second, it threatened the solvency not just of a handful of money center banks, but also of many regional banks, which had joined in syndicated loans. Many of these banks did not appear to have sufficient capital to absorb the losses from unpaid debts of this magnitude. If depositors had become aware of the shortfall, a run on the banks might have begun, which only massive government intervention could have stemmed.

During the summer and autumn of 1982, the United States took the lead in shaping a response to the debt crisis. That response was two-pronged, consisting of short-term crisis management and longer-term stabilization measures. The short-term solution was to inject sufficient liquidity into the payments system to ensure its uninterrupted operation. The longer-term plan, more relevant for our purposes, was to strengthen and recapitalize the international banks, as well as to restructure the economies of the debtor nations, with the help of the International Monetary Fund (IMF). Indeed, it was the heightened demand for the IMF's services in the 1980s that provided policymakers with an instrument for encouraging banks to undertake balance sheet recapitalization; at the same time, that demand would lead to international cooperation with respect to bank capital adequacy.

The story unfolded in the following way. In early 1983, the Reagan administration went to Congress to seek an IMF funding increase. But Congress insisted that the price of that increase would be a new set of banking regulations. In particular, Congress demanded that minimum capital levels be placed on large commercial banks in order to force those with equity positions to share the pain of the debt crisis bailout with US taxpayers.

For their part, the bankers responded that any unilateral increase in their capital requirement would make them uncompetitive with foreign banks, particularly Japanese banks, which held relatively low levels of capital. The solution that Congress hit upon was to demand international convergence of bank capital standards, and, in fact, the legislation that contained the IMF funding increase also included a demand that US financial supervisors pursue such convergence at the international level. This provides a perfect example of the dual pursuit of leveling and stabilizing that lies at the heart of international financial supervision.

The institutional vehicle for pursuing multilateral talks on bank capital adequacy would be the Basel Committee, and the talks proved difficult from the outset. Different countries had adopted different methods for calculating capital and different capital adequacy standards, reflecting in part the peculiarities of their national financial institutions. It seemed absurd to impose on Germany's universal banks the same capital standards the United States used for its commercial banks, and, of course, the risk profiles of these institutions differed.

Given this initial rebuff, in 1987 the United States joined the United Kingdom in announcing a bilateral agreement on bank capital adequacy. This agreement joined the two largest financial markets in a common undertaking and threatened other nations with a zone of exclusion. For the United Kingdom, the bilateral agreement had the added benefit of heading off at the pass any European Community directive on bank capital adequacy, which would naturally reflect the views of the European Communities' other leading powers. Soon thereafter the Japanese signed on, buoyed by a booming Tokyo Stock Exchange that made it seemingly painless for Japanese banks to meet any new capital requirements. Finally, on 10 December 1987, the Basel Committee announced that its members had reached agreement on a proposal for "international convergence of capital measures and capital standards." This agreement, now known as "Basel I" but then called the "Basel Accord," promoted the globalization of risk-based capital standards.

Given current controversies over Basel II, it is useful to recall that Basel I was hardly greeted with universal acclaim when it was first announced.

Ethan B. Kapstein

Critics held, *inter alia,* that it would reallocate assets in banking portfolios and lead to a credit crunch, particularly for small business; that
it was unfair to non-OECD (Organisation for Economic Co-operation
and Development) governments whose bonds were allocated higher risk
weightings; and, perversely, that it would actually make bank balance
sheets riskier in order to compensate for the higher capital requirements.
Even if one rejected these criticisms, it was almost universally recognized
that the Basel Accord's approach to risk management was crude at best
and hardly reflected best practice, at least for the leading money center
banks. As a consequence, it would not take long for calls to revise the
Basel Accord to emerge (Greenspan 2004).

Yet it would also not take long for this "strengthened" post-Basel
financial architecture, with its higher capital standards, to start encoun-
tering new challenges. By the 1990s, banks were once again confident
enough in their capital base and risk management techniques to renew
their global expansion. They were assisted in the process by the lifting
of capital controls that made it easier to access new markets, particularly
in East Asia. But in short order, imbalances in East Asia and in many
other parts of the developing world would place renewed strains on the
international financial system.

MEXICO, ASIA, AND THE INTERNATIONAL
FINANCIAL ARCHITECTURE

This is not the place for a detailed review of the financial crises of the 1990s,
particularly the Mexican peso crisis of 1994–95 and the Asian financial
crisis of 1997–98 and its global spread. As with the 1982 debt crisis,
these shocks incorporated both macro- and microeconomic features.
While each crisis had its unique attributes, what they shared in common
were domestic policies that encouraged macroeconomic imbalances to
accumulate and domestic asset bubbles to form. At the same time, lax
banking regulation and political-economic systems of "crony capitalism"

allowed questionable loans to pile up in weakly capitalized banks. These pathologies went unrecognized for too long by financial agents.

Further, common to banking markets in Mexico and Asia were lending mismatches in terms of both currencies (borrowing in dollars and lending in local currencies) and assets and liabilities (borrowing short and lending long). These mismatches were hardly problematic so long as economies boomed, but as growth slowed, the various risks emerged in sharp relief and investors pulled the plug, although not without significant losses.

Both these financial crises, of course, ultimately led to emergency responses of aid and assistance by the US Treasury, the G10 central banks, and the IMF. Accompanying this lender-of-last-resort function, however, were calls, notably from the US government, for the design of a "new international financial architecture." What was it about the Mexican and Asian crises that led the US Treasury, and particularly its secretary, Robert Rubin, to consider a new financial architecture as a matter of political urgency?

Part of the answer would seem to lie in Rubin's deep-seated concern with the excessive dependence of the global financial system on US financial leadership for its stability. During the Mexican crisis, Rubin and President Bill Clinton had to battle a US Congress that was ultimately unwilling to countenance emergency loans to Mexico, and eventually the Treasury had to act unilaterally by drawing on its Emergency Stabilization Fund (ESF), which of course existed as a kitty to protect the value of the greenback. Rubin came away from the peso crisis – which, after all, occurred quite literally "next door" to the United States – with a grim view of "how little the public understands" of "how critical US leadership is on these international economic matters. The result ... is that public support – and thus political support – for ... international financial-crisis response ... is at best very difficult to obtain" (Rubin 2003: 37). The "lesson" Rubin drew from this was that the United States had no choice but to work closely with other countries, "which often meant making accommodations on our part." At bottom, Rubin felt that financial stability could not rest on US shoulders alone, and that a more durable if more complex architecture was needed, requiring the broader shoulders of the international community (or at least the industrial nations) as a whole.

It was in response to the Asian financial crisis that the finance ministers and central bank governors of twenty-two leading economies met in Washington in April 1998 to promote greater international cooperation with respect to financial market oversight. As one step toward building the new architecture, they created three working groups that were charged with examining: (1) transparency and accountability; (2) ways of strengthening financial systems; and (3) prevention and resolution of international financial crises. Here we focus on the second project, that of strengthening financial systems (for a review of the work in the other areas, see Goldstein 2000).

The core belief of the financial systems working group was that "weak banking systems and poorly developed capital markets contributed to the misallocation of resources that led to the (Asian financial) crisis. Key to the strengthening of domestic financial systems is the implementation of sound practices for supervision, settlement, accounting, and disclosure. This involves close international cooperation and collaboration among those in the official sector who are involved in the supervision of financial systems" (Working Group on Strengthening Financial Systems 1998).

The mission of the Working Group, in short, was to suggest that something like a set of "best practices" existed with respect to financial market oversight and that building a soundly regulated financial system was essential to reducing the likelihood of financial crises. It is notable in this respect that one of the Working Group's recommendations was the creation of a "Financial Sector Policy Forum" that would bring together actors across ministries to discuss financial sector issues; this was a driver behind the establishment in 1999 of the Financial Stability Forum, whose secretariat is currently housed at the BIS.

It is difficult to overemphasize the central place that public officials and analysts gave to financial regulatory failure as a causal driver of the Asian crisis. Noted economist Barry Eichengreen has asserted: "If the Asian crisis has taught us one thing, it is that countries cannot restore exchange rate and balance of payments stability without rectifying deficiencies in their domestic financial systems" (Eichengreen 2000: 184). Yet regulatory failures are normally endogenous; they reflect the exigencies of the domestic political economy. Given that situation, the international community (or at least the members of the G10 nations) had to weigh in and place external pressure on the relevant domestic actors, both firms and government agencies, if reforms were to be carried out. Not surprisingly, those on the receiving end of these pressures were ambivalent about them at best.

That does not mean that financial regulators in emerging markets did not recognize the need for reform. After all, as Morris Goldstein reports, since 1985, "there have been more than 65 episodes where banking problems in emerging economies got so bad that the entire banking system was rendered insolvent. In the Asian countries, we are now looking at fiscal costs of bank recapitalization that range from 10 to 60 percent of GDP" (Goldstein 2000: 29). The implementation of global standards, which emerging economies had little choice but to adopt if they wished to remain plugged into the global economy, therefore became one of the cornerstones of the new international financial architecture.

As Goldstein, among others, has noted, public officials can use several instruments for promoting the implementation of new standards, including market pressures on the one hand and rules and regulations on the other. With respect to market pressures, once a new standard is published, economic agents may adopt it as the basis for forming their own judgments about the behavior of particular institutions. Regulatory instruments can similarly be used as both carrot and stick: as carrot in that regulators can use standards, like capital adequacy standards, as a minimum requirement that must be met if banks (or other financial intermediaries) wish to operate, acquire, expand, or diversify; and, of course, they can also serve as a stick for meting out punishment in the form of fines or limitations on these institutions' licenses to operate.

Regulators in powerful countries like the United States and United Kingdom can also use their standards to shape the terms of market access. To the extent that foreign banks seek access to international money centers like New York and London, they must meet the criteria that these regulators set for host institutions, even in a world where home country control provides the overall supervisory framework. That ultimate authority over market access offers a major inducement for accepting "global" standards.

In the wake of the Asian financial crisis, G10 supervisors and regulators developed a long list of codes and standards – many of which now constitute the Basel Core Principles – that they thought should be adopted on a global basis, again in the interests of creating both a more stable and a more level financial environment. These standards referred to principles of corporate governance and the regulation of banking, insurance, and securities markets. Notably, among these reforms the Working Group expressed its strong support for Basel II, which was already under study by the Basel Committee; we will have more to say about Basel II in a later section.

Advancing the Basel Core Principles globally became a major charge of the IMF and the World Bank, which, along with the BIS, played a significant role in strengthening the regulatory systems of many emerging market economies. Local officials became convinced of the need to accept these principles if they were to become part of the global economy and avoid financial marginalization. Given the high costs associated with adoption of the Principles, and given the weaknesses in many domestic banking institutions, governments called for financial consolidation in order to create intermediaries that could compete at the international level. At the same time, they opened their markets to direct investment by foreign financial firms, placing fresh competitive pressures on local operators. Whether the resulting financial structure has indeed produced both greater stability and a level playing field remains a topic of controversy.

In sum, at least since 1974, financial supervisors have been struggling with the design of a new architecture to meet the dramatic changes that have occurred in markets. That architecture incorporates formal institutions like the BIS, the IMF, and the World Bank; other international supervisory bodies, like the International Organization of Securities Commissions (IOSCO); and informal institutions like the G8 summits and associated meetings of finance ministers and central bankers. These organizations have, in turn, sought to create a new set of regulatory norms for financial markets, or a set of best practices that ought to be followed in the interest of financial stability and a level playing field. These norms have been codified through various principles and practices, notably the adoption of risk-based capital standards. Banks and other financial intermediaries have contributed to this architecture by expressing their own interests and preferences with respect to its design, which supervisors have clearly taken into account. How well the architecture is suited to the new risk environment is the topic of the following section.

CHARTING THE NEW RISK ENVIRONMENT

To the best of our knowledge, there is no broad overview available of the changes that have occurred in the financial risk environment over the past decade or so, even though a number of monographs treat various pieces of that puzzle. In this section, we highlight a paradox that we believe lies at the heart of the contemporary risk environment: the combination – whether poison or elixir – of increasing bank consolidation on the one hand and risk atomization on the other. The question we raise is whether the supervisory architecture, and in particular the Basel II Framework, is well suited to governing or regulating – in the engineering sense of these terms – this structure of risk. And the answer is that we are unconvinced, given the opacity of the risks that we face; an opacity that is especially troubling given all the calls since the Asian crisis for greater financial transparency. We begin the section by addressing the issue of banking consolidation, before turning to the manner in which these large institutions manage their risk profiles. We then ask whether Basel II provides a solid supervisory anchor for this risk environment (recognizing, of course, that Basel II hardly stands alone, but is supplemented by other regulatory instruments).

The 1990s saw a wave of banking consolidation across industrial world banking markets, and, indeed, in many emerging markets as well. Interestingly, most of this activity occurred domestically; cross-border mergers of banking institutions remain exceptional. In the United States, for example, the relaxation of interstate banking regulations in the late 1990s generated a sharp spike in banking consolidation. Indeed, large bank mergers peaked the year after passage of the Riegle-Neal Act in 1997, which allowed interstate bank branching to take place (Group of Ten 2001; Kwan 2004). As a result of this wave of consolidation, the United States now has three banking organizations with over $1 trillion in assets, and the top five banks hold over 20 percent of the nation's deposits (see Figure 3.1). The rationale for these banking mergers and their consequences for competition and efficiency have been assessed in detail elsewhere; here our primary concern is with their effects on the financial risk environment.

No less an authority than Alan Greenspan has viewed this evolution in banking markets as wholly salutary. Speaking before the American Bankers Association in 2004, Greenspan stated that bank consolidation had "greatly strengthened the stability of our financial system. Diversified banking organizations . . . have been able to absorb substantial losses in some lines or weak demand for some products without significant hits to capital" (Greenspan 2004).

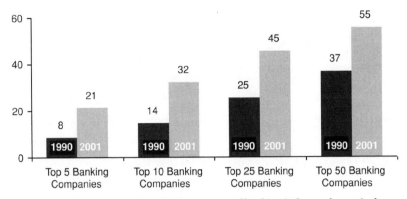

Figure 3.1: Consolidation in US banks. Percent of banking industry domestic deposits held, by group and year.
Source: FDIC Bank Call Reports.

Yet has consolidation really limited systemic risk? The answer is not so clear-cut. To begin with, as Figure 3.2 makes clear, the consolidation trend has certainly not limited the loan losses of US banks. Indeed, consolidation may have led banks to develop greater appetites for risk.

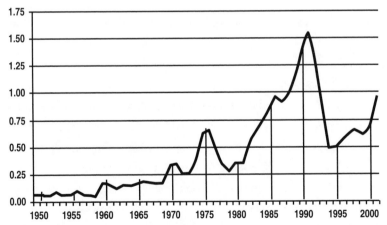

Figure 3.2: Loan losses in US banks. Annual net charge-offs as a percent of average loans.
Source: FDIC Historical Statistics on Banking.

Why would consolidation promote rather than mitigate risk-taking by bank managers? There are several reasons that can be provided. The first pathway to higher risk in large consolidated institutions is through the belief that managers may have that their firms are simply "too big to fail." As two leading academic students of modern banking, Roy Smith and Ingo Walter, have put it: "Not only are these banks 'too big to fail,' they have become 'too big to monitor' and perhaps 'too big to regulate'" (Smith and Walter n.d.). As bank size increases, the likelihood that central bankers will enforce market discipline on poorly managed institutions decreases. If financial stability is a primary concern of regulators, then bank managers may feel confident that public officials will bail them out of crises, even those of their own making. Evidence from bank stock prices indicates that large firms may, in fact, enjoy a "too big to fail" premium.

Second, bank consolidation can create diseconomies of scale, as opposed to the promised efficiencies that normally accompany such mergers and acquisitions. As a consequence, managers may become less rather than more capable of providing their institutions with appropriate governance structures. The breakdown in principal-agent relations could allow poor or unethical managers to go undetected until substantial damage is already done. Hints of this kind of problem have already appeared in several banking institutions around the world.

Third, when regulators or analysts assert that consolidation will promote stability, they must be equating consolidation with diversification. Yet consolidation need not lead to a greater diversification of risks. Take, for example, the Basel II Framework, which adopts a lower risk weighting for mortgages than for many other types of loans. Imagine that a "Basel II" bank decides to specialize in mortgage lending and acquires other firms in this market segment; it would then be greatly exposed to a generalized collapse of housing prices. As Figure 3.3 shows, many banks are placing a greater percentage of their assets in loans as opposed to other securities, and this despite a generalized move to securitize a portion of their loan portfolios.

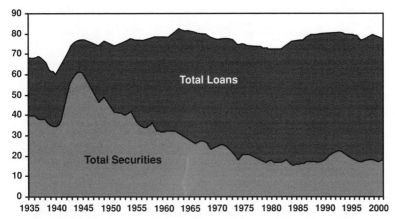

Figure 3.3: The changing composition of bank assets. Total loans and securities as a percent of total assets at year-end.
Source: FDIC Historical Statistics on Banking.

Fourth, and finally, we assume that as banks consolidate, the interdependencies between them will increase as well. The failure of one bank is therefore likely to have serious consequences for others (again see Table 3.2 for the exposure of UK banks to foreign banks). Analysis of bank stock performance already suggests that markets perceive a high degree of interdependency. Thus, as is the case in "classic" bank runs, rumors of poor performance by one big bank could lead to deposit withdrawals from others (see De Nicolò and Kwast 2001). But given the size of these institutions, the lender-of-last-resort function might not be adequately performed by the central bank, and fiscal policy instruments would then be required instead. As we will discuss in our concluding section, this leads to one of our suggestions for possible changes in supervisory structures.

Associated with banking consolidation has been a trend toward asset securitization, though the actual importance of this trend for financial risk diversification remains a topic of inquiry, particularly given the paucity of reliable data. Again, Alan Greenspan believes that securitization has been a great boon to financial stability. He claims that "not only have individual financial institutions become less vulnerable to shocks from underlying risk factors, but also the financial system as a whole has become more resilient" (Greenspan 2004: 6).

Given our limited knowledge of the markets for these new financial products, it is very hard to accept Greenspan's statement as anything more than an article of faith. Indeed, yet another central banker, Sir Andrew Large of the Bank of England, has referred to the "new series of hazards" posed by these instruments. He notes that "credit risk transfer has introduced new holders of credit risk, such as hedge funds and insurance companies, at a time when market depth is untested. Systemically significant issues could increasingly arise from market-related risks, or from single point of failure risks . . . as ever greater volumes of transactions pass through" (Large 2005).

One obvious problem with these instruments and the associated markets is that it is difficult for analysts to get their brains around them conceptually, even with respect to such basic questions as to how large they are and how even to measure their size accurately, to say nothing of risk assessment. As John Plender of the *Financial Times* (15 May 2005) has written: "Where Mr. Greenspan sees dispersion of risk, others see obfuscation." Adam Posen of the Institute for International Economics is certainly correct when he asserts that "the increasing use of derivatives makes ascertaining the true exposure of banks to risk even more challenging," not to mention the exposure of many other financial intermediaries (Posen 2002). If consolidation makes banks "too big to fail," securitization may make them "too hard" to monitor adequately.

To be sure, derivatives play a useful role in financial markets. A credit derivative, for example, is basically a contract purchased by a bank or another financial intermediary to protect itself if a borrower cannot repay a loan or fulfill a lease obligation. There are two major product categories in the credit derivatives market: first, credit default swaps that bear credit risk similar, but not necessarily identical, to that of a bond; and second, collateralized debt obligations (CDOs), whereby the credit risk of a portfolio of underlying exposures is "tranched" into different segments, with differing risk-return characteristics. Clearly, the balanced use of such instruments is helpful to bankers in managing risk exposures.

The increasing demand for credit derivatives that began in the 1990s is understandable for two reasons: first, the environment of falling interest rates, and the resulting quest for higher yields (which of course meant accepting higher risks); and second, the capital adequacy rules that were mandated by Basel I, which required banks to set aside more capital against their commercial loans (although it would probably be an exaggeration to call Basel I a primary *cause* of the growth behind the derivatives market). The use of credit derivatives meant that banks, by passing on the credit risk to other players, could free capital that could be profitably used elsewhere. *It must be emphasized that this shift, which has certainly freed bank capital and thus allowed greater lending activity to take place, has not necessarily reduced systemic risk.*

This securitization and credit transfer trend has only intensified in recent years. Since 2000, Deutsche Bank has reportedly reduced the loans on its books by over 40 percent from 281 to 165 billion euros. Other European banks, such as ABN Amro, Credit Suisse, and UBS, have similarly shrunk the size of their balance sheets. The exposure to risk has been hedged by purchasing credit derivatives. Thus, credit risk has been transferred from banks to the buyers of securities and loans, and to the sellers of credit insurance.

Given this changing financial environment, it was obvious that reforms to Basel I would eventually have to be made, as a tighter linkage between risks – including off-balance sheet risks – and capital had become necessary. Indeed, the main complaint from the banking community that helped launch the Basel II process was that big banks were being forced to hold an inefficient amount of economic capital, given the sophisticated risk analyses they were performing internally. While the 1988 Basel Accord represented an important first step toward recognizing the relationship between the capital that banks held and the risks they took, the risk weightings were presented in a very crude form; for example, a loan to a top-rated company carried the same risk weights as one to a startup enterprise. The major money center banks, therefore, urged members of the Basel Committee to accept their internal models as the basis for a new capital adequacy agreement.

Basel II has undoubtedly gone much further in matching capital and risk, and it has encouraged the continuing development of advanced risk management practices within banks, while making the risks that banks take more transparent to the investing community. This represents a significant advance and should be recognized as such. Still, we reiterate that these risks remain quite opaque in important respects, especially those that remain off-balance sheet. While the spring of 2005 witnessed bold efforts by the Basel Committee – in collaboration with IOSCO – to close some of the analytical gaps with respect to securitization, most analysts agree that the risks sitting out in the derivatives market cannot be calculated with any great precision, at least at the present time. Philip Coggan has rightly said: "The banks say they have sophisticated models that control their risk exposure. But when it comes to more complex instruments, they have yet to be tested" (*Financial Times*, 15 May 2005).

A second area in which Basel II may fall somewhat short of its promise to promote greater financial stability is on the macroeconomic side. As many analysts have already noted, Basel II may have a procyclical bias that could complicate the task of macroeconomic policy during recessions. While some analysts believe this concern to be overblown (Gordy and Howells 2004), others argue that evidence from the recession in the United States during the early 1990s suggests that the original Basel Accord may have provoked a credit crunch in some regions, and that small- and medium-sized enterprises in particular were hurt as a result (Jackson 2002). Along these lines, complicating the task of encouraging banks to hold, for example, greater loan loss reserves as a rainy day fund against future downturns are the very different legal and accounting regimes that still characterize the G10 states. In two domains that are central to financial stability – the risks inherent in increasing financial securitization, and the risks associated with economic downturns – it appears that Basel II still represents a work in progress.

Finally, we note that there are ongoing debates with respect to the effects of bank capital regulations on financial stability. While no less an authority than Tommaso Padoa-Schioppa has declared that "capital adequacy regulation remains *the most important piece of regulation to safeguard financial stability*," empirical support for that assertion is lacking (Padoa-Schioppa 2004). A study by a team from the IMF, for example, has concluded that "credit risk and bank soundness are primarily influenced by macroeconomic and macroprudential factors and that direct influence of . . . Basel Core Principles on credit risk and soundness is insignificant" (Sundararajan, Marston, and Basu 2001: 1). Does this mean we should abandon or loosen bank capital standards? The answer must be no, as there are few regulatory instruments that provide managers with stronger inducements for focusing their minds on their risk-taking activities.

Does Basel II make a significant difference in terms of leveling the international playing field? Diverse opinions have also been expressed on this issue. In some respects, it would appear that Basel II may result in a less level playing field than Basel I for the simple reason that countries are adopting very different approaches to the incorporation of these principles within their domestic banks (see Figure 3.4). In the United States, only the ten or twenty largest banks will become Basel II compliant, while the remainder will retain Basel I standards. Further, in many jurisdictions some banks will adopt the "advanced" approach to Basel II while others will adopt the "foundation" approach. Both within and across nations, then, the competitive effects of Basel II are unclear. While the importance of these differences in capital adequacy approaches can be exaggerated – banks compete on the basis of much more than their capital levels – it is still likely that this issue will continue to resonate for many years to come, as we learn more about the effects of Basel II on both the domestic and international playing fields (for the domestic effects of

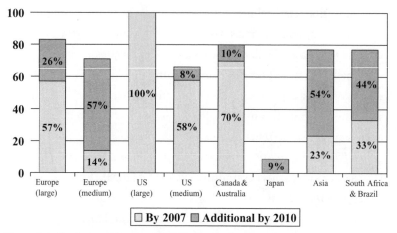

Figure 3.4: Banks targeting Basel II IRB advanced approach.
Note: I thank Professor Ingo Walter for bringing this chart to my attention.
Source: FT Research study commissioned by Accenture, Mercer Oliver Wyman and SAP (2004).

the new Framework may be even more significant from the competitive standpoint than the international ones).

Another area in which Basel II may fail to level the playing field to the satisfaction of some financial intermediaries is with respect to the costs of its incorporation into banking systems, which are judged to be substantial. Again, authorities will respond that these costs must only be borne by the largest financial institutions. Still, it is unlikely that these institutions would accept those costs unless they thought there were competitive benefits associated with the investment. If Basel II ends up driving some smaller players out of business because of the relatively higher capital requirements they might face as compared to the largest banks that adopt the advanced approach – which is perhaps a far-fetched fear – it will have only tilted the playing field in ways that damage financial competition.

Basel II, then, exemplifies the continuing challenges that financial supervisors face in delivering greater stability while trying at the same time to level the competitive playing field. It would be unfairly harsh, and, indeed, patently incorrect, to assert that because Basel II could fall short in important respects, it shows that the supervisors have failed to make important advances with respect to the financial architecture. To the contrary, when examined from an historical perspective, the advances they have made against long odds are nothing short of breathtaking. The work of these officials has contributed to a more risk-oriented financial system, and one in which regulatory arbitrage across capital regimes has been greatly reduced. These are impressive accomplishments that should not be minimized, especially in light of the competing pressures that they have faced.

Still, the extent to which a more resilient and stable financial system has been engineered by humans with imperfect knowledge of the contemporary risk environment remains the great unknown. If history tells us anything about financial markets, it is surely that we have not seen the last crisis, and thus any architecture, as stated earlier, should rightly be conceptualized as a work in progress rather than a polished edifice. Given the strong possibility of future shocks, we turn in the final section to possible innovations that supervisors may wish to contemplate with respect to the financial architecture.

CONCLUSIONS: THE FUTURE OF THE
FINANCIAL ARCHITECTURE

Adam Posen once wrote that "banks are inherently fragile and their supervision is inherently inadequate, making dependence upon banks dangerous" (Posen 2002). One needn't agree with that assessment to appreciate that systemic financial risk remains of significant concern, and that many of the contemporary changes in banking, including consolidation and securitization, have probably done less than we think to reduce it. The emergence of banks with over $1 trillion in assets and a large share of national deposits, coupled with an increasingly opaque market for securities, could be creating a new environment with the capacity to overwhelm the clubby approach to financial regulation that has been built in Basel and elsewhere. The problem is simply that the collapse of a trillion dollar institution, with myriad tentacles of complex financial engagements reaching deeply into firms, markets, and households, will be larger than any central bank can handle, and its negative effects on markets and households will inevitably lead to the politicization of the bailout.

If that is the case, it raises the issue of whether the time has come for financial regulators – who are no doubt fatigued from their Basel II labors – to begin contemplating the possible institutional fixes that someday might have to be made under more stressful circumstances. In particular, we suggest that during future crises it is highly likely that there will be a demand by financial agents for closer cooperation not just between central bankers and financial supervisors, but perhaps with elected officials as well. To the extent that future bailouts may have to draw on treasuries and demand a fiscal policy response, legislators and executives will be intimately involved, for better or for worse.

In some sense, the evolution toward a closer linkage between regulators and legislators is already apparent in the Basel process. After all, the search for international capital adequacy standards was in some respects mandated by the US Congress, and while Basel I itself was not highly politicized there was certainly a much deeper engagement of elected officials with Basel II. In a world of large and complex financial institutions on the one hand and a greater atomization of risk on the other, this sort of political involvement in financial regulation seems almost inevitable.

At the same time, how to build a closer working relationship between "independent" central banks and quasi-independent financial regulators, and between them and elected officials within and across governments, is hardly a straightforward task. This effort must involve not just international institutions like the BIS and IMF, but also foundations, universities, think tanks, and other organizations that bring people together for informal discussions of contemporary political-economic problems. As a starting point, there are several modest steps that can be taken in this direction.

First, central bankers and financial supervisors must speak more openly about the contemporary risk environment, and make clear what it is they do not know or understand. This educative task is essential not just for elected officials, but for all financial intermediaries and agents, including households, which are now facing a dizzying array of financial choices for everything from mortgages to investments to pension plans. While our economic models usually assume rational behavior in the face of more or less perfect information, the history of financial markets suggests that a more nuanced understanding of agent behavior is required.

Second, central bankers and financial supervisors should contemplate playing "war games" or engaging in crisis simulation exercises not only with other government agencies, but with parliamentarians, members of the banking community, and other financial intermediaries as well. While shocks of the September 11 variety suggest, for example, the critical importance of having in place sound continuity plans and procedures, there are many other types of crisis that could be "gamed" in advance, an exercise that could help in revealing systemic strengths and weaknesses. Such games could usefully be played at the international level, perhaps based at the BIS, and could go well beyond the sorts of crisis exercises currently run by central banks and by private financial institutions in terms of their level of sophistication.

Third, and in a related vein, while central bankers and financial regulators meet regularly in places like Basel, there is no similar gathering for elected officials, particularly parliamentarians, who are concerned with financial stability. Creating venues for such activities would make a positive contribution to greater appreciation of financial interdependencies, of risks, and of the need for collective action during crises. These officials, in turn, must be encouraged to educate their own publics about the costs and benefits associated with deepening financial globalization; again, we are reminded of Robert Rubin's admonition that our domestic politics are not "well suited" to the global economy.

Fourth, central bankers and financial regulators must continue to work with elected officials on the sorts of institutional reforms within their home countries that could contribute to greater stability. Overdependence on banks, for example, could be sharply curtailed in this era of competing financial intermediaries. As Adam Posen suggests, if banks represent a significant systemic risk, then limiting their influence may represent a potentially sound regulatory strategy (Posen 2002).

Finally, central bankers and financial supervisors should now consider the "Basel III" changes in regulation that will be needed in light of the potential risks posed by new market developments. In thinking about these changes, the Bank of England has made a useful start with its "matrix approach" that seeks to provide a framework for modeling the sources of threat and the associated supervisory activities required. It is notable, however, that the Bank does not include macroeconomic risks in its matrix, which could be considered a significant oversight (Large 2005).

With respect to individual financial intermediaries, a Basel III framework might consider, *inter alia*, forcing banks to issue subordinated debt, as several analysts have recently proposed.[2] As with Basel II, any of these Basel III changes will likely involve significant input from a variety of agents, who will work with and through their elected officials (the strong interest that elected officials took in Basel II is reflective of this widespread politicization of banking regulation). Again, the important question of the appropriate relationship between legislators and supervisors as the financial architecture is refurbished is one that requires more sustained analysis.

In important respects, our conclusions build on remarks made back in 1996 by a prescient William White, who observed that central bankers and financial regulators around the world may have "more in common"

---

[2] Ingo Walter, personal communication, 29 May 2005.

with each other than they do "with various parts of their national governments. This has a clear advantage in obtaining results. However, it also has dangers in that it can lead to public concerns about the existence of a 'democratic deficit'; that is, important international decisions being made by technocrats rather than politicians" (White 1996: 20–1).

As these comments suggest, one of the great "successes" of financial supervisors over the past thirty years has been to depoliticize the systemic risk environment and to transform crisis management into a technocratic exercise, thereby making financial shocks somewhat easier to manage, by reducing the number and type of players involved in decision making. During future crises, however, there may be greater demands for highly political responses that would involve active intervention by national legislatures and parliaments, alongside financial supervisors and central bank governors, and this could greatly complicate the task of international cooperation. The Mexican peso crisis, for example, may have heralded political problems of this type, and it is for this reason that Robert Rubin believed so deeply in the need for a new international financial architecture. He saw clearly that the legislative process, at least in the United States, might not yield optimal outcomes for dealing with financial crises. A stronger system against crises, therefore, had to be built.

In crucial respects, central bankers and financial supervisors have met Rubin's challenge. The proliferation of standards and codes, and the emphasis placed on safe and sound banking around the world, has undoubtedly led to a more resilient financial system. But it is not yet "shockproof," particularly in the face of the sorts of crises that might reasonably confront us in the future, including either the collapse of very large financial institutions or the widespread distress that could affect markets and households as the assets and financial instruments they hold lose value.

To be sure, central bankers might assume that the atomization of risk means that its holders will face overwhelming collective action problems in responding to a future crisis, thereby reducing political pressures for fiscal responses or major bailouts from the lender of last resort. But such an assumption would form the basis of public policy only at tremendous political peril. It is therefore critical that legislators and publics be educated about the contemporary risk environment before the next crisis occurs. As economic globalization advances, the fundamental role of domestic politics in stabilizing financial markets becomes increasingly apparent.

4

Central Banks, Governments, and the European Monetary Unification Process

ALEXANDRE LAMFALUSSY[1]

PRELIMINARY REMARKS

It was not without hesitation that I accepted the challenge of writing this essay on the evolving relationship between central banks and governments in the European monetary unification process. For one thing, I am not a historian and the formal, narrowly defined beginning of this process goes back to the Hague summit in 1969, when the heads of state or of government "agreed that on the basis of the memorandum presented by the European Commission on 12 February 1969 and in close collaboration with the Commission a plan by stages should be drawn up by the EC Council of ministers during 1970 with a view to the creation of an economic and monetary union." Anything that was conceived more than thirty years ago deserves careful scholarly treatment calling on all the virtues of a reliable historian – even if the scholar is not a professional historian. This is the more so since European monetary cooperation in a broader sense began with the establishment of the European Payments

[1] Catholic University of Louvain, Belgium. Former General Manager of the BIS and former President of the European Monetary Institute. This text was finalized in June 2005.

Union in 1950, well before the emergence of the Common Market and of the European Community. It is arguable that neither the decision taken in The Hague, nor the subsequent Werner Report, nor indeed the long history of the monetary unification process, which has led us to where we are today, can be fully comprehended without referring back to the early 1950s. Much of this scholarly work has already been accomplished and accomplished well. Let me just refer to the collection of papers edited by Alfred Steinherr (*Thirty Years of European Monetary Integration: From the Werner Plan to EMU*, London, Longman, 1994), to Daniel Gros and Niels Thygesen (*European Monetary Integration*, New York, St. Martin's, 1992), and to André Szàsz (*The Road to European Monetary Union*, London, Macmillan, 1999). I have neither the intention nor the ability to compete with them. But I could try to rely on my personal experience and attempt to draw some lessons from my participation in the monetary unification process – if only to stimulate an exchange of views on the current problems in European Monetary Union (EMU).

But what are my credentials for doing this? Here I have encountered some other reasons for being modest: my direct participation in the European monetary unification process was neither continuous nor of the same "quality" all the time. True, I was a member of the Delors Committee, where I could and did play a role, but this took up less than one year; true, first as economic adviser of the BIS and later as its general manager, I was in a good position to observe what was going on within the Committee of the Governors of the Central Banks of the Member States of the European Economic Community (EEC), which was meeting in Basel, and whose secretariat was provided by the Bank for International Settlements (BIS) – but this was observation rather than action; true, the fact that the BIS is a bank allowed me to gain a privileged insight into the crisis mechanics of the critical years of 1992–93, but I did not participate in crisis management meetings. More importantly, I did not take part in the negotiations leading to the Maastricht Treaty, although of course the Treaty took over a very substantial part of the recommendations of the

Delors Report. As opposed to all these "buts," however, I do not have to be unduly modest about my role as the first president of the European Monetary Institute (EMI). Whatever was achieved by the EMI was of course the result of the teamwork of the EC Council of ministers and of the staff of the member central banks and of the Institute itself; but as president I had ample opportunities to wreck, or at least substantially slow down, the realization of the institution-building project. Which I chose not to do. Moreover, during these three and a half years I was directly exposed to a rich variety of political influences and gained a firsthand experience of dealing with high-level civil servants as well as with their political masters, which entitles me to hold some views on the relationship between governments and central banks. This is the reason why most of the comments that follow are strongly influenced by the experience gained during my EMI years.

I propose to group my comments on the relationship between central banks and governments under two headings: institution building and policy mix.

INSTITUTION BUILDING

A major part of the European monetary unification process has had to do with institution building. This observation is valid for the whole process, but it applies especially to periods of accelerating change; and there is little doubt that the quantum jump implied by the introduction of the single currency and the establishment of the European Central Bank (ECB) *was* such a period.

One would think *a priori* (and so I had thought myself) that a period of this kind would provide a propitious environment for bitter conflicts. Specifically, for conflicts between the central banks operating within the EMI structure (which had been put in charge of setting up the ECB, defining the operational infrastructure of the single monetary policy, and preparing the future monetary policy strategy) on the one hand,

and the member governments of the European Union (EU) on the other. But also for conflicts within the central banking community as well as among governments, and for conflicts with the Commission, guardian of the treaties. So many vested interests were at stake. Countries had to give up their monetary sovereignty (even though most of them had already lost it in practice). The National Central Banks (NCBs) were invited to cooperate in a sort of merger process as a result of which they swapped their ability to carry out "their" monetary policy for their governors having one vote in the future ECB's decision-making body. They might have considered this a net loss, even though most of them had already tied their currency to the deutsche mark (DM) without having any say in the Bundesbank's decisions. Even the Commission was about to lose some of its power: there would no longer be a commissioner in charge of monetary affairs. Last but not least, one could not expect generalized popular support for losing one's country's national currency (even though the citizens of a great number of European countries could hardly derive great pride from the past performance of their national currencies).

These forebodings proved unfounded. The road leading to 1 January 1999 – the beginning of Stage III – was on occasion somewhat bumpy, but there were no major conflicts of the kind that could have fatally jeopardized the implementation of the single currency: neither between the EMI Council and the governments, nor among governments, nor inside the EMI, nor indeed between any of these and the Commission. I myself was not excessively optimistic about the outcome when I was appointed president of the EMI, but I became gradually more and more confident, and by the winter of 1995–96 I had acquired the conviction that we were on the right track. Market sentiment was also beginning to change at that time; witness the downward convergence of long-term interest rates. This was not the case for the majority of our American friends, who argued, first, that it had been foolish to conceive the single currency project; at a second stage, when they could no longer ignore the determination of our politicians to go ahead, they predicted that implementation would fail; and when implementation was about to be achieved, they were beginning to foretell that the system would shortly be blown apart by market forces.

There can be little doubt that the institution-building phase of the single currency project has been successful – this much, I would guess, has by now been accepted even by those who dislike(d) the project or those who (not without reason) harbor some misgivings about current developments. And by institution-building phase I do not refer only to the period ending on 1 January 1999, but also to the one that ended during the early weeks of 2002 with the exchange of banknotes. But the absence of disruptive conflicts, however important it was, does not fully explain this success story. First, because the absence of these conflicts itself requires an explanation. Second, because the enterprise was a unique event for which there had been no genuine historical precedent; it amounted to the merging of the monetary policy functions of eleven central banks, all of which had a long history behind them and were operating in highly complex monetary and financial systems. A lot of things could have gone wrong in this process, even without the disruptive influence of vested interests. How is it that they did not go wrong?

My explanation is that we have been well served by the exceptional convergence of several facts and influences. In what follows, I will try to list them, but not in their order of importance because I have no clue what that order is.

First, the initiators of the project were the governments themselves – and at the highest level: the heads of state or of government (as it should be). This was the case when, in The Hague, they started the process; this was again the case when, in Hanover in June 1988, they recalled that "in adopting the Single Act, the Member States of the Community confirmed the objective of progressive realization of economic and monetary union" and therefore decided to set up the Delors Committee, which was given the "task of studying and proposing concrete stages leading towards this union." Finally, at the Maastricht summit (December 1991) they adopted the Treaty on European Union, which, among many other provisions, decided the creation of the European System of Central Banks, of its central institution, the ECB, and of a new currency, the ecu, to replace the national currencies of the member countries. The ratification process took almost two years but, after granting an opt-out clause to the United Kingdom and an opt-in clause to Denmark, the Treaty entered into force in November 1993. So the initiative was clearly a political one; not simply because the initiators were heads of government, but also because, at decisive moments, the political motivation played a major role. This had already been the case in the earlier years, but it became quite decisive at the time of the negotiations preceding the Maastricht Treaty. With such a political commitment, the highest political authorities acquired a vested interest in a successful implementation process.

Second, it is worth noting that the political leaders entrusted the central bankers right from the beginning with a major role in the preparation of the Maastricht Treaty, starting when they decided to set up the Delors Committee, the membership of which was overwhelmingly of central banking extraction. Jacques Delors was not only a good Chairman, but he also possessed the political wisdom to accept that the majority of the meetings, and practically all the preparatory work for the meetings, would take place at the BIS, with both rapporteurs being central bankers. Subsequently, the Dublin summit (June 1990) mandated the Committee of EC Governors to draft a statute for the ESCB (European System of Central Banks) to be submitted to the Intergovernmental conference on EMU.

Third, the institution-building process was governed by the Maastricht Treaty, which set out a roadmap in great detail, reasonably clearly described what should be the division of labor between the Council, the Commission and the central bankers of the EMI and of the ECB, and, most importantly, set 1 January 1999 as the latest date on which the single monetary policy should start operating. Time constraint – as I, and later

Wim Duisenberg, had the privilege to learn – turned out to be a barbarian but most effective instrument for finding compromises in matters that were not regulated by the Treaty (I propose to give a major example). Finally, while the Treaty left open a number of issues, it was (almost) clear on two subjects that could have created serious conflicts between governments and central bankers. The independence of the ECB – and before that of the EMI – was well defined; and so were the convergence criteria for accession to EMU. Among these criteria, the fiscal ones, and naturally the inflation criterion, were of crucial importance for preventing major conflicts between governments and central banks.

Fourth, let me make a few remarks on how it was possible to avoid major disruptive conflicts *among* the central banks. There was, of course, the time constraint just mentioned. At the EMI in 1994 we devised a somewhat pompously titled "master plan" that set out for each of the monthly Council meetings the topics on which decisions *had* to be taken in order to ensure that the single monetary policy would become operationally feasible on 1 January 1999. Given the long, but variable, lead times necessary for implementing measures, and the interactions between them, this was a highly complex procedure, which, moreover, required appropriate deadlines for the various subcommittees that prepared the Council decisions. We included, of course, precautionary safety margins and made appropriate adjustments, but this technique served as a useful monthly reminder of the Treaty obligations imposed on the EMI. In addition, the discussions, and the search for constructive compromises, received increasingly powerful support from the EMI staff, which grew from about two dozen members taken over from the secretariat of the Committee of EC Governors to more than 400 by the time I relinquished my position as president in mid-1997. Most of the staff, and all those in key positions, came from the member central banks, but within months they had acquired the "multilateral" frame of mind so indispensable for making realistic proposals to reconcile conflicting views held by member central banks (and not to forget: most of the Council decisions had

159

to be unanimous). Achieving progress would have been impossible if, instead of a solid institutional structure, the work had had to be carried out within a cooperative framework. Finally, I have to pay tribute to all Council members. They were given an institution-building mandate, and they fulfilled their obligation, even when some of them had misgivings about the feasibility, or even the desirability, of the project.

At the same time, the absence of major conflicts and the relatively smooth development of the institution-building process owe quite a lot both to the facts and figures relating to the economic situation prevailing at that time in Europe, and to the changing perception of how macro-economic policy should operate. As regards the first factor, these facts and figures concern mainly the deterioration of the fiscal indicators. As noted in the first *Annual Report* of the EMI (April 1995): "The early 1990s marked a sharp reversal of trends in general government deficits in the Union. Following a prolonged period of decreasing deficits, fiscal balances deteriorated significantly from 1989 onwards. After standing at 5 percent of GDP in 1992, deficits in the Union reached 6 percent of GDP in 1993, the highest level on record since the foundation of the European Community." The deficits began to decline in 1994, but in 1996 still stood at 4.4 percent of GDP. As a result, general government gross debt, which had stood at 56 percent of GDP in 1991, reached 73.5 percent in 1996. This was such an obviously unsustainable development that in all likelihood it would have triggered policy reactions, though perhaps not with sufficient vigor. The constraint of the convergence criteria emerged at the right time.

As for macroeconomic policy, Keynesian demand management went out of fashion after the stagflation experience of the 1970s – and not only in Europe – many years before the revival of the EMU initiative. This resulted in a dramatic decline in the rate of inflation in Europe, which started after the observation of very high inflation rates, which peaked in 1974 at slightly above 14 percent. As observed in the second *Annual Report* of the EMI (April 1996): "Average EU inflation has declined successively from 10.5 percent in 1980–84, to 4.4 percent in 1985–89, to 4.1 percent in 1990–95, and to 3 percent in the past two years." Even more significantly, the (unweighted) standard deviation of national CPI inflation, which had been 6.5 percent on average during 1972–82, had fallen to 2 percent by 1995. This goes a long way toward explaining the relatively serene atmosphere prevailing in the Economic and Financial Affairs Council (Ecofin) Council meetings that I attended. To which one has to add the fact that the regained respect for both inflation fighting and the inflation-fighting capability of monetary policy has been accompanied by a gradual, but general, move toward granting policymaking independence to central banks – and this, too, began well before Maastricht. It is, of course, true that the Federal Republic of Germany played a major role in shaping the definition of the ECB's independence (which in fact was defined more strictly than that of the Bundesbank, although not more strictly than what had become over time the German practice), but these requests fell on receptive ears in the case of the majority of member countries. The time was ripe for moving collectively in this direction.

Let me conclude these comments by recalling the story of the scenario of the changeover to the single currency. This is a good illustration of how it was possible to achieve decisive progress in an area which the Treaty left undecided, without unnecessarily spectacular conflicts between the Council, the Commission, and the EMI, which all had their part to play. Indeed, while it was quite clear that the irrevocable pegging of exchange rates vis-à-vis each other and vis-à-vis the ecu and the implementation of a single monetary policy had to start at the latest on 1 January 1999, as regards the introduction of the single currency the Treaty simply said that the "Council shall, acting according to the same procedure [which meant "on a proposal from the Commission and after consulting the ECB"], also take the other measures necessary for the rapid introduction of the ecu as the single currency of those Member States" (the "those" refers to the member states that passed the hurdle of the convergence criteria).

By early 1995 it had gradually become clear that unless agreement was reached on a precise changeover scenario, the credibility of the whole undertaking would suffer. How could market participants prepare themselves for the changeover in a timely manner, unless they knew what was going to happen and when? Or perhaps nothing would happen anyhow? (A question I heard often from quite a few market participants, and not only Americans.)

The Commission took up the challenge first, by publishing on 31 May 1995 a Green Paper on "*The Practical Arrangements for the Introduction of the Single Currency.*" The EMI, which was supposed to be consulted instead of the not-yet existent ECB, was somewhat behind. During the spring it undertook an extensive EU-wide survey of the banking community, covering nearly 400 credit institutions, on the detailed technical implications of the changeover. This was indispensable for drawing operational conclusions, of which we prepared a preliminary version for the informal autumn meeting of Ecofin, scheduled to take place in Valencia under Spanish presidency (the final, formal EMI report, titled "*The Changeover to the Single Currency,*" was published on 14 November 1995).

The Valencia meeting (29–30 September 1995) was a crucial one. A number of informal decisions were reached, possible compromises were outlined – to be submitted for formal decisions to the November Ecofin meeting and to the December Madrid summit. The main objection to the Commission's Green Paper, coming principally from Germany but supported also by other countries, was that it wanted to achieve at a very early stage a volume of transactions denominated in the single currency that would reach a "critical mass" (thereby ensuring "no return") and, if necessary, to do so through regulation. At a time when public opinion was barely familiar with the whole process, it was deemed dangerously counterproductive to signal four to five years ahead the list of transactions that would have to be denominated in the single currency, announcing only too clearly the ultimate disappearance of the national currency units. The alternatives, therefore, seemed to be *either* an early announcement

162

of a number of mandatory changeovers, which would have enhanced credibility at the risk of creating a political backlash, or leaving practically all the changeovers to the very end of a three-year period, which would have appeased those who feared this backlash but at the same time could have undermined the credibility of the whole process. In other words, the choice appeared to be between an early "big bang" and one that would occur more or less simultaneously with the exchange of banknotes. The challenge, then, was to find a way around this unappealing choice.

In discussions within the EMI, I began to argue that all monetary policy operations by the future ESCB should be carried out from the very first day in ecu, which meant that all accounts held by counterparties with the ESCB would have to be denominated in ecu, yet the banks and all private market participants would retain their right to undertake their changeover at the time of their liking, but naturally at the latest at the beginning of the banknote exchange. I thought (and after some discussion it turned out that I was right) that even the most hesitant members of my Council would realize that *not* doing this would have made monetary policy operations remarkably cumbersome (although not impossible technically) and would have exposed the central bankers to the criticism that they themselves had some doubt about the final outcome of the process. I also thought that any such decision implied that the entire interbank market would start operating instantaneously in ecu – not by decree, but for obvious practical reasons.

The second initial change I considered essential was that, right at the beginning, governments should denominate in ecu new tradable debt issues by the public sector, for the same credibility reason that applied to monetary policy decisions – knowing full well, of course, that any such decision would have to be accompanied by the conversion of the outstanding stock of public debt into ecu. Once we had agreed among ourselves on the decision to be taken by the Governing Council of the future ECB, all of us saw that this was a practical necessity for conduct-ing a smooth monetary policy (it would not have been impossible, just ridiculously unpractical, to operate with repos otherwise). At the same time, it was obvious that we should keep a low profile on an issue that, ultimately, had to be decided by the governments. But this did not prevent me from outlining the argument to a number of ministers.

Interestingly, the final decision in favor of denominating all new tradable government debt issues in the single currency was triggered, as so often happens in intergovernmental negotiations, by a deal that would seem strange to any distant, outside observer. The Germans did not like the idea (even though they acknowledged the logic of the argument), but accepted it in the end in exchange for the French agreeing to swap the name ecu for euro.

The changeover scenario contained a large number of less controversial but quite important decisions: the formal acceptance of dates, the carefully worded legal definition of the euro (as a result of which the national currency units would on 1 January 1999 become the nondecimal components of the euro), the commitment by the NCBs to provide conversion facilities during a three-year period to those financial institutions that had not been able to equip themselves with such facilities, a timetable for the changeover of the public administrations, and so on. Combined with the two key decisions, they formed a coherent whole, which radically enhanced the credibility of implementing the single currency project, without, however, imposing an early changeover on private market participants by decree. In the spring of 1996, I concluded one of my presentations to a group of European banking CEOs thus: "You may still have some doubts, but you would be well advised to insure yourself against the risk that the single monetary policy will effectively start operating on 1 January 1999." A year before, they would have taken this remark as a joke; this time they did not smile, but looked genuinely interested.

The package that was finally adopted by the Madrid summit, on the recommendation of the (formal) Ecofin meeting of 27 November 1995, was fully compatible with the detailed report issued by the EMI on

14 November. Little mention was made of the earlier Green Paper drafted by the Commission. This, in a sense, was unfair. It was the Commission that had got the ball rolling, and for this initiative it deserved praise. Moreover, the "critical mass" concept was far from being a silly one. But the EMI played a decisive role by formally proposing one key measure, suggesting a second, and putting in place a number of practical ones, which crucially contributed to the fact that, for the financial markets, the euro became an early reality – without having to resort to administrative regulations.

THE POLICY MIX

During my EMI years, not only institution building, but also macropolicy decisions were characterized by the absence of major, disruptive conflicts between the central banks and the governments involved. This applied certainly to the relationship between the EMI Council and Ecofin, but also to the relationship between most of the NCBs and their respective governments, although in the latter case there *were* instances or periods of conflict (one significant example was provided by France). For the central banks, there were two main reasons for not being unduly worried by actual, or prospective, policy misbehavior by governments. One was the declining trend of inflation. The other was the existence of the fiscal convergence criteria, which governments *did* try to respect. Yet even in a period that by today's standards could be regarded as having been relatively peaceful, we were beginning to perceive causes for concern. Both in the *1996 Convergence Report* published by the EMI (in November 1996) and in the Institute's *1996 Annual Report* (published in April 1997) you may find numerous examples of concern expressed regarding several developments: the slowness of the pace of reduction of fiscal deficits; the recourse to one-off measures; the temptation to raise taxes rather than reducing expenditure; and, most importantly, the little attention paid to the sustainability of the deficit reduction measures (the *Convergence*

Report contains a detailed analysis of a development that received far less attention at that time than it does today: the growing fiscal burden of old-age pensions).

As regards governments, their traditional inclination to blame central banks for poor economic performance was also tempered by two factors: on the one hand, by the declining trend of long-term interest rates (which had started at the beginning of the 1990s and was interrupted only in 1994 for a short period); and, on the other, by their formal commitment, as a result of the ratification of the Maastricht Treaty, to respect central bank independence. It would have been strange if they had chosen to ignore this commitment so quickly – especially since this was in fact the "sixth" convergence criterion, compliance with which conditioned access to EMU, and could therefore not be taken lightly.

More than six years have now elapsed since the beginning of the end of the institution-building process on 1 January 1999 and more than three years since its unquestionable end. These are short periods when compared to the more than thirty-five years that have elapsed since the Hague summit, and even shorter if you trace back the origins of European monetary cooperation to the establishment of the European Payments Union in 1950. Yet we have been watching significant changes in the relationship between central banks and governments during these periods; and these changes have not been for the better. Hardly a week passes without a head of state or of government publicly questioning the appropriateness of the monetary policy stance decided by the Governing Council of the ECB, and suggesting that the ECB should take as its model the Federal Reserve of the United States – thereby flatly disregarding Article 107 of the Treaty, which unequivocally states that "The Community institutions and bodies and the governments of the Member States undertake not to seek to influence the members of the decision-making bodies of the ECB or of the national central banks in the performance of their tasks." Similarly, the cavalier way in which an increasing number of member states have dealt with the constraints of the Stability and Growth Pact suggests that they have conveniently forgotten that this pact was explicitly designed (not in prehistoric times, but in 1997) to preserve the constraining elements of the fiscal convergence criteria *after* accession to EMU, precisely because uncontrolled fiscal laxity could severely undermine the ECB's ability to fulfill its prime responsibility of maintaining price stability. No wonder this triggered reactions not only from the President of the ECB, but also from practically all the NCBs – reactions that were not to the liking of the governments concerned. No wonder either that when the head of government of one of the large countries attributes all the hardships of his country simultaneously to the introduction of the euro and the high level of the ECB's interest rates, central bankers feel it appropriate to argue that their country's problems have nothing to do with monetary policy. This hardly amounts to an environment that would favor a balanced and constructive exchange of views on optimal policy mixes (note the plural).

What has gone wrong since the second half of the 1990s?

It is easy to see with hindsight that, after the completion of the "heroic" institution-building phase, some deterioration in the political environment should not have come as a surprise. Managing the successful implementation of the single currency required considerable efforts on the part of politicians – efforts that could not be expected to be sustained. The success may have given the impression that the difficult part of the process was behind us, whereas it simply implied that the nature of the challenges had changed: we now had to "live" with EMU. On top of this, within a few years there has been a generational change in the political elite in the majority of countries and, most importantly, in three of the largest countries (but not only there). This stands in stark contrast *both* to what had been happening in the political world during the decade following the signing of the Maastricht Treaty *and* to the continuity still prevailing in the world of central banking. A personal note: when I meet members of the ESCB (at various levels) today, I expect to know at least two-thirds of them, whereas when I meet politicians, or even high-ranking civil servants, the proportion is below one-quarter – and even this is to be attributed to my recent activity relating to the reform of the regulatory process in the European securities markets rather than to my more distant EMI experience.

A much heavier responsibility for the deteriorating relationship between European governments and European central bankers lies with the worsening performance of the economy in the euro area, especially in comparison with the United States. The single most important fact in this respect has been the decline in Europe of the rate of growth of labor productivity (as measured by output per hour). For the EU 15 the deterioration has been dramatic, in comparison both with the European past and with the performance of the United States. Between 1985 and 1995 the average annual rate of growth was 2.2 percent, which allowed a sizeable catching up for the United States, where productivity rose at that time at an average rate barely exceeding 1 percent. Since the middle of the 1990s, however, this relationship has been radically reversed; and during the years 2000–04 the US figure came close to 3 percent, while its European counterpart declined to 1 percent (and this figure would be even lower if the United Kingdom was excluded from the total). As estimated by the BIS (*74th Annual Report*, p. 20), more sophisticated calculations of total factor productivity (TFP) developments confirm this dismal story. I find convincing the arguments put forward in the report that this discrepancy cannot be solely attributed to greater use of information technology equipment in the United States: "much of the acceleration in the trend TFP in the United States could well have come from the previous deregulation of markets for goods and services" (p. 21). Central bankers, looking at these figures, have come to the conclusion (which I share) that there is precious little that monetary policy can do to alleviate these supply-side inefficiencies. Supply-side reforms are the responsibility of governments.

But this is arguably not the full story. That in the medium to long run these productivity developments are bound to put a brake on European growth is beyond doubt. But it is true that other factors are also at work; and in a shorter perspective they seem to play a more important role. One is the relatively low rate of participation of the European population in the labor force; another is the high rate of unemployment; and the third is that Europeans tend to work fewer hours per year than their American counterparts. These three facts can be summed up in one sentence: fewer Europeans work fewer hours than Americans, which explains to a large extent why European income per head of population is lagging behind the American equivalent. No wonder that governments, and quite a few academics, argue that even if you define potential output in a quite restrictive way, there is a negative output gap that could be reduced by an acceleration in the very modest rate of growth of European domestic demand. And, so runs the argument, since central bankers are so vocal in opposing fiscal laxity, they should engineer this acceleration by pursuing a more aggressive monetary policy. By doing this, they would also help alleviate the danger that the so strongly anticipated US policy adjustment measures – cutting the country's fiscal deficit and raising the propensity to save of its households – will end up creating a slump in the world economy (which, incidentally, is about the last thing that Europe needs).

This is a serious debate that *has* to be pursued, but how can this be done within the framework of our current institutional arrangements?

It is at this point that I turn to the third group of reasons that bear a responsibility for it not being possible to pursue this debate in an environment conducive to constructive solutions. The major weakness of our current institutional arrangements can be summed up in a few words: that while the m-leg of the economic and monetary union is solidly established, its e-leg is not. Let me remind you that I had misgivings about (what one might summarily call) the "missing federal finance minister issue" from the very beginning of my active participation in the monetary unification process. You may find the expression of my misgivings in a paper (for the preparation of which I received Claudio Borio's active assistance) submitted to the Delors Committee and published in an annex to the report itself (*"Macro-Coordination of Fiscal Policies in an Economic and Monetary Union in Europe,"* January 1989).

Let me briefly elaborate on how I see this problem today.

One problem would not necessarily be solved by having a large federal budget and a powerful federal finance minister: the destabilizing emergence of a "globally" excessive fiscal deficit. No doubt, there is a powerful secretary of the Treasury and a large federal budget in the United States, yet few of us would argue that the current and prospective American public sector deficit is an optimal one. Nor would I argue that such a situation would by itself prevent the emergence of differences, even of major differences, between national (or "state") fiscal balances. To avoid this happening, you need additional arrangements: you cannot dispense with something akin to the poorly managed Stability and Growth Pact. A large federal budget would, however, represent one major advantage. It would provide a framework for more or less automatic transfer mechanisms that could help alleviate the politically and socially disruptive impact of differences between the growth performances of the member countries. Whether this would be a good or a bad thing would, however, depend on the origin of these differences: probably a good thing if we had to deal with country-specific external shocks – but a rather bad thing if the differences are of the countries' own making. And since my suspicion is that the emerging differences between the growth performances within Euroland can to a large extent be attributed to policy decisions (or the lack of them) by individual countries, I come to the conclusion that we should not expect much help from any move toward macroeconomic fiscal federalism – which in any case is highly unlikely to happen.

I would therefore today put less exclusive stress on the need for macropolicy coordination than I did sixteen years ago, but would rather emphasize the desperate need to accelerate – and collectively accelerate – the micro- or supply-side reforms, of which we have so far seen only timid, and very uneven, beginnings. It is in this particular area that the e-leg should be strengthened.

170

CONCLUDING REMARKS

It would be disingenuous on my part not to briefly outline, by way of conclusion, where I stand in my "stylized" summary of the current debate between European central bankers and their governments.

Let me start by saying that I share the concern of those who would like to see a pickup in the lackluster rate of growth of domestic demand in Euroland. But what are the policy means of achieving this?

Forget about monetary policy – however tempting it might be to ask for "more responsive" policy reactions by the ECB. Anyone who cares to take a glance at the monetary statistics published by the ECB is bound to notice the currently relatively high rate of growth of broad money. You also have to bear in mind that this is not a new development: between mid-2001 and late 2003, M3 had been growing at a yearly rate of around 8 percent. As a result, Euroland now enjoys a comfortable "money gap" – even if allowance is made for the earlier portfolio shifts from equity into money. By calling attention to these figures, I do not want to imply that I see a danger of such "excess" liquidity putting upward pressure on consumer prices in the foreseeable future – although I would not rule out that it could have an undesirable impact on asset prices, at least in some countries. All I am trying to say is that, with such a high degree of liquidity and with the currently prevailing very low nominal and real interest rates throughout the whole yield curve, it would require a generous dose of imagination to believe that a relaxation of monetary policy could significantly stimulate domestic investment and consumption. I do not possess such imagination. Moreover, in a world flooded by dollar liquidity, a liquidity-generating European monetary policy would surely not contribute to global financial stability.

What about fiscal policy? It would seem difficult to argue that a relaxation of the fiscal policy stance could provide no stimulus whatsoever to domestic demand in Euroland. Initially, and for a short period, it possibly could – but at a price. Public opinion is no longer ignorant to the point of not realizing that any such relaxation would come on top of the irrespon-sible handling, by the largest member countries, of their commitment to the Stability and Growth Pact. This has seriously undermined the credi-bility of future fiscal policy commitments. It is easy to lose credibility, but very hard to regain it. And this has happened at a time when the same public opinion has become acutely aware of the need to reform our health care and social security systems and to draw the appropriate conclusions for our pension systems from the aging prospects of our populations. With the level of taxation well exceeding any reasonable level, it would seem difficult not to expect an increase in the burden of public debt. No wonder that the citizens of Euroland are not very keen to abandon their high propensity to save.

The upshot of all this is that the use of the two traditional macropolicy tools for stimulating domestic demand would be unlikely to yield sizeable and lasting results, but would surely pile up trouble for the future. So what to do? The short answer is: try to exert an influence on investment and consumption by other means.

As regards investment, two objectives should be simultaneously pur-sued. First, to nurture an "investment-friendly" climate across the full range of the enterprise sector, but with special attention to small- and medium-sized firms, which as a group are the only ones likely to create jobs. The core concern in this field (in addition to the obvious need to reduce the administrative, fiscal, and regulatory impediments that hin-der entrepreneurial initiatives) is to encourage risk-taking, which in plain language means increasing the rewards in case of success in comparison with the penalties in case of failure. The second objective is to raise not only the level of, but also the return on, investment, that is, the reverse incremental capital/output ratio. This is what I regard as one of the major lessons to be drawn from the US experience.

As regards consumption, the key word is "confidence," or rather the lack of it. Many of our citizens are worried about their future because, on the one hand, they are fully aware that our "European model" (the solidarity features to which they are deeply attached) badly needs repair, but, on the other hand, they either do not see the beginning of a credible reform process or they fear its outcome. Our politicians face the historical challenge of having to relieve these often conflicting anxieties. They will not succeed in their endeavors unless the reform programs enjoy wide popular support, which, in turn, requires broadly based consultation of all stakeholders. The bulk of the reforms will have to be conceived, agreed upon, and carried out within national borders – but, with Euroland being a politically motivated collective endeavor, confidence building would gain much through agreement on broad principles at the European level. Quite a challenge for the policymakers of the economic and monetary union's e-leg.

5

The Future of Central Bank Cooperation[1]

BETH A. SIMMONS[2]

Central bank cooperation has a long history. From the episodic efforts to support the nineteenth century gold standard, to the personal interactions of interwar central bankers, to the institutionalized postwar efforts to maintain fixed exchange rates, to the post-Bretton Woods progress in developing standards for prudential bank regulation, central bankers have progressively consulted and coordinated their activities. Such cooperation has always been shaped by a few perennial parameters. Can central bankers agree on theory (end-means relationships)? To what extent can they agree on goals (social purpose)? Do they have the capacity (technical and institutional) to achieve their collective goals? Does the broader political environment facilitate or impede cooperation?

It is easy to assume, in writing a paper on the "future of central bank cooperation," that such cooperation is (1) easily observable (implicit in the assumption that a non-participant can meaningfully write about it), and (2) a good thing. Neither of these assumptions is without controversy,

[1] The author would like to acknowledge the excellent research assistance of Alexander Noonan and Adrian Yung Hwei Ow. All errors remain her own.
[2] Harvard University.

however. First, central bank cooperation is *factually* controversial. Looking over the historical record, there are important disagreements over *whether*, in fact, central bankers have cooperated at various historical moments. The passage of time does not seem to have settled the debate over whether, for example, central bankers in the nineteenth century were mutually cooperative or merely opportunistic.[3] Much depends on how one defines cooperation. The dictionary defines it as "joint operation or action"; its antonym is "competition." Joint action can be shallow or deep; deep cooperation is marked by policy adjustments that differ from those that would have been taken unilaterally, and that are taken specifically to address a collective good or mutual interest (Keohane 1984; Downs, Rocke, and Barsoom 1996).

"Deep" central bank cooperation can be *normatively* controversial as well. Theoretical controversies rage about whether – and the extent to which – exchange rate or monetary policy coordination actually improves outcomes over well-designed unilateral policies (Obstfeld and Rogoff 2002). Moreover, to countries that are excluded from decision making, policy coordination may look more like a cartel than cooperation. Global standards for the supervision and regulation of internationally active banks, for example, can be interpreted as serving disproportionately the interests of major banks in the leading jurisdictions. Some of the more profound forms of central bank cooperation can be expected to raise domestic political controversies as well: there are bound to be domestic voices concerned that collective interests might sacrifice an important national interest. The historical reluctance of the United States to officially allow the Federal Reserve to participate in the activities

---

[3] Barry Eichengreen, for example, has developed an explanation for the success (stability) of the nineteenth century gold standard that rests largely on the "linchpin" of international cooperation (Eichengreen 1992). Other scholars have responded that nineteenth century cooperation was little more than *ad hoc* specific actions taken for self-gain but lacking any institutionalization and taken without any perception of supporting a public good (Flandreau 1997).

of the Bank for International Settlements (BIS) largely reflects such a concern.[4]

Despite these concerns, central banks have accomplished a lot through collective effort, which bodes well for the future. Collectively produced and shared information is increasingly rich and user-friendly. Central bank independence from regular government interference is fairly (though not universally) robust, reducing (though not eliminating) political frictions. Cooperation in some areas appears to be cumulative, involving positive feedback loops through which central bankers continue to develop and improve on past achievements, successfully learning while doing despite an increasingly complex global financial environment. In their collective regulatory capacity, for example, it is hard to imagine a return to the free-for-all that existed prior to the 1980s. Additionally, central banks also seem to have developed a reasonably robust response to financial crises, though efforts here have plateaued far short of acting as lenders of last resort. The ability of central bankers to assemble very short-term financial packages to contain crises (as a bridge to more substantial – and more conditional – International Monetary Fund [IMF] assistance) has been an important example of the rapid response of which central banks may be uniquely capable. We are a very long way from 1931.

However, in areas such as setting exchange rates or other macroeconomic policies, central bank cooperation is as difficult and controversial as ever. At the theoretical level, there are important debates over whether

---

[4] In deciding not to allow Fed participation in the BIS at its founding, the Hoover administration felt constrained by Congressional sentiments of this kind. In Stimson's words, the Fed would be barred from participating "to prevent our friends on the Hill from running amuck" (Stimson to Hoover, 8 June 1929, as quoted by Costigliola 1973: 478). Similarly in 1994, in hearings that touched on whether the Fed should take up its seat on the Board of the BIS, the subcommittee Chair expressed concern "whether this would put the Federal Reserve at some point in time . . . in conflict with the domestic independence they exercise." Rep. Paul Kanjorski, Chair, US Monetary Policy. *Hearing of the Economic Growth and Credit Formation Subcommittee of the House Banking Committee.* Witness: Alan Greenspan. Federal News Service, 22 July 1994.

central banks should do anything other than tend to domestic price stability. Optimism in the 1980s on the joint gains to be made from coordinating monetary policies has given way to greater skepticism that such coordination could ever really "get it right." Legitimate questions have even been raised about the efficacy of official international intervention in foreign exchange markets of the major floating currencies. Moreover, with the imbalances reflected in rapidly expanding Asian, and particularly Chinese, dollar reserves, the global political economy is changing in ways that will challenge existing institutions and practices.

This chapter explores the future of central bank cooperation along a continuum from "easy" to "difficult." The first section lays the foundation for assessing future collaboration by observing the central banks and governors themselves. The second examines what I have been able to find on the state of the presentation and sharing of information among central banks. The trajectory here, I argue, is really quite positive. The third section discusses cooperative standard setting, and the fourth looks at extraordinary emergency central bank assistance. Finally, I examine the most difficult issue facing central bank cooperation in the near future: imbalance at the core of the international economy. I conclude with some observations about the political–economic and institutional environment.

PLAYERS AND INSTITUTIONS: AN OVERVIEW

Before we look into cooperation itself, it is useful to have a look at the players involved. The number of central banks has increased tremendously over the past century, as the number of independent countries has grown, and as more countries have established monetary authorities (see Figure 5.1). Membership in the BIS has grown over time as well, even exceeding overall central bank growth since 1995.

In addition to the number of member banks, the prospects for cooperation are often assumed to depend on the time horizons of the players.

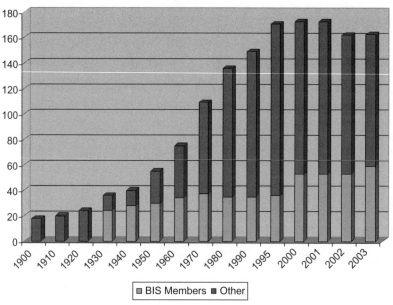

Figure 5.1: Number of central banks, 1900–2003.
Sources: Morgan Stanley, Central Bank Directory (2004); Bank for International Settlements.

Worldwide, most, but not all, central bank governors have a definite term of office ranging from three to eight years, with five-year terms the most common (see Table 5.1). On the whole, BIS member governors tend to have longer statutory terms than do non-members. Governors that have

Table 5.1: *Central bank governors' terms of office (number of banks, worldwide)*

Term in years	Not available	Indefinite	8 Years	7 Years	6 Years	5 Years	4 Years	3 Years or less
G20 members	1	2	1	2	3	6	4	0
BIS members, not including G20	1	2	1	6	15	9	0	1
Non-BIS members	24	17	0	4	8	46	9	14
Total	**26**	**21**	**2**	**12**	**26**	**61**	**13**	**15**

Note: Data current as of 2004.
Sources: Morgan Stanley, Central Bank Directory (2004); Bank for International Settlements.

Table 5.2: *How central bank governors' terms end*

	1997	1998	1999	2000	2001	2002	2003	2004	Average
At end of term	8	11	12	6	7	12	5	11	**9**
Before end of term	11	5	15	7	6	7	17	14	**10.25**
Indefinite term	2	5	5	2	3	2	3	3	**3.125**
Unknown term	4	8	5	8	9	4	1	2	**5.125**
New governor	–	–	–	–	–	–	3	2	**2.5**
Total	**25**	**29**	**37**	**23**	**25**	**25**	**29**	**32**	**28.125**

Source: Morgan Stanley, Central Bank Directory (2004).

"indefinite terms" – which I interpret as serving at the pleasure of the government – are much less likely to be BIS members than those with definite terms.

However, actual terms in office can vary significantly from official terms and in recent years more central bank governors have tended to leave office *before the end of their term* (if one is specified) than at the end of their term (see Table 5.2). Multiple terms and early terminations account for significant deviations from formal term provisions. Figure 5.2 gives a sense of how long central bank governors of the G10 and G20 have actually remained in office during the postwar period. During these years, governors from the G10 countries have held their posts for a little over an average of eight years. Governors of the remaining G20 countries, on the other hand, have generally held their positions for under five years. Actual term heterogeneity is much higher among the remaining G20 members than the G10 as well.[5]

---

[5] The standard deviation for central bank governors' terms for the G10 is 2.55; for the remainder of the G20 it is 3.24.

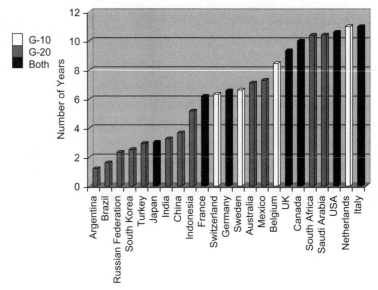

Figure 5.2: Average tenure in office, governors of G10 and G20 countries, postwar period.

The broader institutional context in which central banks operate has been changing in important ways as well. The home states of BIS member banks for most of the postwar years were converging toward democratic governance. Using a common measure of democratic participation, the "polity score,"[6] we can see that a big positive shift (as well as a strong reduction in the standard deviation) took place with the democratic consolidation of Eastern Europe in the 1990s. Since 1990, however, the significant expansion of membership to Latin American and Asian countries reverses both of these trends (see Figure 5.3).

The changing political organization of BIS member states raises the possibility of some states trying to exert political control over central bank governors. While evidence is hard to come by, it is at least possible to look

---

[6] The polity score is a commonly used measure of the degree of democracy that includes components measuring the extent of the franchise, political competition, free elections, and checks on executive power. See http://www.cidcm.umd.edu/inscr/polity/.

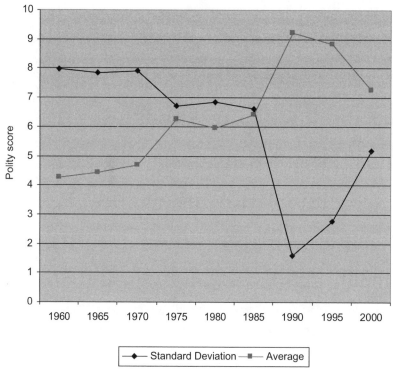

Figure 5.3: Democratization in BIS member countries (excluding Bosnia & Herzegovina, Hong Kong SAR, Iceland, and Serbia & Montenegro).

at the relationship between elections and the turnover of governors (see Figure 5.4). Among BIS members, election years and replacement of central bank governors appear practically to take a random walk. About 20 percent of all election years are also years in which the governor of the central bank is replaced within six months before or after an election. Never does the number of such coincident years exceed four, consistent with the received wisdom that most of the BIS member banks, at least in the democracies, enjoy a high degree of political independence.

If we focus in for a moment on the G10 group of central bankers, there are some other interesting points that are potentially relevant for cooperation emerge. Suppose we take a snapshot of the background

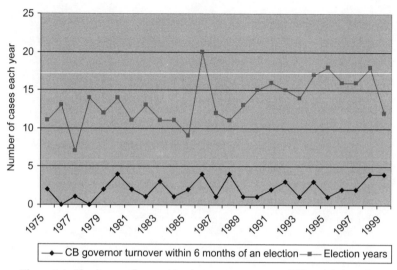

Figure 5.4: Elections and central bank governor turnover, BIS members only.

characteristics of the ten (actually eleven) governors for 1990, 2000, and 2005, coding for whether each has had experience as the following (note these are not mutually exclusive):

- Staff of the Ministry of Finance/Treasury
- Other government position
- Industry experience
- Private finance experience
- Academic background
- Worked at the IMF
- Worked at the Organisation for Economic Co-operation and Development (OECD)

Coding for each for the G10 governors and calculating and then summing the standard deviation reveals a noticeable increase in homogeneity of backgrounds over time (see Figure 5.5).

The notable shift in the governors' backgrounds, however, is more interesting than the aggregate dispersion. Over these fifteen years, G10

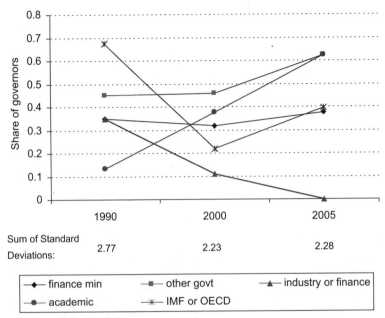

Figure 5.5: Background of G10 central bank governors, 1990, 2000, and 2005.
Source: Author's classifications based on various biographical encyclopedias and central bank websites.

central bank governors are much less likely to have an industry or private financial background. They are somewhat less likely to have worked for an international economic organization, though there has been a slight increase in this proportion between 2000 and 2005. Experience in the finance ministry has just about held constant, while "other" government experience has increased somewhat. But the most significant trend to be revealed by a look at these bios is the *sharp and persistent rise in academic background.* In 1990, only one out of ten governors had spent much (post-PhD) time in the academy. Among the current G10 governors, six were once academics (to some degree).

This survey seems to suggest that central bankers are "structurally" and attitudinally fairly well placed to take a cooperative approach to monetary and financial problems, and may be even more so in the future.

Cooperation seems most likely among the obvious candidates: the G10, and to a lesser extent the G20 and the rest of the BIS members. Bankers associated with these institutions, especially the G10, are more likely to have longer terms (*de jure* and *de facto*) and hence longer time horizons. Their polities and economies are much more homogeneous than are other groupings. Up to the early 1990s, BIS members increasingly enjoyed the legitimacy that comes with democratic governance, while the political cycles and bank staffing cycles tend to run quite separately within these countries. G10 governors are increasingly likely to be academics, interested in learning and persuasion; possibly more open than others to the power of evidence and reasoned argument. Of course, as Bordo points out in his comments that follow, the increased sophistication of central bankers may also improve their handling of monetary policy, reducing the *need* for international cooperation in the future.

In any case, this cozy homogeneity alone will not provide ready answers to some of the most difficult problems that will face central bank cooperation in the future. Globalization has brought a plethora of heterogeneous players to the fore. The interconnectedness of financial markets will make it increasingly difficult to handle systemic risks from a narrow decision-making base. Tectonic plates are shifting in the global economy as China – increasingly powerful, steadfastly heterodox – seeks influence and the protection of her interests. However, rather than delve immediately into an analysis of cooperative approaches to address the East-West economic imbalance, I turn first to a far simpler problem: information sharing.

SHALLOW COOPERATION: INFORMATION SHARING

It is hard to imagine central bankers accomplishing much in common without sharing information that is relevant to economic and regulatory policymaking in an increasingly interdependent world. The major central banks have been exchanging policy-relevant information for the better part of a century. In fact, information gathering and dissemination was one of the primary purposes of the BIS; I have argued elsewhere that one of the crucial initial functions of the Bank was to provide credible information about Germany's capacity to pay reparations in order to overcome informational asymmetries between Germany and her creditors (Simmons 1993). Practically every commentary on the BIS acknowledges the continuing role the institution plays with respect to information generation and sharing among central banks (Howell 1993; Baer 2000; Fratianni and Pattison 2001; Bernholz 2003).

Good economic and financial information is something easily taken for granted these days. Financial crises have revealed serious weaknesses, but have also created demands for more transparency and disclosure. The BIS has assisted in the development of principles of transparency in central banking,[7] and the International Monetary Fund has issued a series of "*Reports on the Observance of Standards and Codes*"[8] that use these principles as a guideline. For their part, IMF members can submit to voluntary reviews, which can be quite revealing. To analyze how well BIS members performed in this regard, I read through sections of the reports for the three areas most relevant to central banking: monetary policy, banking supervision, and data dissemination (see Figure 5.6 and Table 5.3). Most members of the BIS rate in the "good" to "excellent" range when it comes to providing routine information regarding their monetary and financial/supervisory policies as well as accessible economic data.[9]

The main point is that quality information in a standard format is increasingly available so that more and more central bankers are in a better position to compare and discuss economic and financial conditions. Moreover, this relatively new emphasis on transparency may have

---

[7] These principles can be found at http://www.imf.org/external/np/exr/facts/mtransp .htm.

[8] These reports are located at http://www.imf.org/external/np/rosc/rosc.asp.

[9] For a study that argues that cooperation with these standards varies according to the extent of cooperation of private agents, see Mosley (2003).

Beth A. Simmons

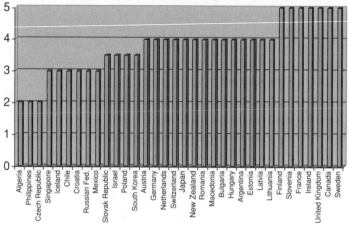

A. **Transparency in Banking Policy & Supervision**
Not reporting: Australia, Brazil, China, Greece, Turkey, India, Italy, Norway, Portugal, South Africa, Spain, United States

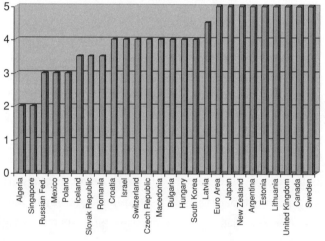

B. **Monetary Policy Transparency**
Not Reporting: Australia, Brazil, Chile, China, India, Norway, Philippines, Slovenia, South Africa, Turkey, United States

Figure 5.6: Central bank transparency.
Note: (1 = poor, 2 = many shortcomings, 3 = some shortcomings, 4 = good, 5 = excellent.
Source: Author's ratings based on information provided in reports rendered by the IMF staff. Reports can be found at: http://www.imf.org.

C. **Data Quality**
Reports not found on IMF website: Algeria, Australia, Austria, Chile, China, Finland, Germany, Greece, Iceland, India, Italy, Netherlands, Norway, Portugal, Philippines, Singapore, Slovenia, South Africa, Spain, Turkey, United States

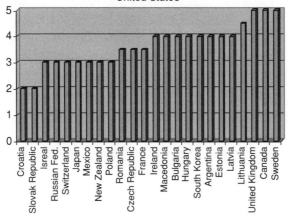

Figure 5.6 (*continued*)

helped to alter normative expectations about information generation and disclosure more generally. Along with the information the BIS has helped collect and interpret from reporting private banks ever since the early 1960s, these transparency exercises have done a good deal to raise expectations about the quality and availability of information.

Information sharing is not just about data, of course. After all, if all the information central banks ever needed could be posted on a website, there would be much less reason to spend time in Basel. At least two other kinds of information are crucial to cooperation: theoretical information and information about policy plans and preferences. The former involves a discussion about the theories underlying concepts that are not directly observable in the hard numbers. "Potential output," the "natural rate of unemployment," and the "equilibrium interest rate" are not directly measured; they are theoretical constructs that respond to new theoretical developments (Kozicki 2004). One of the most influential papers on

Table 5.3: *Countries that subscribe to the IMF Special Data Dissemination Standard (SDDS)*

Argentina	Egypt, Arab Republic of	Kazakhstan	Romania
Armenia	El Salvador	Korea (Republic of)	Russian Federation
Australia	Estonia	Kyrgyz Republic	Singapore
Austria	Finland	Latvia	Slovak Republic
Belarus, Republic of	France	Lithuania	Slovenia
Belgium	Germany	Luxembourg	South Africa
Brazil	Greece	Malaysia	Spain
Bulgaria	Hong Kong, SAR, PRC	Mexico	Sweden
Canada	Hungary	Moldova, Republic of	Switzerland
Chile	Iceland	Morocco	Thailand
Colombia	India	Netherlands	Tunisia
Costa Rica	Indonesia	Norway	Turkey
Croatia	Ireland	Peru	Ukraine
Czech Republic	Israel	Philippines	United Kingdom
Denmark	Italy	Poland	United States
Ecuador	Japan	Portugal	Uruguay

Note: The SDDS is a standard for the level of coverage, integrity, accessibility, and quality of economic and financial data. Countries that subscribe to the SDDS promise to make public accurate and timely information across eighteen categories of economic data, listed on http://dsbb.imf.org/Applications/web/sddsdatadimensions/. The list of member countries is available at http://dsbb.imf.org/Applications/web/sddscountrylist/.

policy coordination in the past twenty years has shown that where various national monetary policy authorities are not working from the same models – the same basic understandings of how the economic world works – they are less likely to be able to improve joint welfare (Frankel and Rockett 1988). Information sharing of this theoretical nature is an opportunity to learn and to persuade, to take a collective look at a situation and draw on broader wisdom to better understand economic reality.

Finally, information sharing is about "showing one's hand." It is about communicating policy preferences and the intensity with which they are held. As such, it is part of the natural bargaining process precedent to policy coordination. Information sharing of this kind is an exercise in giving notice, sometimes subtly, concerning policy choices that are being, or will soon be, implemented. It is important to note that in the absence of efforts to coordinate policies, mere notification can reduce rather than enhance joint welfare. After all, an uncoordinated reaction to being informed of an undesired policy choice in another country could be to redouble the efforts to counter its effects – a classic case of working at cross purposes. In the absence of international coordination, it is possible for information to induce governments to pursue their own inefficient policies even more vigorously (Ghosh and Masson 1994: 172).

Generally, *information sharing is the easiest possible form of "cooperation."* Indeed, over the course of the past century it is difficult to think of an instance in which a lack of shared information *alone* led to a breakdown in more profound forms of central bank cooperation on policy.[10] This is not to say there have been no instances of "policy regret" as new information comes to light, but this is a problem in virtually all areas of monetary policymaking where knowledge is uncertain, projected data undergoes significant revision (Orphanides and Williams 2003; Kozicki 2004), or where information of a proprietary nature may be difficult to share. Finally, effective cooperation in today's (and even more so, tomorrow's) global economy will require the efficient and effective use of *real-time* information. These are important difficulties, no doubt. Yet I believe that information sharing is likely to continue to be one area in which central bank cooperation will become increasingly routinized. Of course, information alone does not settle difficult issues such as *what constitutes wise policy, who bears the risks, and who adjusts.* These issues will continue to complicate central bank policy cooperation in the future.

---

[10] There have been cases of hostile policy actions, plans of which presumably central banks did not share with one another before their implementation. Richard Cooper (2005a) cites the example of concerted French withdrawal of gold from Germany in 1929 during Young Plan negotiations. One might also include French conversion of dollars into gold in the 1960s. These are cases of hostile intent, rather than informational failure.

Beth A. Simmons

GLOBAL FINANCIAL STABILITY: INFORMATION
AND REGULATORY COORDINATION

One of the prime innovations in central bank cooperation in the past
two decades has been the collective attention given to the problem of the
systemic stability of the interbank financial system. The forces that gave
rise to this attention are likely to accelerate in the future. Institutional
consolidations and the globalization of financial markets are likely to
continue to increase the interdependencies among major organizations,
extending and intensifying systemic linkages. It will become increasingly
difficult to think in terms of "national banking systems," as the complex
web of connections across institutions, markets, and countries intensifies.
With these changes we are likely to witness new sources of systemic risk
and financial instability that private firms simply do not have the incentive
to internalize (Hoenig 2004). As many analysts have noted, central banks –
acting in their regulatory and supervisory capacity – can provide a real
public service by devising and disseminating standards and practices that
minimize the systemic risks associated with highly leveraged and highly
interdependent banking institutions.

Critiques of the Basel Accord are easy to come by, but beginning
in the 1980s central banks have successfully agreed to standards that
address systemic risks.[11] Some say the original Accord was foisted upon
a reluctant G10 by the Anglo-Americans (Kapstein 1989, 1992; Oatley
and Nabors 1998); others note that it was hardly appropriate for banks in
emerging markets, where much of the instability was likely to originate.
Practically everyone has acknowledged the crude bluntness of the original
Accord, with its undifferentiated 8 percent prudential capital requirement
(Ferguson 2003).

---

[11] For a good review of the theoretical literature, see Santos (2001). For a discussion of the
domestic politics underlying the harmonization of regulatory approaches, see Singer
(2004).

What is interesting, however, is that the combination of external standard setting and internal enforcement has "caught on" in a rather convincing way. In my view, a surprising number of countries – many of which did not participate in fashioning the original Basel Accord (or its successor) and are not formally obligated to adopt it – indeed have done so (Simmons 2001; Ho 2002). It is widely viewed as having broadly achieved its primary purpose: the promotion of stability in world financial markets (Ferguson 2003).

Cooperation among central banks in the supervision and regulation of internationally active banks is not as "easy" as information sharing, though we shall continue to see a lot of progressive and, for the most part, successful activity (despite the varying roles central banks have in bank supervision and regulation). The key to this issue area is that standards of this nature are a *coordination problem*. The initial regulatory decision involves important distributive issues, but once these are resolved and a standard is accepted by an important core set of regulators, peripheral regulators have no interest in eschewing the core's standard. Admittedly, market power and expertise play a huge role in the initial decision of *which* standard ought to become global, but once that is decided by a group as influential as the Basel Committee on Banking Supervision (which in turn is influenced by the preferences of a powerful subset), the incentives to strike out in another regulatory direction are relatively weak.

As for why, the central reason is the perceived nature of market pressures that encourage the adoption of "global standards." International banking is characterized by information asymmetries that provide an opening for opportunistic behavior. The adoption of a stringent regulatory and supervisory regime conveys information on the quality of a firm as a counterparty to an agreement. In this environment, an appropriate prudential and supervisory regime is a competitive advantage that other jurisdictions have an incentive to copy. In describing why they chose to adopt the original 1988 Accord on capital adequacy standards, for example, Bernard W. Fraser, Governor of the Reserve Bank

191

of Australia, remarked that, "there is considerable [market] pressure on others to follow – otherwise their banks risk being perceived as somewhat inferior institutions in competitive situations" (Fraser 1995: 26). The same perceptions seem to surround adoption of the revised Basel II Framework. Standard and Poor's website claims that "firms can use the regulatory imperatives of Basel II as an opportunity to push ahead of the competition . . . By using Basel II and other mandates as the catalyst for an enterprise-wide examination and refinement of its infrastructure and processes, a firm can achieve significant operational efficiencies and improvements."[12] Similarly, Canadian consulting firms urge Canadian banks to adopt Basel II to "give themselves a competitive, high-performance advantage."[13]

This is not the place (and I am not the person) to debate the technical merits of various approaches to the supervision and regulation of internationally active banks.[14] Rather it is the place to make the point that the *politics* of coordinated approaches to systemic risks are reinforced to some extent by competitive market forces. Still, two kinds of problems remain. The first is that claiming to have adopted "international standards" and "best practices" may very well be a pooling equilibrium, a cheap signal that officials in both well-regulated and not-so-well-regulated jurisdictions may have an incentive to try to send. Thus, the reinforcing competitive mechanism I describe cannot work without a high degree of transparency regarding the extent of domestic implementation of these standards. While enforcement is generally recognized to be domestic, cooperative institutions such as the Basel Committee should continue to stand ready to verify (and publicize) compliance.

---

[12] See http://www.gtnews.com/article/5891.cfm (accessed on 30 May 2005).

[13] http://www.accenture.com/xd/xd.asp?it=caweb&xd=locations%5Ccanada%5Cinsights%5Cpov%5Cbasel2_rewards.xml (accessed on 30 May 2005).

[14] The literature is immense. For a discussion of precommitment approaches versus "formulas," see Estrella (1998). On the macroeconomic effects of Basel II, see Tanaka (2003) and Griffith-Jones and Spratt (2001).

The second issue that may plague cooperation in this area is the nature and legitimacy of the standards themselves. Essentially, a small core of powerful and technically sophisticated regulators with input from the largest internationally active banks have defined what "international standards" and "best practices" mean.[15] I have no doubt the Basel Committee has the regulatory and financial expertise to develop such standards. I have somewhat less confidence that its standards are viewed universally as legitimate, or even appropriate, for banks the world over.[16] Canadian and Australian bank regulators may readily succumb to "competitive pressures" to adopt the recommendations of the Basel Committee, but will Indonesia (banking crises, 1992–99), Malaysia (banking crises 1985–88, 1997–98), or India (banking crises 1991–98)? Will Chinese[17] or Islamic regulators[18] adopt Basel recommendations? Commentators have

---

[15] The Committee's members come from Belgium, Canada, France, Germany, Italy, Japan, Luxembourg, the Netherlands, Spain, Sweden, Switzerland, the United Kingdom, and the United States.

[16] It is important to note that the actual standards adopted have serious *distributed* implications. The original Basel Accord, some have maintained, was politically biased in granting OECD members a 0% weight for their country credit risk, while non-OECD countries had a 100% weight. This led to the financially difficult-to-justify situation in which Turkish debt would get a 0% weight and Singaporean debt a 100% weight. See Fratianni and Pattison (2001: 208).

[17] In China, for example, the China Banking Regulatory Commission (CBRC) has said that it will wait until China's banks are fully compliant with Basel I before making the second stage a requirement. The lack of regulatory take-up in the region is one reason that, overall, its banks are behind those in other parts of the world in implementation. In 2004, KPMG, the accounting firm, surveyed banking clients around the world on the status of their Basel II implementations. It found that 16 percent of Asian financial institutions surveyed had no Basel II implementation plans, the highest for any region. Another roadblock for the Asian financial institutions is that, even if many desire to opt for the more sophisticated IRB approach, they lack the information required to build the databases for the credit risk models. According to Peter Poon, EDS sales director for Hong Kong SAR: "Credit assessment, particularly among small- to medium-sized enterprises, is still based on the relationship between the loan officer and the client – not a very systematic tool." See article by Niles Lo, "Late for the Basel," *CFO Asia*, May 2005; available at http://www.cfoasia.com/archives/200505-05.htm.

[18] On the appropriateness of Basel-type approaches to Islamic banking systems, see Muljawan, Dar, and Hall (2004).

noted that developing countries lack not only the technical capacity to implement the new Framework (Basel II) but the "political will" as well (Chami, Khan, and Sharma 2003). Political will may well remain weak as long as standards are propagated without the serious participation of regulators from developing-country jurisdictions.

These questions will come to the fore in the future because the further integration of financial markets will push them there. One of the key findings of the research on banking crises is that these crises are typically preceded by capital account liberalization (Kaminsky and Reinhart 1999).[19] Economists now have a pretty good idea of the factors that lead countries into banking crises: problems ensue following a period of expansion built on credit fueled by strong capital inflows and an overvalued currency, followed by a recession. Capital account liberalization – on the agenda in the (distant?) future in China, for example – will create conditions that will challenge developing-country banks. In the future, systemic consequences stemming from consolidation, which some predict as the result of more stringent reporting requirements, and intensification of these banks' international activities will be potentially important.

Of course, financial stability requires concerted efforts that go beyond central bank cooperation. It will involve central banks, but also other bank and securities regulators – hence the creation of the Financial Stability Forum (FSF) in 1999. The FSF's purpose is to promote international financial stability through information exchange and international cooperation in financial supervision and surveillance. To this end, it primarily involves authorities from the "significant international financial centers"[20] as well as international financial institutions, sector-specific international groupings of regulators and supervisors, committees of

---

[19] For a review of the literature on currency and banking crises, see Breuer (2004).
[20] Australia, Canada, France, Germany, Hong Kong SAR, Italy, Japan, the Netherlands, Singapore, the United Kingdom, and the United States.

central bank experts, and well-organized "special interest groups."[21] Creating a permanent meeting forum for major regulators is an important achievement, but in the future there is likely to be a growing tension between the need for efficiency, which calls for an intimate gathering of the major players (Crockett 2001a);[22] and global authority, which calls for much wider participation, especially on the part of Asian and Latin American representatives (Fratianni and Pattison 2001).

Financial stability will also require monitoring much more information than seems to be currently available, which is not principally a problem of central bank cooperation as much as it is the ability of central banks and other regulators to get useful information from private financial entities. The Special Data Dissemination Standard (see Table 5.3) is a start, and the high frequency data this standard requires may eventually be forthcoming from firms. As long as reporting remains voluntary, however, central banks' ability to address global financial stability will depend on the kind of cooperation they are able to elicit from firms operating in their own jurisdictions.

URGENT ACTION: EMERGENCY LIQUIDITY

Central banks have a long, if episodic, history of coming to one another's aid in a liquidity emergency. Early examples include the Baring crisis of 1890, the sterling crisis of 1906, and the American financial panic of 1907 (Eichengreen 1992). Within a year of its founding, the BIS had extended

---

[21] International Monetary Fund, World Bank, Bank for International Settlements, Organisation for Economic Co-operation and Development, Basel Committee on Banking Supervision, International Accounting Standards Board, International Association of Insurance Supervisors, International Organisation of Securities Commissions, Committee on Payment and Settlement Systems, Committee on the Global Financial System, and European Central Bank.

[22] On the issue of expanding membership, Andrew Crockett comes down clearly on the side of keeping the Forum small: "Expanding the membership would [be] at the cost of increasing the size of the Forum, and therefore reducing the informality and making it more difficult to discuss."

short-term credits to the central banks of Austria, Yugoslavia, Hungary, and Germany totaling some 750 million Swiss francs ($145 million), although such funds were recognized as paltry compared to the looming financial disasters that avalanched throughout Central Europe in 1931 (Fraser 1936). In addition, the BIS organized informal consortia of central banks to extend emergency credits and, by the late 1930s, had developed facilities for reciprocal credits among central banks (BIS 1938). In addition to a range of liquidity schemes arranged during the Bretton Woods period (Cooper 2005a), the BIS arranged special support credits for the Italian lira (1964) and the French franc (1968), alongside two so-called Group Arrangements (1966 and 1968) and a third backstop agreement (1976) to support sterling. In the 1980s and 1990s, the BIS extended short-term liquidity to central banks in Eastern Europe, Latin America, and Africa – regardless of whether they were members of the organization at the time (Howell 1995) – in anticipation of longer-term loans under negotiation with the IMF.

Short-term credits to central banks in immediate need of liquidity is one of the things central banks are advantageously positioned to provide (Fratianni and Pattison 2001). Decisions on these kinds of arrangements can be made quickly, and without the political scrutiny that government loans might receive. These loans, in contrast to those made by the IMF, do not include any explicit policy conditionality, making them easier to negotiate. Central banks hardly have a monopoly in this area, however. In Asia, for example, the Chiang Mai initiative – an agreement to provide reserve swaps to increase liquidity in case of currency attacks – is primarily a product of cooperation between the ministries of finance, merely to be executed by their central banks.[23]

---

[23] For the series of bilateral arrangements negotiated by Japan's Ministry of Finance, see http://www.mof.go.jp/jouhou/kokkin/pcmie.htm. As of late 2003, thirteen bilateral swap arrangements had been concluded worth a combined $32.5 billion – a relatively small amount given the magnitude of borrowing during the Asian crisis.

Meanwhile, in the West central banks are increasingly recognizing the need to reach understandings on access to liquidity in non-financial crises. After the terrorist attacks on 9/11, the Federal Reserve established thirty-day reciprocal swap arrangements with the European Central Bank (ECB) – which drew on the swap facility on September 12, 13, and 14, 2001 – and the Bank of England, and temporarily augmented its existing swap facility with the Bank of Canada (Federal Reserve Board 2001). Because global capital markets are tightly integrated and because these markets respond negatively to major attacks and terrorist events, central banks in the future will have to develop disaster recovery plans – including, but not limited to, the appropriate provision of liquidity – in case of surprise cataclysmic events of a political nature (Chen and Siems 2004).

As a result, it may very well fall to central bankers to act as financial "first responders" well into the future. Rapid financial and capital account liberalization may mean more currency crises in the future, reinforced by the unpredictable self-fulfilling behavior of market actors (Wyplosz 1998: 71). In the event of political attacks, which are even more difficult to forecast, central banks may increasingly play the role of lender of *first* resort.

"MACROMANAGEMENT": EXCHANGE RATES AND MONETARY POLICY COORDINATION

The future of central bank cooperation is the least certain in the broad area of "macropolicy," by which I mean both exchange rate policy and, more ambitiously, monetary policy. Cooperation in these areas raises a number of issues that are difficult to resolve. Varying theoretical perspectives lead to different policy prescriptions. Evidence that coordination in these areas has "worked" as expected is mixed. Most importantly, since cooperation implies implementing policies with serious economic consequences that might not have been chosen on domestic grounds alone, the issues involved tend to be much more politically charged than any of those discussed so far. Now we are wading into issues of truly "deep" coordination, and the prospect of central bank cooperation is concomitantly less likely.

The actual coordination of macropolicies has always been difficult for central banks to engineer. The Federal Reserve cooperated to facilitate Britain's return to gold in 1924–25 by reducing interest rates, but was not willing to do so in 1928–29 when speculative profits were drawing money to New York (Clarke 1967: 151). Exchange rate commitments went by the wayside in the early 1970s because they were inconsistent with the basic orientation of United States monetary and fiscal policies. Anna Schwartz bluntly opines: "Coordination is a fair-weather instrument because countries have independent interests that they will not sacrifice for the sake of the collectivity" (Schwartz 2000: 23). Many would agree with Kenneth Rogoff's assessment, that "Currency volatility is the price we pay for having independent monetary policies" (Rogoff 2005: 74). The recent trajectory of economic theory, policy experience, and the reassertion of national priorities suggest central bank cooperation in these areas will be difficult to pull off.

Coordinated Intervention: Managing Exchange Rates and their Volatility

Monetary authorities may consider that foreign exchange intervention influences exchange rates for a number of reasons: when markets are perceived to be disorderly, when the medium-term level of the exchange rate is perceived to be too high or too low, and sometimes at the behest of foreign authorities who want to coordinate policies (Neely 2000; Schwartz 2000). Of course, relative to the size of foreign exchange markets, any single authority's intervention resources are likely to be small, and in some cases unilateral intervention may be too difficult for market actors to interpret. Coordinating intervention with foreign central banks is supposed to improve the impact of the intervention, not only by increasing the resources used but, more importantly, by sending a clearer signal to the market that the central banks have credible "inside information" about the economy and that they want to convey it as clearly and truthfully to the market as is possible to do.[24] They may also want to coordinate intervention in order to avoid working at cross purposes; that is, to preclude the possibility that their own signals will be offset or overpowered by signals from other, more credible central banks (Dominguez 1990: 127).

For starters, it is important to note that central banks are not institutionally at liberty to design and execute exchange rate policies in an unconstrained way. Policies are typically designed in treasury departments or finance ministries; central banks may be thought of as the "junior agency" in the management of exchange rate regimes (Schwartz 2000).[25] In fact, managing the exchange rate is not an explicit part of the mandate of the major central banks; rather their primary charge is price stability. According to its Statute, the "primary objective of the ESCB shall be to maintain price stability." And: "without prejudice to the objective of price stability, the ESCB shall support the general economic policies in the Community with a view to contributing to the achievement of the objectives of the Community as laid down in Article 2 [of the Treaty on European Union]" (Treaty Article 105.1).[26] The Bank of Japan's Statutes stipulate that "the Bank of Japan's missions are to maintain price stability and to ensure the stability of the financial system, thereby laying the foundations for sound economic development."[27] And as for the

---

[24] Some have even argued that central banks may "agree to coordinate intervention operations in order to free-ride off other central banks' reputations for providing informative signals" (Dominguez 1990: 127).

[25] For a good comparison of the relative responsibilities in the United States, Japan, and Germany (now irrelevant with the creation of the ECB), see Henning (1994).

[26] The objectives of the Union (Article 2 of the Treaty on European Union) are a high level of employment and sustainable and non-inflationary growth. See the ECB website, http://www.ecb.int/ecb/orga/tasks/html/index.en.html.

[27] Bank of Japan website, http://www.boj.or.jp/en/.

Federal Reserve: "The Board of Governors of the Federal Reserve System and the Federal Open Market Committee shall maintain *long* run growth of the monetary and credit aggregates commensurate with the economy's long run potential to increase production, so as to promote effectively the goals of maximum employment, stable prices, and moderate long term interest rates."[28] Since none of these banks are specifically tasked to defend or stabilize a currency, exchange rate policy coordination is likely to take a back seat to their primary mission.

Consensus regarding the usefulness of coordinated exchange rate intervention seems to have withered over the past decade. First, there is often no clear consensus on what constitutes an "appropriate" exchange rate, largely due to a lack of robust models of exchange rate determination to inspire coordinated action (Truman 2005). Second, the empirical research has turned up quite mixed results concerning the "success" of intervention,[29] though coordinated intervention seems to have somewhat larger effects than unilateral operations.[30] The effects of intervention (United States, Europe, and Japan) do not seem to be as significant post-1989 as they were in the 1980s, and the ability of intervention to reduce volatility has even been questioned recently.[31] Some research suggests

---

[28] 12 USC 225a. As added by act of 16 November 1977 (91 Stat. 1387) and amended by acts of 27 October 1978 (92 Stat. 1897); 23 August 1988 (102 Stat. 1375); and 27 December 2000 (114 Stat. 3028), as found at the Fed website: http://www.federalreserve.gov/generalinfo/fract/sect02a.htm.

[29] For a general review of the effects of central bank intervention on exchange rates, see Sarno and Taylor (2001). Recent research on effectiveness of central bank intervention on exchange rates includes Evans and Lyons (2001) and Kearns and Rigobon (2002).

[30] Coordinated intervention has been shown to have larger and longer-lasting effects, at least for the 1985–87 period (Dominguez 1990). Recent research in the dollar-yen market also suggests that small unilateral operations are not likely to be an effective policy tool, though coordinated intervention sometimes delivers significant effects on the exchange rate in the short run (less than a month) (Fatum and Hutchison 2003).

[31] Dominguez's (1998) results suggest that reported Fed intervention reduced volatility in the period 1985 through 1988 and *increased* volatility over the period 1989 through 1991. Since 1989, she finds there is little to no evidence that central bank intervention in the foreign exchange markets delivers noticeable reductions in market uncertainty, at least when measured as volatility in rates (Dominguez 2003b).

that market players have been skeptical of the effects of intervention: the stability following the Louvre Accord was largely attributed by market actors to fundamentals, not exchange rate management (Rosenberg 1993). Third, theoretical developments in macroeconomics over the past decade (Obstfeld and Rogoff 1995) have thrown the assumption of gains from cooperation into question (Clarida, Gali, and Gertler 2001). Meanwhile, the debate over exchange rate price "pass-through" has led many to wonder if volatile exchange rates are really such a problem. Empirical research has revealed that exchange rate volatility greatly exceeds consumer price volatility and, to a lesser degree, import price volatility (Betts and Devereux 2000; Bacchetta and van Wincoop 2002). If exchange rate volatility does not have much effect on price stability,[32] why should it be a high priority of central banks?

Precisely which of these considerations is influencing decisions to intervene is not clear, but what is clear is that both the Federal Reserve and the ECB have drastically cut back on the practice. The last major coordinated intervention by the Fed, the ECB, and the Japanese Ministry of Finance – to support the euro – was in September 2000. Prior to that, no coordinated intervention had occurred since August 1995,[33] when the US Treasury coordinated intervention with the central banks of Japan, Germany, and Switzerland to keep pushing the dollar higher by buying the currency on the exchange markets. Proposals to stabilize "tripolar" exchange rates exist, but given current trends they are not likely to inform central bank cooperation in the foreseeable future.[34]

---

[32] While many doubt the relevance of the "direct" effect of exchange rate volatility for the achievement of price stability, the indirect effects – sometimes referred to as "second round" effects – and aggregate demand effects might be more important. This is an unresolved empirical issue.

[33] The United States also bought yen in 1998.

[34] Among the best known are the target zone schemes of Williamson (1986, 1994, 1998), McKinnon (1998), and Bergsten (1999; http://financialservices.house.gov/banking/52199ber.htm). Economic critiques of these kinds of goals are well known (Schwartz 2000). Thinking futuristically, Richard Cooper (2000) has proposed a common currency

Beth A. Simmons

The Problem of China: A Coordinated Move to Flexibility?

"Quadra-polar" exchange rates (among the dollar, euro, yen, and Chinese yuan) are a distinct and serious issue. In essence, it is a problem of extreme global imbalance among the major economies, not just an exchange rate issue. The ingredients in this imbalance include the burgeoning US fiscal and current account deficits, Europe's relatively slow growth, and Asia's (especially China's) relatively high savings rates. The imbalance has accumulated at least partially because the yuan remains linked to the dollar, at the cost of massive purchases of low yielding US debt by the Chinese central bank. At these exchange rates, a massive inflow of capital from abroad – totaling some $2 billion every working day, and growing – finances American consumption. The dramatic shift over the past few decades in the proportion of reserves held by major central banks can be seen by comparing the reserves of Japan, China, and the Republic of Korea against those of the rest of the G10 (see Figure 5.7).

The basic facts of this imbalance are undisputed. Where policymakers and analysts disagree is over its seriousness, its sustainability, and how best to (and *who* should) adjust. Optimistic assessments view the imbalance as sustainable, even logical, given China's need to attract high quality capital in the form of foreign direct investment (Dooley, Folkerts-Landau, and Garber 2003, 2004a). The central bargain is stable, some have argued, since many Asian central banks (especially China's) are willing to intervene on a massive scale to prevent currency revaluation and finance the US deficit (Dooley, Folkerts-Landau, and Garber 2004b). The only real alternative for the Asian countries is to hold dollars (and finance US deficits) since the basically unhedgeable exchange rate risk for dollar asset holders would be intolerable were Asian currencies to appreciate (McKinnon

for Europe, Japan, and the United States. The instability of a "tripolar" exchange rate system has long drawn proposals for some form of nominal anchor; see, for example, the discussion in Berner (1993).

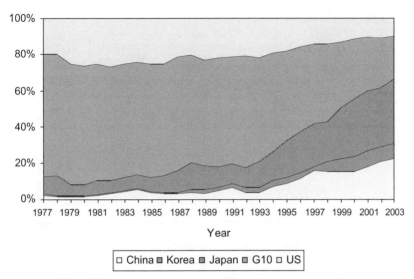

Figure 5.7: Share of total reserves held by the major economies.

and Schnabl 2004a, 2004b). Federal Reserve Chairman Ben Bernanke believes the imbalance emanates from a "glut" of global savings, and the inherent attractiveness of the US market to foreign investors, citing "no reason why the whole process [of reducing the imbalance] should not proceed smoothly" (Cooper 2004; Bernanke 2005). Moreover, Michael Bordo points out that while today's imbalance is large compared to earlier periods that ended in serious recessions (the interwar gold standard and the twilight years of the Bretton Woods system, for example), the fundamentals of the international monetary regime today are stronger, and the major monetary authorities are better equipped to deal with the process of readjustment (Bordo 2005).

That said, many others believe the imbalances are unsustainable and have begun to propose various exit strategies. Paul Volcker (2005) has called the imbalances "as dangerous and intractable as any I can remember" and calls for US fiscal discipline. The IMF (2004), citing "reasons to be concerned that this [imbalance] cannot last," calls for a cooperative strategy to achieve fiscal consolidation and greater exchange rate

flexibility, while expressing concern about the effects of rising US interest rates on emerging markets. The consensus view among economists
(to the extent there is one) is that some combination of deficit reduction in the United States, structural adjustment to improve growth in
Europe, and currency appreciation in China are needed to avoid a disruptive correction (Eichengreen 2004b; Summers 2004; Roubini and Setser
2005).

My purpose here is not to recite the economics of these various policy
options, but rather to place the future of central bank cooperation in this
awkward context. What cooperative dilemmas will central bankers face
in dealing with the imbalances in the global economy? First, there may be
some difficulty in working out these issues in a G7 context. China is not,
after all, a regular member of this group and the Governor of the People's
Bank of China does not regularly attend the meetings of G7 finance
ministers and central bankers. Although a key player, China is outside
a major institutional loop, sometimes invited (October 2004, February
2005), occasionally spurning invitations to take part (April 2005). The
People's Bank of China was also a latecomer to the BIS, only joining in
1996.

The key point is that the People's Bank of China is not very well
integrated – some would say, not well "socialized" – into institutional
channels where the exchange rate issue might be cooperatively handled.
This is an important point, especially since recent social science research
shows that when China *does* become systematically involved in international or regional institutions, there is a significant change in the nature of
the discourse among Chinese leaders and bureaucrats that evinces much
more sensitivity to multilateral issues and China's interests in cooperative
solutions to problems (Johnston 2002).

For its part, the G7 meetings of finance ministers and central bankers
do not appear to have made noticeable progress in handling the problem
of these imbalances. The first communiqué to deal with exchange rate
flexibility resulted from the Dubai meeting (September 2003), but all the

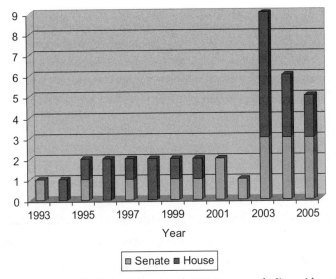

Figure 5.8: Number of bills introduced in the US Congress dealing with exchange rates.
Note: First quarter data only.

United States contributed to the "growth agenda" at that meeting was tax cuts and the hope of tort reform! The same statement on exchange rates was recycled for the communiqués of the next three meetings, though with language conveying greater urgency with respect to fiscal debts and restructuring to enhance growth.[35]

Meanwhile, the dollar/yuan exchange rate is beginning to raise political pressures in the United States for more unilateral action and Congress is beginning to pressure the administration to act. Figure 5.8 displays the number of bills introduced in Congress (House and Senate) that are

[35] "We reaffirm that exchange rates should reflect economic fundamentals. Excess volatility and disorderly movements in exchange rates are undesirable for economic growth. We continue to monitor exchange markets closely and cooperate as appropriate. In this context, we emphasise that more flexibility in exchange rates is desirable for major countries or economic areas that lack such flexibility to promote smooth and widespread adjustments in the international financial system, based on market mechanisms." See http://www.g8.utoronto.ca/summit/index.htm for all G7-G8 communiqués. This point is also made by Truman (2005).

substantially about the value of the dollar. The spike beginning in 2003 and continuing through 2005 (note these are bills introduced in the first quarter of 2005 alone) is almost completely accounted for by the problem of "currency manipulation" by China.

On July 21, 2005, China surprised financial markets by unpegging the yuan from its long-standing rate of 8.28 yuan to the dollar, responding in part to repeated calls for flexibility. The unpegging had two components – an immediate 2 percent revaluation, which lowered the exchange rate to 8.11 yuan to the dollar, and the introduction of a "managed float," which would unlink the yuan from the dollar, and peg it instead to a basket of currencies whose composition is undisclosed. The People's Bank of China has stated that the yuan will be allowed to trade in a tight daily band of 0.3 percent against the dollar, giving room perhaps for a continued adjustment of the yuan's value. Yet hopes for a larger readjustment have remained unfulfilled, as the current value of the yuan hovers around a rate of 8.09 to the dollar, barely 0.24 percent from its value at the time of the revaluation.[36]

China's recent policy may or may not assuage political pressures in the United States agitating for more meaningful (some might say, precipitous) change. In the spring of 2005, Senators Charles Schumer (Democrat, New York) and Lindsey Graham (Republican, South Carolina) introduced a bill that would impose a tariff on Chinese exports to the United States if Beijing continues to keep the value of the yuan "artificially low" compared with the dollar. The minimal movement in the yuan may mean that such domestic pressures will persist. In an interesting rhetorical turn, "free trade" is being identified with and defined as a "free float."[37] Even if the Schumer-Graham bill was withdrawn in September 2006, the

---

[36] Rate of RMB to USD on 5 November 2005, http://www.oanda.com/convert/classic.
[37] In an 8 June 2005 op-ed piece in *The New York Times*, Schumer and Graham wrote: "Remember, a major tenet of free trade is that currencies need to be free to float in value against other currencies" (p. A-25).

presence, persistence, and rhetoric of this bill and others like it raise risks of ill-advised unilateralism.

Imbalances of this scale also complicate the Federal Reserve's primary task – the conduct of monetary policy. Some evidence suggests that Asia's massive purchases of treasury bills are weakening the Fed's ability to modulate US monetary policy. Recently, treasury yields have weakened, even as official rates have increased. Demand from Asia, according to some studies, has kept US interest rates anywhere from 40 to 100 basis points below where they would otherwise be in the absence of central bank demand (Bernanke, Reinhart, and Sack 2004). "Monetary policy is most effective when it is clearly targeted, and it can't be used to fix *everything*" (Rogoff 2003: 57), but if official demand for securities continues unabated, the Fed will soon have to worry whether monetary policy can do *anything*.

The economic imbalances between the United States and Asia raise some cooperative issues not directly confronted in the past. Asia's apparent willingness to hold huge quantities of US securities (with a very low yield) raises a potential collective action problem among several Asian central banks. As Barry Eichengreen (2004b) has noted in an important working paper, the large reserve holders are much less cohesive as a group than were the group of European holders of dollar assets toward the end the Bretton Woods period. India, China, Republic of Korea, Taiwan (Republic of China), and Japan have very different interests, but they do have one thing in common: they do not want to be the last holder of significant quantities of depreciated dollars. Some of the smaller holders may defect early in anticipation of depreciation to come, triggering a general sell-off in no country's interest. As a group, they face a collective action problem: how to avoid disorderly flight from the dollar that would involve huge capital losses. Part of the problem Asian central banks face is their weak record of regional cooperation and thin network of cooperative institutions (ASEAN, APEC, and the Asian Bellagio Group come to mind) needed to support collaboration. Central bank cooperation in Asia is in its infancy and observers seem in agreement that "the political and technical issues involved in a collective currency policy means that [cooperation] may be a long way off."[38]

As Asia transforms, as China and India grow and create regional centers of demand, and as democratizing Asian polities become less satisfied with financing Western (especially American) consumption, the special position of the dollar is bound to change. The difficulties of cooperative monetary and exchange rate management are rife: Asian central banks tend to be far less independent of government control, the level of mutual trust is far lower, communications and cultural differences persist, and the security environment is much more tense than has been the case between the Western countries in the postwar years. Nonetheless, central bankers from Asia will increasingly have to be dealt with as full-fledged partners, not occasional visitors summoned to Western dominated institutions.

CONCLUSIONS

"Futurology" is a notably precarious exercise; no one has an accurate model of economic, political, or other developments into the future. But central bank cooperation has adapted remarkably well to the demands of the times. From the efforts of individual bankers such as Montagu Norman and Benjamin Strong in the 1920s to achieve and help maintain a general return to the gold standard, to the efforts of central bankers in the 1960s to "lubricate" the Bretton Woods system of fixed but adjustable exchange rates, to the work of central bankers to develop and propagate supervisory standards for internationally active banks since the late 1980s, central bankers have been problem oriented. Cooperation among them has been shaped by the economic conditions they have encountered,

---

[38] William Pesek Jr., "Commentary: The buck, one day, may stop at Asian central banks." *International Herald Tribune Online*, Bloomberg News, 3 March 2005.

the theoretical lenses through which they view the world, and even the political context in which they operate. Nothing better illustrates this proposition than the history of the BIS itself (Fratianni and Pattison 2001).

Central banks have successfully cooperated where it has been possible for them to do so. The informational landscape has largely been transformed and policies better informed by intensified standards of information provision. These efforts will continue to pay important dividends into the future, especially when banks, without a long history of mutual trust, need to work increasingly closely.[39] If there is one thing that can damage cooperative efforts it is mistrust, which flourishes in an environment of policy opacity. As central banks intensify their cooperation, there will be a growing demand to be able to verify good faith efforts to comply with agreements. Fostering a norm of transparency will make possible – though not necessarily easy – future cooperative efforts.

The most significant challenge for central bankers in the future will be to adjust to the changed economic realities vis-à-vis Asia. Asian countries are latecomers to the core institutions of central bank cooperation. For example, a consortium of banks represented Japan when it first joined the BIS in 1930. Japan then relinquished membership in the context of the San Francisco Peace Treaty of 1951, but regained representation when the Bank of Japan joined the BIS in 1970, shortly before fixed rates collapsed. The central banks of the People's Republic of China and of India only joined the BIS in 1996; that of the Republic of Korea in 1997. Despite the fact that Taiwan (Republic of China) holds more foreign exchange reserves than all of Latin America, it is not a member of the BIS, though this is more an issue of politics than economics. In the future, Europeans and Americans might reconsider much more actively supporting regional cooperative arrangements in Asia, even if they operate

---

[39] As an aside, the author notes that the IMF has posted only one *Report on the Observance of Standards and Codes* for the United States and none for China.

independently from their Western counterparts. In 2004, retiring Federal Reserve Chairman Alan Greenspan told a European banking conference in Frankfurt that he sees no need for more cooperation between US, European, and Japanese central banks. The banks are already doing "as much as is necessary" in terms of cooperation, he said.[40] In the very near future, it will be important to be able to say the same for trans-Pacific central bank cooperation.

[40] "Greenspan says no need for closer US, EU, Japan central bank cooperation." *AFX News Limited*, 19 November 2004.

6

Interdependence and Cooperation: An Endangered Pair?

TOMMASO PADOA-SCHIOPPA[1]

The editors of this volume have kindly asked me to share some thoughts on a topic that has occupied most of my professional life, namely international economic interdependence and cooperation. The gist of these thoughts – which I have developed through multiple experiences in the fields of central banking and policymaking – is the fallacy of the "house in order" precept as an adequate rule to deal with the policy issues raised by economic interdependence. I reiterate: "as an adequate rule to deal with interdependence" and not "as a desirable precept *per se.*"

Compared to the general title of this volume, my comments have a broader scope and a narrower focus. A broader scope because I refer to "international policy" in general, not to "central banks" only. The intention here is not to avoid being specific about central banks, but rather to place central bank cooperation in the only context in which – I think – it can be properly approached.

The focus is, however, narrower because I concentrate on the philosophy, or perhaps the ideology, of interdependence and cooperation, not on its technicalities or its analytics. Cooperation is the word chosen

[1] Former member of the Executive Board of the European Central Bank.

by the editors of this volume. Coordination is an equally common term used in the literature, which, surprisingly, lacks a rigorous and agreed glossary in this field. To elaborate, a taxonomy would be a task in itself. In what follows I use "cooperation" and "coordination" as loosely interchangeable words, meaning the process whereby different policymakers work together for a common purpose.

The world in which I was educated and started professional life was strongly marked by a special combination – say, a pair – of economic interdependence and cooperation. The memory was fresh not only of World War II, but also of the economic evils that had preceded and perhaps facilitated it: the dramatic halt of the long expansion of the 1920s, the rise of nationalism, the collapse of world trade, mass unemployment, financial crises, and competitive devaluations.

The acceptance, and even the promotion, of interdependence was seen as a way to prosperity and as an antidote to aggressive policies. There was a bias in favor of international cooperation because this was seen as an economic corollary, or perhaps rather a lemma, of interdependence, a key foundation of a world freed from past grief.

It is remarkable that for many years no significant voice from political or academic society questioned either term of the pair or their juxtaposition. Politically and intellectually, such questioning would have appeared as incorrect because the cooperation bias was so strong.

From this point of departure – fixed by the experience of the 1930s and 1940s – the market and the policy components of the pair moved in rather different ways. Interdependence galloped, cooperation slogged. The strong pro-cooperation attitude gradually faded, while a different mindset gained ground.

Consider interdependence. The first striking trend was its phenomenal *deepening*. The fact that decade after decade international trade grew at about twice the rate of growth of world GDP is the most visible indicator of this trend. As Adam Smith discovered and elementary textbooks have taught ever since, division of labor made people and nations at the same time less self-sufficient, more mutually dependent, and richer. The *widening* of interdependence, however, was no less striking. It was a *geographical* widening, as the number of active participants in the global division of labor increased to the point of including almost every country of the planet. But it was also an *economic* – or functional – widening, as cross border mobility and exchanges extended from the original fields of finished goods and raw materials to intermediate goods, services, capital, and labor. All in all it is not an exaggeration to say that today interdependence *across* nations is far greater than interdependence *within* nations was two or three generations ago.

Consider now cooperation. "Slogging" may sound like a harsh and undeserved word and let me say immediately that I presume to fully acknowledge – and even to have occasionally contributed to – some remarkable progress in international cooperation over the last three decades. Membership in international organizations, institutions, and forums – be they the International Monetary Fund (IMF), the World Bank, or the Organisation for Economic Co-operation and Development (OECD), not to mention the Bank for International Settlements (BIS) itself – grew in line with the geographical widening of interdependence. New forums such as the Basel Committee on Banking Supervision (BCBS), the Committee on Payment and Settlement Systems (CPSS), and the Financial Stability Forum (FSF) were created. The agenda of cooperation widened to include fields like banking supervision, securities regulation, or payment systems, which were previously the preserve of national authorities.

Still, there are good reasons, in my view, to maintain my choice of words. The inevitable collapse of the Bretton Woods regime deprived the international system of a strong and accepted mechanism to impose adjustment of imbalances. The ideology of unrestricted national sovereignty made a powerful comeback. Most of all, cooperation did not progress at the same phenomenal pace at which interdependence did. The gap between needs and accomplishments actually widened.

213

Given this, I would like to discuss the intellectual argument under-pinning what I have called the "slogging" of cooperation.

To be sure, the key reason for the slogging is not an intellectual argu-ment, but rather a hard fact; the fact that an increase in *policy cooperation* faces formidable obstacles that do not exist for *economic integration*. The two terms of the pair – interdependence and cooperation – are indeed driven by different agents, subject to different constraints, and moved by different aims. Interdependence is driven by the self-interest of firms and households, which maximize utility functions with no regard for political borders. There is no equivalent self-interest for the actors of policy coop-eration, which are mainly entrusted with the task of pursuing a national interest, directly elected by the citizens or accountable to elected bodies. This fundamental asymmetry explains the different speeds at which the two terms have evolved.

These are facts. But the influence of ideas should not be underesti-mated. The intellectual argument developed by policymakers and schol-ars to provide a rationalization of the widening of the gap can be put under the general name of "house-in-order doctrine."

The house-in-order doctrine states that if each and every national policy player kept its house in order, then the world itself would be in order. In this case, there is no special need for policy cooperation or coordination, no need for any prior commitment to act together, no need for collective decisions resulting from a policy give-and-take. At most, what is needed in addition to good housekeeping is a regular exchange of information.

The doctrine is not formulated in the literature in the way I have stated it, but rather popularized by economists and policymakers. It is a collection of arguments, rather than a single economic theorem. Yet it can often be encountered in policy documents of national and interna-tional institutions, as well as in the non-technical writings of prominent economists.

Moreover, the doctrine claims powerful academic credentials. So, let me now turn to such claims and briefly examine the two main ones.

The first claim of the house in order doctrine is to be the legitimate heir of the tradition of economic liberalism. Already John Stuart Mill had argued that "it is in general a necessary condition of free institutions that the boundaries of governments should coincide in the main with those of nationalities." And the *Zollverein* advocated by Friedrich List was internally market oriented and externally protectionist.

Later, in the mid-twentieth century, the main argument against international policy coordination was that this would create an international leviathan increasing government intervention.

This argument, however, does not stand against the compelling theoretical argumentation of leading liberal thinkers and is inconsistent with the lesson of history. As to theoretical thinking, such eminent liberal economists as Hayek, Einaudi, and Robbins have conclusively demonstrated the difference between the decision on how activist the state should be in economic policy and the allocation of power across different levels of government. On the first, they favor strong limits to public intervention, but on the second, they espouse the creation of an international level of government for its peacekeeping and wealth-generating impact.

With the swing in the pendulum of ideas and policies away from activism, two pairs of attitudes have been arbitrarily formed: government intervention *cum* international cooperation, on the one side; market orientation *cum* national egoism on the other. It has been wrongly argued by Friedman and his followers that rejecting the form of policy activism that was dubbed "Keynesianism" needed to automatically entail opposition to the cooperative spirit that characterized the post-World War II years. In reality, describing international cooperation as an exclusive feature of an interventionist state is a major conceptual mistake. It confuses the sphere of economics with the sphere of politics. To combine the concept of the minimal state with that of a strong, and yet limited, supranational level of government is certainly more congenial to the legacy of liberal thinking than to any other economic or political doctrine. Such a government should be imbued with the power to enforce free trade, openness of economic frontiers, non-discrimination, and the international rule of law.

As to history, it would be wrong to attribute the collapse of the pre-1914 world to the rise of illiberal domestic policies. At the time, the role of the state in economic and social policies was still minimal. And even before liberal economic policies deteriorated, the foreign policies of the nation-states had taken a turn toward militarism. Already in the mid-nineteenth century, a split had emerged between liberal domestic policies and an aggressive foreign policy. In the period before 1914, very little was left of the combination of political, economic, and cultural elements of the golden years of the nineteenth century. The shot of a pistol was sufficient to make the edifice crumble. World War I was the effect of the unsustainability of the preceding order, not the cause of its fall.

The second claim of the house-in-order doctrine is the robust discovery of recent economic research supporting the proposition that international policy cooperation is not desirable and may be counterproductive.

Scrutiny of this recent literature is somewhat awkward for a policymaker not regularly frequenting the research laboratory and, at best, only familiar with penultimate generation analytical tools. The body of literature is large and still growing, often analytically sophisticated and difficult to read. Yet, let me state in simple terms the three reasons why the recommendation to refrain from structured international policy coordination looks ill conceived to me.

The first reason is that the scholarly debate is far from concluded. It is in the typical phase in which different results are collected presenting different conclusions, which are strictly dependent on the chosen assumptions. There is no "general theory" for the time being. For every paper advising against cooperation there is another paper re-commending it.

The second and far more important reason is that the debate is, by con-struction, somehow off the mark. Indeed, most of the literature explores circumstances in which cooperation produces a better or an inferior out-come compared to the result produced by "going it alone." One is tempted to ask: "And so what?" What is the ultimate value of this collection of examples? The optimal policy *line* and the optimal policy *level* must not be confused and require different types of investigation. I wonder if this literature is not simply discovering the obvious, and namely, that a pol-icymaker or a government can make mistakes. But is this a reason to do without it? Is the fact that the US Fed presumably made policy mistakes in the 1930s a good argument to conclude that a central bank should not have been created?

The third and related reason is the failure to rigorously define the non-coordination regime. Often, the anticooperation authors loosely speak of policy competition as the alternative. Of course, "competition" sounds better than "conflict." But, how to draw the line that separates the two? What we know is that the distinction is exceedingly difficult and contro-versial both analytically and practically. What we also know, however, is that competition, unlike conflict, requires a strong framework of agreed and enforceable rules. And how could this strong framework come into existence if not through an extraordinary cooperative effort by the would-be competitors?

My impression is that scholars sometimes forget to strip down their ideological conviction and leave it at the door before entering the labo-ratory. And let me add that it is somewhat amazing to see authors like Rogoff using completely different linguistic and analytical precautions in the "pop" and in the "lab" versions of their thinking. One may ask: Which of the two inspires the other?

Let me conclude. Policymaking consists, by definition, of pursuing the public interest. But what does "public" mean? It may mean different things for different communities, and if the optimum government is to be neither below nor above the level at which an interest needs to be recognized as public, then a multitier government is necessary. The choice of the appropriate level relates to the definition of the area in which a good is in fact public, that is, whether it is a local public good or whether, at the other extreme, it is a world public good.

As interdependence broadens and deepens so does the "public" domain because the economic and the political order are fundamentally interlinked. Here is the sense of the pair. Policy coordination is the way to deal with this broadening and deepening in a world in which political borders exist and the nation-state preserves the largest portion of public power. Inevitably, cooperation among national public actors entails a reduction in the independent decision-making power of national institutions.

The reluctance to confer portions of the national power to international forums and institutions is based on a model of sovereignty according to which government should remain undivided, be kept as a single and monolithic block. This model originated with the Westphalian order, took strength from the Jacobin movement during the French Revolution, and was increasingly engrafted in the course of the nineteenth century, first with the idea that nation and state should coincide, then with the rise of representative government and the advent of universal suffrage. But it was this same evolution that set the conditions for the rise of nationalism and the catastrophe of 1914–45.

While the memory was still fresh, the lessons from history and politics impregnated the thinking of economists and the attitudes of policymakers; hence, the balance on which the pair was set in shaping the post-World War II world. As time passes, however, memories grow dim and the risk augments that the pair will shift off balance.

Just as politicians, according to Keynes, are the slaves of some defunct economist, so economists and officials tend to be the slaves of some defunct historian or political thinker. They risk neglecting the fact that in a globalized world, unlimited national autonomy does not exist any longer and that sovereignty can in fact be regained – rather than lost – when delegating tasks to supranational forums and institutions. As Robert Cooper puts it in his recent *The Breaking of Nations*: "For the post-modern state, sovereignty is a seat at the table" (Cooper 2003: 44).

Bibliography

Allen, A. M. (1938). "The principles of statutory regulation," in A. M. Allen et al. (eds.), *Commercial Banking Legislation and Control.* London: Macmillan.

Alston, P. (1997). "The myopia of the handmaidens: International lawyers and globalization." *European Journal of International Law,* 8(3), 435–41.

Apel, E. (2002). *European Monetary Integration 1958–2002.* London: Routledge.

Bacchetta, P. and E. van Wincoop (2002). "Why Do Consumer Prices React less than Import Prices to Exchange Rates?" *NBER Working Paper* No. 9352.

Baer, G. D. (1994). "The Committee of Governors as a Forum for European Central Bank Cooperation," in A. Bakker et al. (eds.), *Monetary Stability through International Cooperation: Essays in Honour of André Szász,* Amsterdam: De Nederlandsche Bank, pp. 147–57.

Baer, G. D. (1999). "Sixty-five years of central bank cooperation at the Bank for International Settlements," in C.-L. Holtfrerich, J. Reis, and G. Toniolo (eds.), *The Emergence of Modern Central Banking from 1918 to the Present.* Aldershot: Ashgate, pp. 341–61.

Baer, G. D. (2000). "The role of the Bank for International Settlements in the 1930s and 1990s," in R. Tilly and P. J. J. Welfens (eds.), *Economic Globalisation, International Organisations and Crisis Management: Contemporary and Historical Perspectives on Growth, Impact and Evolution of Major Organisations in an Interdependent World.* Heidelberg: Springer.

Baffi, P. (2002). *The Origins of Central Bank Cooperation.* Bari-Roma: Laterza.

Bank for International Settlements (1931–2004). Various *Annual Reports.* Basel: BIS.

Bibliography

Bank for International Settlements (1935). *5th Annual Report.* Basel: BIS.

Bank for International Settlements (1938). *8th Annual Report.* Basel: BIS.

Bank for International Settlements (1978). *48th Annual Report.* Basel: BIS.

Bank for International Settlements (1980). *The BIS and the Basle Meetings, published on the Occasion of the Fiftieth Anniversary 1930–80.* Basel: BIS.

Bank for International Settlements (1983). *53rd Annual Report.* Basel: BIS.

Bank for International Settlements (1984). *54th Annual Report.* Basel: BIS, pp. 151–2.

Bank for International Settlements (1994). "Chapter VIII: Payment and settlement systems: Trends and risk management," in *64th Annual Report.* Basel: BIS, pp. 172–92.

Bank for International Settlements (1997). "Chapter VIII: The evolution of central banking," in *67st Annual Report,* Basel: BIS, pp. 140–60.

Bank for International Settlements (2005). "Chapter VI: Financial markets," in *75th Annual Report.* Basel: BIS, pp. 97–119.

Bell, P. W. (1956). *The Sterling Area in the Postwar World.* Oxford: Clarendon Press.

Berger, H., J. de Haan and S. Eijffinger (2001). "Central bank independence: An update of theory and evidence." *Journal of Economic Surveys,* 15(1), 3–40.

Bernanke, B. S. (2000). *Essays on the Great Depression.* Princeton: Princeton University Press.

Bernanke, B. S., V. R. Reinhart and B. P. Sack (2004). "Monetary policy alternatives at the zero bound: An empirical assessment." *Finance and Economics Discussion Series* 2004–48. Washington DC: Board of Governors of the Federal Reserve System.

Bernanke, B. S. (2005, April 14). "The Global Saving Glut and the US Current Account Deficit." Speech delivered at Homer Jones Lecture, St. Louis, MO.

Berner, R. (1993). "Do we need a single nominal anchor in today's tripolar world?" *Journal of Asian Economics,* 4(2), 387–96.

Bernholz, P. (2003). "The Bank for International Settlements: Which activities can be justified from a normative economic perspective?" in J.-R. Chen (ed.), *The Role of International Institutions in Globalisation: The Challenges of Reform.* Cheltenham-Northampton: Edward Elgar.

Betts, C. and M. B. Devereux (2000). "Exchange rate dynamics in a model of pricing-to-market." *Journal of International Economics,* 50(1), 215–44.

Bloomfield, A. I. (1959). *Monetary Policy under the International Gold Standard, 1880–1914.* New York: Federal Reserve Bank of New York.

Bordo, M. D., B. Eichengreen and D. Irwin (1999). "*Is globalization today really different than globalization a hundred years ago?*" Preliminary version, prepared

Bibliography

for the Brookings Trade Policy Forum on Governing in a Global Economy, Washington DC, April 15–16. Revised version published in *Brookings Trade Policy Forum*, 1999.

Bordo, M. D. and A. J. Schwartz (2000). "Measuring real economic effects of bailouts: Historical perspectives on how countries in financial distress have fared with and without bailouts." *Carnegie Rochester Conference Series on Public Policy*, 53, 81–161.

Bordo, M. D., B. Eichengreen, D. Klingebiel and M. S. Martinez-Peria (2001). "Is the crisis problem growing more severe? Financial crises: Lessons from the last 120 years." *Economic Policy*, 32, 51–82.

Bordo, M. D. and M. Flandreau (2001). "Core, periphery, exchange rate regimes and globalization." *NBER Working Papers* No. 8584.

Bordo, M. D (2005). "Comment on Beth Simmon's paper *The Future of Central Bank Cooperation*." Paper presented at the Fourth BIS Annual Conference: *Past and Future of Central Bank Cooperation*. Basel: BIS, June 27–29.

Borio, C. and P. Van den Bergh (1993). "The nature and management of payment system risks: An international perspective." *BIS Economic Papers* No. 36.

Borio, C. (1995). "Payment and settlement systems: Trends and risk management," in G. Kaufman (ed.), *Research in Financial Services Private and Public Policy*, vol. 7. Greenwich, CT: JAI Press, pp. 87–110.

Borio, C. and P. Lowe (2002). "Asset prices, financial and monetary stability: Exploring the nexus." *BIS Working Papers* No. 114.

Borio, C. and W. R. White (2003). "Whither monetary and financial stability? The implications of evolving policy regimes," in *Monetary Policy and Uncertainty: Adapting to a Changing Economy. A Symposium Sponsored by the Federal Reserve Bank of Kansas City*, pp. 131–211. Also available as *BIS Working Papers* No. 147, February 2004.

Borio, C. (2004). "*The Search for the Elusive Twin Goals of Monetary and Financial Stability*." mimeo. Basel: BIS.

Breuer, J. B. (2004). "An exegesis on currency and banking crises." *Journal of Economic Surveys*, 18(3), 293–320.

Bryant, R. C. (1987). "Intergovernmental coordination of economic policies: An interim stocktaking," in *International Monetary Cooperation: Essays in Honor of Henry C. Wallich*, Princeton Essays in International Finance No. 169. Princeton: Princeton University, International Finance Section.

Bryant, R. C. (2003). *Turbulent Waters*. Washington DC: Brookings Institution.

Cairncross, A. and B. Eichengreen (2003). *Sterling in Decline: The Devaluations of 1931, 1949 and 1967*, 2nd ed. New York: Palgrave Macmillan.

Bibliography

Camdessus, M. (1998, May 8). "Toward a New Financial Architecture for a Globalized World." Speech delivered by the Managing Director of the International Monetary Fund at the Royal Institute for International Affairs, London. (Available online at http://www.imf.org/external/np/speeches/1998/050898.htm.)

Capie, F. (2003). "Central banking," in J. Mokyr (ed.), *The Oxford Encyclopedia of Economic History*. Oxford: Oxford University Press, pp. 372–77.

Chami, R., M. S. Khan and S. Sharma (2003). "Emerging issues in banking regulation." *IMF Working Papers*. Washington DC: IMF.

Chandler, L. V. (1958). *Benjamin Strong: Central Banker*. Washington DC: Brookings Institution.

Chen, A. H. and T. F. Siems (2004). "The effects of terrorism on global capital markets." *European Journal of Political Economy*, 20(2), 349–66.

Clapham, J. H. (1944). *The Bank of England: A History*. Cambridge: Cambridge University Press.

Clarida, R., J. Gali and M. Gertler (2001). "Optimal monetary policy in open versus closed economies: An integrated approach." *The American Economic Review*, 91(2), 248–52.

Clarke, S. V. O. (1967). *Central Bank Cooperation 1924–1931*. New York: Federal Reserve Bank of New York.

Coombs, C. A. (1976). *The Arena of International Finance*. New York: John Wiley, p. 29.

Cooper, R. N. (1982). "The gold standard: Historical facts and future prospects." *Brookings Papers on Economic Activity*, 1982(1), 1–56.

Cooper, R. N. (1985). "Economic interdependence and the coordination of economic policies," in R. W. Jones and P. B. Kenen (eds.), *Handbook of International Economics*, vol. 2. Amsterdam: Elsevier.

Cooper, R. N. (2000). "Toward a common currency?" *International Finance*, 3(2), 287–308.

Cooper, R. N. and J. S. Little (2000). "US monetary policy in an integrating world: 1960–2000," in R. W. Kopcke and L. E. Browne (eds.), *The Evolution of Monetary Policy and the Federal Reserve System over the Past Thirty Years*. Boston: Federal Reserve Bank of Boston. (See also *New England Economic Review*, 2001, No. 3.)

Cooper, R. N. (2004). "US deficit: It is not only sustainable, it is logical." *Financial Times*, October 31, p. A15.

Cooper, R. N. (2005a). "*Almost a century of central bank Cooperation.*" Paper presented at the Fourth BIS Annual Conference: *Past and Future of Central Bank Cooperation*. Basel: BIS, June 27–29. (See also chap. 2 of this volume.)

Bibliography

Cooper, R. N. (2005b). "A half century of development," in F. Bourguignon and B. Pleskovic (eds.), *Lessons of Experience, Annual World Bank Conference on Development Economics 2005*. Washington DC: World Bank.

Cooper, Robert (2003). *The Breaking of Nations: Order and Chaos in the Twenty-first Century*. London: Atlantic Books.

Costigliola, F. C. (1973). *The Politics of Financial Stabilisation: American Reconstruction Policy in Europe, 1924–30*. Ithaca: Cornell University.

Crockett, A. D. (2001a). "Running the bank of central banks." *The International Economy*, May/June, pp. 20–23, 48.

Crockett, A. D. (2001b). "Monetary policy and financial stability." *BIS Speeches*, February 13.

Crockett, A. D. (2002). "Globalisation." House of Lords testimony for Report on Globalisation, Select Committee on Economic Affairs. HL paper 143 (Session 2001–02). London: The Stationary Office Limited.

Cukierman, A. (1992). *Central Bank Strategy, Credibility and Independence: Theory and Evidence*. Cambridge: The MIT Press.

De Bandt, O. and P. Hartmann (2000). "Systemic risk: A survey." European Central Bank, *Working Paper Series* No. 35.

De Cecco, M. (1974). *Money and Empire*. Oxford: Blackwell.

De Gregorio, J., B. Eichengreen, T. Ito and C. Wyplosz (1999). "An independent and accountable IMF." *Geneva Reports on the World Economy*, No. 1, September. Geneva: ICMB.

De Kock, M. (1974). *Central Banking*, 4th ed. New York: St. Martin's Press.

DeLong, J. B. (1999, March 16). "Why we need – and why there will not be – a new international financial architecture." Speech delivered at the World Affairs Council.

De Nicolò, G. and M. Kwast (2001). *Systemic Risk and Financial Consolidation: Are they Related?* Unpublished manuscript.

Dominguez, K. M. (1990). "Market responses to coordinated central bank intervention." *Carnegie-Rochester Conference Series on Public Policy*, 32, 121–63.

Dominguez, K. M. and J. A. Frankel (1993). *Does Foreign Exchange Intervention Work?* Washington DC: IIE.

Dominguez, K. M. (1998). "Central bank intervention and exchange rate volatility." *Journal of International Money and Finance*, 17(1), 161–90.

Dominguez, K. M. (2003a). "Foreign exchange intervention: Did it work in the 1990s?" in C. F. Bergsten and J. Williamson (eds.), *Dollar Overvaluation and the World Economy*. Washington DC: IIE, pp. 217–45.

Bibliography

Dominguez, K. M. (2003b). "When do central bank interventions influence intra-daily and longer-term exchange rate movements?" *NBER Working Paper* No. 9875.

Dooley, M. P., D. Folkerts-Landau and P. Garber (2003). "An essay on the revived Bretton Woods system." *NBER Working Paper* No. 9971.

Dooley, M. P., D. Folkerts-Landau and P. Garber (2004a). "Direct investment, rising real wages and the absorption of excess labor in the periphery." *NBER Working Paper* No. 10626.

Dooley, M. P., D. Folkerts-Landau and P. Garber (2004b). "The revived Bretton Woods system: The effects of periphery intervention and reserve management on interest rates & exchange rates in center countries." *NBER Working Paper* No. 10332.

Downs, G. W., D. M. Rocke and P. N. Barsoom (1996). "Is the good news about compliance good news about cooperation?" *International Organization*, 50(3), 379–406.

Eatwell, J. and L. Taylor (2000). *Global Finance at Risk: The Case for International Regulation.* Cambridge: Polity Press.

Eichengreen, B. (1985). *The Gold Standard in Theory and History.* New York-London: Methuen.

Eichengreen, B. (1992). *Golden Fetters, the Gold Standard and the Great Depression, 1919–39.* New York: Oxford University Press, p. 160.

Eichengreen, B. (1993). *Reconstructing Europe's Trade and Payments: The European Payments Union.* Manchester: Manchester University Press.

Eichengreen, B. (1995). "Central bank cooperation and exchange rate commitments: The classical and interwar gold standards compared." *Financial History Review*, 2(2), 99–118.

Eichengreen, B. (1996). *Globalizing Capital: A History of the International Monetary System.* Princeton: Princeton University Press.

Eichengreen, B. (2000). "The International Monetary Fund in the wake of the Asian crisis," in G. Noble and J. Ravenhill (eds.), *The Asian Financial Crisis and the Architecture of Global Finance.* New York: Cambridge University Press.

Eichengreen, B. (2004a). "Financial Instability," in Bjorn Lomborg (ed.). *Global Crises, Global Solutions,* New York: Cambridge University Press.

Eichengreen, B. (2004b). "Global imbalances and the lessons of Bretton Woods." *NBER Working Paper* No. 10497.

Einzig, P. (1930). *The Bank for International Settlements.* London: Macmillan.

Estrella, A. (1998). "Formulas or supervision? Remarks on the future of regulatory capital." *Economic Policy Review*, 4(3), 191–200.

Bibliography

Evans, M. D. D. and R. K. Lyons (2001). "Portfolio balance, price impact, and secret intervention." *NBER Working Paper* No. 8356.

Fatum, R. and M. Hutchison (2003). "Effectiveness of official daily foreign exchange market intervention operations in Japan." *NBER Working Paper* No. 9648.

Federal Reserve Board (2001). "Treasury and Federal Reserve Foreign Exchange Operations," in *Federal Reserve Bulletin*, December, pp. 757–62.

Federal Reserve Board (n.d.). "Quarterly reports on foreign exchange intervention," in *Federal Reserve Bulletin*, various monthly editions.

Feenstra, R. C. (1998). "Integration of trade and disintegration of production in the global economy." *Journal of Economic Perspectives*, 12(4), 31–50.

Ferguson, R. W., Jr. (2003). "Capital standards for banks: The Evolving Basel Accord." *Federal Reserve Bulletin*, September, 89(9), 395–405.

Fischer, S. (1998, September 10). "Economic crises and the financial sector." Speech delivered at the Conference on Deposit Insurance, Washington, DC. (Available online at http://www.imf.org)

Flandreau, M. (1997). "Central bank cooperation in historical perspective: A skeptical view." *Economic History Review*, 50(4), 735–63.

Frankel, J. A. and K. E. Rockett (1988). "International macroeconomic policy coordination when policymakers do not agree on the true model." *The American Economic Review*, 78(3), 318–40.

Fraser, B. W. (1995, September 25). "Central Bank Cooperation in the Asian Region." Remarks to the 24th Conference of Economists, Adelaide. *Reserve Bank of Australia Bulletin*, October, pp. 21–8.

Fraser, L. (1936). "The international bank and its future." *Foreign Affairs*, 14(3), 453–64.

Fratianni, M. and J. Pattison (2001). "Review essay: The Bank for International Settlements: An assessment of its role in international monetary and financial policy coordination." *Open Economies Review*, 12(2), 197–222.

Funibashi, Y. (1989). *Managing the Dollar: From the Plaza to the Louvre*, 2nd ed. Washington DC: IIE.

Galati, G. and W. Melick (2002). "Central bank intervention and market expectations." *BIS Papers* No. 10.

Galati, G. (2002). "Settlement risk in foreign exchange markets and CLS Bank." *BIS Quarterly Review*, December, pp. 55–66.

Gallarotti, G. M. (1995). *The Anatomy of an International Monetary Regime: The Classical Gold Standard, 1880–1914*. Oxford: Oxford University Press.

Ghosh, A. R. and P. R. Masson (1994). *Economic Cooperation in an Uncertain World*. Cambridge: Blackwell.

Bibliography

Giannini, C. (2002). *L'età delle banche centrali*. Bologna: Il Mulino.

Gilbert, M. (1980). *Quest for World Monetary Order: The Gold-Dollar System and its Aftermath*. New York: John Wiley, p. 132.

Giovannini, A. (1988). "How do fixed-exchange-rate regimes work: The evidence from the gold standard, Bretton Woods and the EMS." *CEPR Discussion Paper Series* No. 282.

Giovanoli, M. (2000). "A new architecture for the global financial market: Legal aspects of international financial standard setting," in M. Giovanoli (ed.), *International Monetary Law: Issues for the New Millennium*. Oxford: Oxford University Press, pp. 3–60.

Goldstein, M. and P. Turner (1996). "Banking crises in emerging economies: Origins and policy options." *BIS Economic Papers* No. 46.

Goldstein, M. (2000). "Strengthening the international financial architecture: Where do we stand?" Peterson Institute for International Economics, *Working Paper Series* WP-008. (Available online at http://www.iie.com)

Goodhart, C. A. E. (1992). "Alternative monetary standards," in K. Dowd and M. K. Lewis (eds.), *Current Issues in Financial and Monetary Economics*. Houndmills-Basingstoke: Macmillan, pp. 15–41.

Goodhart, C. A. E. and P. J. R. Delargy (1998). "Financial crises: Plus ça change, plus c'est la même chose." *International Finance*, 1, 261–87.

Gordy, M. and B. Howells (2004). "*Procyclicality in Basel II*," Federal Reserve Board of the United States.

Greenspan, A. (1992, October 14). "International Financial Integration." Speech delivered at the Federation of Bankers Association of Japan.

Greenspan, A. (2004, October 5). "Banking." Speech delivered at the American Bankers Association, New York. (Available online at http://fraser.stlouisfed.org.)

Griffith-Jones, S. and S. Spratt (2001). "The pro-cyclical effects of the new Basel Accord," in J. J. Teunissen (ed.), *New Challenges of Crisis Prevention: Addressing Economic Imbalances in the North and Boom-Bust Cycles in the South*. The Hague: Forum on Debt and Development.

Gros, D. and N. Thygesen (1998). *European Monetary Integration*, 2nd ed. London: Longman.

Group of Ten (1997). *Financial Stability in emerging market economies: A Strategy for the Formulation, Adoption and Implementation of Sound Principles and Practices to Strengthen Financial Systems*. Basel: BIS.

Group of Ten (2001). *Report on Consolidation in the Financial Industry*. Basel: BIS.

Bibliography

Henning, C. R. (1994). *Currencies and Politics in the United States, Germany, and Japan.* Washington DC: IIE.

Herring, R. J and R. E. Litan (1995). *Financial Regulation in the Global Economy.* Washington DC: Brookings Institution.

Hillgenberg, H. (1999). "A fresh look at soft law." *European Journal of International Law,* 10(3), 499–515.

Hirsch, F. (1965). *The Pound Sterling: A Polemic.* London: Victor Gollancz.

Ho, D. E. (2002). "Compliance and international soft law: Why do countries implement the Basle Accord?" *Journal of International Economic Law,* 5(3), 647–88.

Hoenig, T. M. (2004). "Exploring the macro-prudential aspects of financial sector supervision." *Federal Reserve Bank of Kansas City – Economic Review,* 89(2), 5–17.

Holthausen, C. and T. Ronde (2004). "Cooperation in international banking supervision." *European Central Bank, Working Paper Series* No. 316.

Howell, K. (1993). "The role of the Bank for International Settlements in central bank cooperation." *Journal of European Economic History,* 22(2), 367–80.

Howell, K. (1995). "The evolution and goals of lending to developing countries by the Bank for International Settlements." *Journal of Economic Studies,* 22(6), 69–80.

International Monetary Fund (2004). *World Economic Outlook.* Washington DC: IMF.

Jackson, P. (2002). *"International financial regulation and stability."* Paper presented to the Judge Institute, Cambridge. (Also available online at http://www.bankofengland.co.uk.)

James, H. (1996). *International Monetary Cooperation since Bretton Woods.* Washington DC-Oxford: IMF and Oxford University Press.

James, H. (2001). *The End of Globalization: Lessons from the Great Depression.* Cambridge: Harvard University Press.

Johnston, A. I. (2002). "The social effects of international institutions on domestic (foreign policy) actors," in D. Drezner (ed.). *Locating the Proper Authorities: The Interaction of Domestic and International Institutions.* Ann Arbor: University of Michigan Press.

Jurgensen, P. (1983). *"Report of the Working Group on Exchange Market Intervention (Jurgensen Report)."* Working Group Report.

Kahler, M. (2000). *"Private capital central banks and international monetary governance."* Paper prepared for the Political Economy of International Finance Research Group Meeting, Cambridge, MA.

Bibliography

Kahler, M. (2004). "Defining accountability up: The global economic multilaterals." *Government and Opposition*, 39(2), 132–58.

Kaminsky, G. L. and C. M. Reinhart (1999). "The twin crises: The causes of banking and balance-of-payments problems." *American Economic Review*, 89(3), 473–500.

Kane, E. (2001). "Relevance and need for international regulatory standards." *Brookings-Wharton Papers on Financial Services*, pp. 87–115.

Kapstein, E. B. (1989). "Resolving the regulator's dilemma: International coordination of banking regulations." *International Organization*, 43(2), 323–47.

Kapstein, E. B. (1991). *Supervising International Banks: Origins and Implications of the Basle Accord.* Princeton: Princeton Essays in International Finance.

Kapstein, E. B. (1992). "Between power and purpose: Central bankers and the politics of regulatory convergence." *International Organization*, 46(1), 265–87.

Kapstein, E. B. (1994). *Governing the Global Economy: International Financial and the State.* Cambridge-London: Harvard University Press.

Kapstein, E. B. (2005). "*Architects of stability? International cooperation among financial supervisors.*" Paper presented at the Fourth BIS Annual Conference: *Past and Future of Central Bank Cooperation*, Basel: BIS, June 27–29. (See also chap. 3 of this volume.)

Kearns, J. and R. Rigobon (2002). "Identifying the efficacy of central bank interventions: The Australian case." *NBER Working Paper* No. 9062.

Keohane, R. O. (1984). *After Hegemony: Cooperation and Discord in the World Political Economy.* Princeton: Princeton University Press.

Keohane, R. O. and J. S. Nye Jr. (2001). "Democracy, accountability and global governance." *Politics Research Group Working Paper* No. 01–04, Harvard University.

Kindleberger, C. (1987). *The World in Depression, 1929–39*, 2nd ed. London: Penguin.

Kindleberger, C. (1996). *Manias, Panics and Crashes*, 3rd ed. Cambridge: Cambridge University Press.

Kozicki, S. (2004). "How do data revisions affect the evaluation and conduct of monetary policy?" Federal Reserve Bank of Kansas City, *Economic Review*, 89(1), 5–38.

Kraft, J. (1984). *The Mexican Rescue.* New York: G-30.

Kwan, Simon (2004). "Banking consolidation." *FRBSF, Economic Letter.*

Laidler, D. (1999). *Fabricating the Keynesian Revolution.* Cambridge: Cambridge University Press.

Lamfalussy, A. (1994). "Central banking in transition," in F. Capie, C. Goldhart, S. Fischer, and N. Schnadt (eds.), *The Future of Central Banking, The Tercentenary*

Bibliography

Symposium of the Bank of England. Cambridge: Cambridge University Press, pp. 330–41.

Lamfalussy, A. (2000). *Financial Crises in EME Markets.* Yale University Press.

Lamfalussy, A. (2001). "Reflections on the regulation of European securities markets." *SUERF Studies,* No. 14.

Lamfalussy, A. (2005). *"Central banks, governments and the European monetary unification process."* Paper presented at the Fourth BIS Annual Conference: *Past and Future of Central Bank Cooperation.* Basel: BIS, June 27–29. (See also chap. 4 of this volume)

Langley, P. (2002). *"What's 'new' about the New International Financial Architecture?"* Paper presented at the International Studies Association Annual Convention, March 25–27.

Large, A. (2005, March 18). "A framework for financial stability." Speech delivered at the International Conference on Financial Stability and Implications of Basel II, Istanbul. (Available online at http://www.bankofengland.co.uk.)

Ma, G. and E. Remolona (2005). "Opening markets through a regional bond fund: Lessons from ABF2." *BIS Quarterly Review,* June, pp. 81–92.

Maddison, A. (2001). *The World Economy: A Millennial Perspective.* Paris: OECD Development Centre.

Maier, C. S. (1988). *In search of Stability: Explorations in Historical Political Economy.* Cambridge: Cambridge University Press.

Maisel, S. (1973). *Managing the Dollar.* New York: Norton.

McCauley, R. (2005). "Distinguishing global official dollar reserves from official holdings of US assets." *BIS Quarterly Review,* September, pp. 57–72.

McKinnon, R. and G. Schnabl (2004a). "The return to soft dollar pegging in East Asia: Mitigating conflicted virtue." *International Finance,* 7(2), 169–201.

McKinnon, R. and G. Schnabl (2004b). "The East Asian dollar standard, fear of floating, and original sin." *Review of Development Economics,* 8(3), 331–60.

Meltzer, A. (2003). *A History of the Federal Reserve, vol. 1, 1914–1951.* Chicago: University of Chicago Press.

Moreau, E. (1991). *The Golden Franc: Memoirs of a Governor of the Bank of France: The Stabilization of the Franc.* Boulder: Westview Press. (Originally published in French in 1955.)

Mosley, L. (2003). "Attempting global standards: National governments, international finance, and the IMF's data regime." *Review of International Political Economy,* 10(2), 331–62.

Muljawan, D., H. A. Dar and M. J. B. Hall (2004). "A capital adequacy framework for Islamic banks: The need to reconcile depositors' risk aversion with managers' risk taking." *Applied Financial Economics,* 14(6), 429–41.

Bibliography

Neely, C. J. (2000). "The practice of central bank intervention: Looking under the hood." *Federal Reserve Bank of St. Louis Review*, 83(3), 1–10.

O'Rourke, K. H. and J. G. Williamson (1999). *Globalization and History: The Evolution of a Nineteenth-Century Atlantic Economy.* Cambridge: MIT Press.

Oatley, T. and R. Nabors (1998). "Redistributive cooperation: Market failure, wealth transfers and the Basel Accord." *International Organization*, 52(1), 35–54.

Obstfeld, M. and K. S. Rogoff (1995). "Exchange rate dynamics redux." *The Journal of Political Economy*, 103(3), 624–60.

Obstfeld, M. and K. S. Rogoff (2002). "Global implications of self-oriented national monetary rules." *The Quarterly Journal of Economics*, 117(2), 503–35.

Orphanides, A. and J. C. Williams (2003). "Imperfect knowledge, inflation expectations, and monetary policy." *NBER Working Paper* No. 9884.

Padoa-Schioppa, T. and F. Saccomanni (1994). "Managing a market-led global financial system," in *Managing the World Economy: Fifty Years After Bretton Woods.* Washington DC: IIE, pp. 235–68.

Padoa-Schioppa, T. (2004, March 22). "The evolving European financial landscape: Integration and regulation." Remarks to the Groupe Caisse des Dépôts/KfW, Berlin. (Available online at http://www.ecb.int.)

Peltzman, S. (1976). "Toward a more general theory of regulation." *Journal of Law and Economics*, 19, 211–40.

Picciotto, S. (1997). "Networks in international economic integration: Fragmented states and the dilemmas of neo-liberalism." *Northwestern Journal of International Law and Business*, 17(2/3), 1014–56.

Posen, A. (2002). "*A strategy to prevent future crises.*" Unpublished manuscript, IIE, 6 October.

Putnam, R. (1988). "Diplomacy and domestic politics: The logic of two-level games." *International Organization*, 42(3), 427–60.

Quintyn, M. and M. W. Taylor (2003). "Regulatory and supervisory independence and financial stability." *CESifo Economic Studies*, 49(2), 259–94.

Rogoff, K. S. (1985). "Can international monetary cooperation be counterproductive?" *Journal of International Economics*, 18, 199–217.

Rogoff, K. S. (2003). "A vote against grandiose schemes." *Finance and Development*, 40(1), pp. 56–7.

Rogoff, K. S. (2005). "Let it ride." *Foreign Policy*, 147 (March/April), pp. 74–5.

Rosenberg, M. R. (1993). "Is G-7 coordinated intervention responsible for greater stability of exchange rates?" *Journal of Asian Economics*, 4(2), 397–405.

Bibliography

Roubini, N. and B. Setser (2005). "*Will the Bretton Woods 2 regime unravel soon? The risk of a hard landing in 2005–2006.*" (Available online at http://pages.stern. nyu.edu/~nroubini/papers/BW2-Unraveling-Roubini-Setser.pdf.)

Rubin, R. E. (2003). *In an Uncertain World.* New York: Random House.

Saccomanni, F. (2002). "Tigri globali, domatori nazionali. Il difficile rapporto tra finanza globale e autorità monetarie nazionali." *Studi e Ricerche,* Bologna: Il Mulino, p. 312.

Santos, J. A. C. (2001). "Bank capital regulation in contemporary banking theory: A review of the literature." *Financial Markets, Institutions & Instruments,* 10(2), 41–84.

Sarno, L. and M. P. Taylor (2001). "Official intervention in the foreign exchange market: Is it effective and, if so, how does it work?" *Journal of Economic Literature,* 39(3), 839–68.

Sayers, R. (1976). *The Bank of England 1891–1944.* Cambridge: Cambridge University Press.

Schacht, H. H. G. (1956). *Confessions of "The Old Wizard."* Boston: Houghton Mifflin.

Schloss, H. H. (1958). *The Bank for International Settlements.* Amsterdam: North-Holland.

Schneider, B. (2001, April 11). "International financial architecture: Have we done enough to set it right?" Speech delivered at the Overseas Development Institute.

Schwartz, A. J. (2000). "The rise and fall of foreign exchange market intervention." *NBER Working Paper* No. 7751.

Siebert, H. (2003). "Should G-7 policy coordination be revived?" *The International Economy,* Fall.

Simmons, B. A. (1993). "Why innovate? Founding the Bank for International Settlements, 1929–30." *World Politics,* 45(3), 361–405.

Simmons, B. A. (1994). *Who Adjusts: Domestic Sources of Foreign Economic Policy during the Interwar Years.* Princeton: Princeton University Press.

Simmons, B. A. (1996). "Rulers of the game: Central bank independence during the interwar years." *International Organization,* 50(3), 407–43.

Simmons, B. A. (2001). "The international politics of harmonization: The case of capital market regulation." *International Organization,* 55(3), 589–620.

Singer, D. A. (2004). "Capital rules: The domestic politics of international regulatory harmonization." *International Organization,* 58(3), 531–65.

Slaughter, A.-M. (1997). "The real world order." *Foreign Affairs,* 76(5), 183–97.

Slaughter, A.-M. (2000). "Governing the global economy through government networks," in M. Byers (ed.), *The Role of Law in International Politics: Essays*

Bibliography

in International Relations and International Law. Oxford: Oxford University Press, pp. 177–205.

Slaughter, A.-M. (2004). "Disaggregated sovereignty: Towards the public accountability of global government networks." *Government and Opposition*, 39(2), 159–90.

Smith, R. and I. Walter (n.d.). *"Megabanks: Too big to fail, too big to monitor, too big to regulate?"* New York University, unpublished manuscript.

Solomon, R. (1977). *The International Monetary System, 1945–1976.* New York: Harper & Row.

Solomon, R. (1999). *Money on the Move.* Princeton: Princeton University Press.

Summers, L. H. (2004, October 3). "The US current account deficit and the global economy." Speech delivered at The Per Jacobsson Lecture, Washington DC.

Sundararajan, V., D. Marston and R. Basu (2001, May). "Financial system standards and financial stability: The case of the Basel Core Principles." *IMF Working Paper* WP/01/62.

Tanaka, M. (2003). "The macroeconomic implications of the new Basel Accord." *Cesifo Economic Studies*, 49(2), 217–32.

Tew, B. (1970). *International Monetary Cooperation 1945–1970.* London: Hutchinson & Co.

Toniolo, G., with the assistance of P. Clement (2005). *Central Bank Cooperation at the Bank for International Settlements, 1930–1973.* Cambridge-New York: Cambridge University Press.

Truman, E. M. (2003). "A critical review of coordination efforts in the past," in H. Siebert (ed.), *Macroeconomic Policies in the World Economy.* Heidelberg: Springer.

Truman, E. M. (2005). "The euro and prospects for policy coordination," in A. S. Posen (ed.), *The Euro at Five: Ready for a Global Role?* Washington DC: IIE.

Van Walre de Bordes, J. (1924). *The Austrian Crown: Its Depreciation and Stabilization.* London: P. S. King & Son.

Volcker, P. and T. Gyohten (1992). *Changing Fortunes: The World's Money and the Threat to American Leadership.* New York: Times Books.

Volcker, P. (2005). "An economy on thin ice." *Washington Post*, April 10, p. 7.

White, W. R. (1996). "International agreements in the area of banking and finance: Accomplishments and outstanding issues." *BIS Working Papers* No. 38.

White, W. R. (2000). "What have we learned from recent financial crises and policy responses?" *BIS Working Papers* No. 84.

Bibliography

Wooldridge, P. (2002). "Globalising international banking." *BIS Quarterly Review*, March, pp. 41–51.

Working Group on Strengthening Financial Systems (1998). *Report of the Working Group on Strengthening Financial Systems.* (Available online at http://www.bis.org)

Wyplosz, C. (1998). "Globalised financial markets and financial crises," in J. J. Teunissen (ed.), *Regulatory and Supervisory Challenges in a New Era of Global Finance.* The Hague: Forum on Debt and Development.

Zaring, D. (1998). "International law by other means: The twilight existence of international financial regulatory organizations." *Texas International Law Journal*, 33, 281–330.

Index

Index

Index

Index

Index

Index

Index

Index

United Kingdom, 84, 87, 88, 131
    abandonment of the ERM, 105
    and the European monetary unification
        process, 158
    central bank loans to the, 88
United States, 5, 31, 42, 45, 53, 86, 87, 89, 91,
    92, 99, 120–123, 126, 129, 131, 138, 145,
    170, 204, 206
    role in the debt crisis of 1982, 130

Valencia meeting (1995), 162
Volcker, Paul, 96, 99, 101

Werner Plan (1970), 103
Werner Report (1970), 58, 154
"window-dressing", 94, 98

Wolff, Julius, 30
Working Group on Strengthening Financial
    Systems, 134
World Bank, 2, 39, 44, 67, 98, 136, 137, 213
    and membership to the FSF, 195
World Trade Organization (WTO), 65
World War I, 3, 4, 25, 27, 31, 32, 216. *See also*
    German reparations
World War II, 25, 36, 81, 82, 84, 85
WTO. *See* World Trade Organization

Young Plan (1929), 76, 78, 189
Yugoslavia, 83, 196

Zhixiang, Zhang, 106
Zijlstra, Jelle, 96

Other titles in the series (*continued from page iii*)